DE[Y AND EDUCATION
REC [ED

P[
Cha[
Subject to

http[

Democracy and Education Reconsidered reflects on the continued importance of what is arguably the most internationally influential book on education written in the twentieth century. In celebration of the 100th anniversary of publication, this volume highlights the enduring relevance of John Dewey's seminal *Democracy and Education* while also examining the need to reconstruct and re-contextualize Dewey's educational philosophy for our time. The authors propose ways of revising Dewey's thought in light of the challenges facing contemporary education and society, and address other themes not touched upon heavily in Dewey's work, such as racism, feminism, post-industrial capitalism, and liquid modernity. Drawing on theories of interactive constructivism, Garrison, Neubert, and Reich integrate Dewey's philosophy with more recent trends in scholarship, including pragmatism, post-structuralism, constructivism, and the works of other key philosophers and scholars.

Jim Garrison is Professor of Philosophy of Education at Virginia Tech in Blacksburg, Virginia.

Stefan Neubert is Privatdozent (PR Dr.) at the Faculty of Human Sciences, University of Cologne.

Kersten Reich is Professor of Educational Research at the University of Cologne.

DEMOCRACY AND EDUCATION RECONSIDERED

Dewey After One Hundred Years

Jim Garrison, Stefan Neubert, and Kersten Reich

Routledge
Taylor & Francis Group

NEW YORK AND LONDON

First published 2016
by Routledge
711 Third Avenue, New York, NY 10017

and by Routledge
2 Park Square, Milton Park, Abingdon, Oxon, OX14 4RN

Routledge is an imprint of the Taylor & Francis Group, an informa business

Library of Congress Cataloging in Publication Data
Garrison, James W., 1949–
Democracy and education reconsidered : Dewey after one hundred years/ Jim Garrison, Stefan Neubert, and Kersten Reich.
pages cm
Includes bibliographical references and index.
1. Dewey, John, 1859–1952—Criticism and interpretation. 2. Education—Philosophy. 3. Education—Social aspects. 4. Education and democracy. I. Neubert, Stefan. II. Reich, Kersten. III. Title.
LB875.D5G368 2016
370.1—dc23
2015025280

ISBN: 978-1-138-93949-3 (hbk)
ISBN: 978-1-138-93950-9 (pbk)
ISBN: 978-1-315-67489-6 (ebk)

Typeset in Bembo and Stone Sans
by Florence Production Ltd, Stoodleigh, Devon, UK

Printed and bound in the United States of America by Publishers Graphics, LLC on sustainably sourced paper.

CONTENTS

INTRODUCTION

Many consider John Dewey's 1916 book *Democracy and Education* the most influential work on education published in the twentieth century. Translated into over 25 languages including Arabic, Spanish, Gujarati, Hebrew, German, Chinese, Marathi, Japanese, Serbo-Croatian, and Bulgarian, we may certainly call it a global educational classic that continues to draw the ire of critics while inspiring a new generation of educators around the world. Our goal in the pages to follow is to reconsider *Democracy and Education* today, 100 years after its publication. Fully appreciating the philosophical depth of *Democracy and Education* will allow us, among other things, to address the following question: Why is it that Dewey's influence on actual school practice remains surprisingly minimal or unrecognized even while his educational writings have been widely read, discussed, and even advocated by those claiming to support educational reform? Our intention is to expose and reconstruct the theoretical richness of Dewey's educational thought for our time and to point out in what regards Dewey is still challenging educational practices. It is fully in the spirit of Dewey that our leading intention consists in overcoming the gap between educational thought and practice, philosophy and schooling, science and everyday experience.

Our reconsiderations will take many forms. First, of the 37 volumes comprising the Early (5 volumes), Middle (14 volumes), and Later (17 volumes) *Collected Works of John Dewey 1882–1953*, *Democracy and Education* occurs just beyond the midpoint of *The Middle Works* (volume 9 of 14). There is also the more recent Supplementary Volume 1: 1884–1951 that contains material overlooked in the compilation of the first 37 volumes.[1] Known as the philosopher of reconstruction, Dewey slowly and deliberately reconstructed himself throughout his career. His subsequent writings contain many reconstructions and redirections of his thinking, e.g., as concerns his theories of experience (LW 1), communication (LW 1), culture

(MW 12, MW 14), art (LW 10), logics (LW 12), politics (The Public and Its Problems, LW 2: 200–372; Liberalism and Social Action, LW 11: 1–66; Freedom and Culture, LW 13: 63–188), and anticipatory steps to the linguistic turn (LW 16). He considerably expanded his positions on, for example, experience, communication, democracy, values, inquiry, morality, and with all that: education.

Going back to a book published a century ago offers a number of crucial opportunities. In many respects, Dewey was ahead of his time and close to ours. He already recognized the tensional relation between cultural improvements offered by science and technology in modern life and the risks and dark sides of modernization and globalization that haunt many critical debates today. Unlike many of his contemporary admirers of modernization, he stridently rejects scientism, positivism, reductionism, and such. For instance, he vociferously disposes of the theory-versus-fact and fact-versus-value dualisms. Indeed, he dismisses many entrenched epistemological dualisms such as the knower-versus-known, subject-versus-object, and mind-versus-body. From classical Western philosophy, he retained one thing especially important for educators: the notion of potential. However, he reconstructed that notion in a pragmatic sense that valued process over outcome and emerging constructions over fixed ends.

On the political side, Dewey decries many of the tenets of classical democratic liberalism including egoistic, ahistorical, and atomistic individualism. He also rejects innate free will along with innate rationality such as that advocated by Kantians as much as Utilitarians, especially that of the hedonistic maximizing of pleasure while minimizing pain variety. He also rejects the classical liberal confinement of the role of the state in securing the social good. There can also be no doubt that Dewey was personally committed to some form of socialism, although he strongly rejected Marxist communism. Instead of the typical early twentieth-century divide between capitalist and communist positions, he advocated the search for a third way of social reconstruction based on democracy as participatory and pluralistic experience on all levels of human interaction and communication.

One only has to look at contemporary global education driven by international economic competition keyed in the leading and emerging post-industrial nations to the Programme for International Student Assessment (PISA) financed by the Organisation for Economic Co-operation and Development (OECD). In many ways, educational standardization does for the refinement of raw human capital in the twenty-first century into interchangeable parts for the global production function what industrial production did for the refinement of raw materials as interchangeable parts in the nineteenth century.

In an earlier book (Garrison, Neubert & Reich, 2012), we recontexualized Dewey in terms of several prominent late-twentieth-century thinkers. We especially concentrated on the writings of the neo-pragmatist Richard Rorty, the more or less post-structuralist (or post-modernist) critiques of Pierre Bourdieu, Michel Foucault, Jacques Derrida, Emmanuel Levinas, and finally, Zygmunt Bauman. Here we take a different approach. Working closely on essential parts of Dewey's text, we intend to put Dewey into critical and creative encounters with relevant challenges of education in our time. We hope that this project may provide opportunities for readers to reconsider and perhaps reconstruct *Democracy and Education* for themselves and their own unique context.

The impact of *Democracy and Education*, at the time of its publication, was simultaneously in the dimensions of education and politics. We read the book today as a classic in both fields. We think it is unfortunate that many readers have underestimated the political and philosophical relevance of the book. This especially holds in a time like ours when many take democracy as something given and self-maintaining. Dewey, in *Democracy and Education*, and still more insistently in his later texts on political philosophy like *The Public and Its Problems* or *Liberalism and Social Action*, understood democracy as a challenge for continual reconstruction—as something to be preserved and developed. If we reconsider *Democracy and Education* today, we must do so through the lens of his challenging political positions since the 1920s, for instance with regard to the contradictions of democracy and capitalism, individualism and solidarity, compartmentaliza- tion of life and democratic communication, corporate power and democratic participation, vested interests and public decision making.

In addition, his increasing emphasis on artistic creation and aesthetic appreciation marks another important transformation in the later Dewey. We will attend to Dewey's aesthetic turn along with other developments, including his increasing emphasis on how meaning and knowing grow from the embodied and impassioned conditions of life, the nature of technology, and the transactional- ism that is central to his last book, *Knowing and the Known*, authored with Arthur Bentley. In his autobiographical essay, "From Absolutism to Experimentalism," Dewey complains:

> Although a book called *Democracy and Education* was for many years that in which my philosophy, such as it is, was most fully expounded, I do not know that philosophic critics, as distinct from teachers, have ever had recourse to it. I have wondered whether such facts signified that philos- ophers in general, although they are themselves usually teachers, have not taken education with sufficient seriousness for it to occur to them that any rational person could actually think it possible that philosophizing should focus about education as the supreme human interest in which, moreover, other problems, cosmological, moral, logical, come to a head.
>
> (LW 5: 156)

Here, Dewey scolds philosophers for their failure to appreciate education. On the other hand, few in education attend to the fact that most of Dewey's publications were on the traditional topics of philosophy (e.g., epistemology, metaphysics, anthropology, morality, logic, and, later, aesthetics) for an audience of specialists in the field. While few philosophers even today appreciate the importance of education for understanding philosophy, most educators fail to realize the philosophical depth of Dewey's thinking about education.

In our book, we will reconsider Dewey by drawing on his philosophical work before and especially after the publication of *Democracy and Education*. Indeed, because he writes so much less on education after 1916, this is necessary to carry out the kind of reconsideration we intend. We will call attention to diverse educational, social, cultural, and philosophical themes and connections in Dewey. In the first eight chapters, we proceed in roughly the same way. This is the part of our book where we give a substantial reconsideration that is fairly close to Dewey's text. First, we strive to extract the core meaning of those chapters of *Democracy and Education* upon which we focus. Second, we enrich the argumentation by drawing on carefully selected sections of his other writings. Third, we recontextualize the Deweyan positions with regard to contemporary situations, conditions, and debates. This part focuses on what seems to us the most important challenge for today. Fourth, we close by citing Dewey's summary from his respective chapters followed by our own summary.

At the beginning of each chapter, we will indicate the chapters of *Democracy and Education* to which our chapter refers. Starting with Chapter 9 we loosen our grip to the original text by turning deliberately to three core challenges in contemporary educational discourses; namely, we discuss issues of "class, race, gender, and disability" in Chapter 9, "capitals as contexts of education" in Chapter 10, and "ways to democratic inclusion" in Chapter 11. We do so on the basis of selected readings from the later Dewey and of the argumentation of our foregoing chapters, which is to say that we try to respond to these issues and challenges from what we think can be a reconsidered and reconstructed Deweyan perspective for our time. The closing Chapter 12 of our book comes back more closely to Dewey's text again.

Upon the whole, our Chapters 1–8 correspond with Dewey's Chapters 1–14 of *Democracy and Education*. At the start of his Chapter 24, Dewey explains that he has divided his book in three parts. The third part begins after Chapter 17. We briefly discuss Chapter 15 on "Play and Work in the Curriculum" in our Chapter 10. Chapters 16 and 17 of *Democracy and Education* are concerned with specific subject matters (i.e., geography, history, and science), which we preferred not to single out for special attention compared to mathematics, social studies, and such. Of Chapters 18–23, Dewey tells us "the discussion took for granted the democratic criteria and its application to social life"; hence, these chapters consider "the present limitations of its [democracies] actual realization" (MW 9: 332). Our Chapters 9–11 do the same for our time.

Our closing Chapter 12, "Philosophy as Education: From Pragmatism to Constructivism" corresponds to Dewey's Chapter 24, "Philosophy of Education." It offers readers a conclusion that strongly argues for a renewed awareness of the necessary connections between education and philosophical reflection to over-come vested reductionisms—like thinking in numbers more than experiences and contexts, learning for the test instead of learning for life, privileging standardization over context—that have become predominant in many fields of educational research today.

As authors of this book, we agree that pragmatism and social (or cultural) constructivism are companions in contemporary education. We believe Dewey was one of the most important predecessors of what today we call constructivism in education (see Hickman, Neubert & Reich, 2009). Two of the present authors, Kersten Reich and Stefan Neubert, are proponents of the Cologne program of interactive constructivism.[2] Jim Garrison writes extensively on Dewey's social constructivism and finds the critical reflections on Dewey's constructivism offered by the Cologne constructivists a creative extension of his thinking suitably adapted to our times.[3]

Constructivist approaches have proliferated during the last decades not only in learning theory but also in the social sciences and cultural theory. Interactive constructivism is a program that puts emphasis on the necessary social and cultural dimensions. Among other things, its perspectives are relevant for education, and more generally the social sciences and humanities, because they provide at least the following three advantages that can be subsumed, for reasons of convenience, under the labels of "constructions," "methods," and "practices."

Like pragmatism, interactive constructivism values the constructive side of human knowledge and provides a model for explaining the mutual interrelation between observing, acting, and participating in lived cultures as necessary contexts of learning and educational growth. Both pragmatism and interactive constructivism have very broad approaches to experience and education, taking account of discursive diversity and the singularity of events, along with social and cultural contexts of constructions that steadily undergo transformation in response to social and cultural changes. They both take pains to consider the following tension: If we overemphasize the aspect of constructions, we are readily inclined to a rather subjectivist approach that neglects the cultural contexts of constructions.[4] However, to underestimate the individually constructive side will render us oblivious to the constructive powers necessary for releasing our creative, spontaneous, and innovative processes. With regard to democracy and education, Dewey already had a clear implicit understanding that both sides need to be properly recognized. In interactive constructivism, we use the terms observer, participant, and agent to articulate a theoretical understanding of this tension. The constructive side in education and learning appears most obviously in the learners' role as observers who participate in the active construction of their learning. Living in culture, we are always participants, observers, and agents simultaneously. We may only distinguish them for the purpose of abstract analysis, but we may never cleave them entirely apart in concrete practice. As participants, we are constrained by the expectations, conventions, norms, and standards that are involved in cultural practices, routines, and institutions. Culture always has us before we have it. This involvement frames and often limits our experiences, opportunities of acting, and of observing. We are always participants in culture when we are observers, whether distant observers or self-observers. As observers, we still have the freedom to choose between different perspectives according to our selective interests. Therefore, in the role of observers there is always a diversity of perspectives and possible interpretations. However, even as the most deconstructive and reconstructive observers, we never cease being cultural agents that must respond to cultural norms and constructions. As agents, we live in the world of action where we must respond to the challenges of diverse situations and realize our own intentions in cooperation, communication, and conflict with other agents, groups, institutions and so on. The role of the agent, therefore, refers to aspects of learning by doing in connection with cultural participation.

Failure to consider all three roles together leads to a reductionist understanding of learning and education. A narrow focus only on observation easily leads to a merely subjectivist understanding of education and learning. A narrow focus only on participation overemphasizes a one-sided adaptive and affirmative understanding of socialization. A narrow focus only on action reduces experience to doing for the sake of doing without taking larger conditions and consequences into account.

Pragmatism and interactive constructivism do not restrict their methodological approaches to narrow procedures of warranting truth claims, trying to exhaust all disturbing elements by reduction in order to secure ultimate unambiguousness and validity in the frame of a scientific interpretive community. Rather, they explore methods in their interrelation with constructions and practices in cultural contexts. In this connection, they call attention to the ineradicable indeterminacy of knowledge that remains despite all methodical sophistication. Overemphasizing methodological aspects easily leads us into methodical rigidity, which often only blocks innovations. Nonetheless, to neglect the methodological side will lead to arbitrariness. Democracy and education need clear and elaborated methodological approaches and methodical tools as developed in Deweyan pragmatism as well as in interactive constructivism. The reader will find in the following book a systematic network of theoretical concepts and perspectives that provide methodological orientations for research on democracy and education, as well as a suggestion of methods for educational and democratic practices in teaching and learning.

Pragmatism and interactive constructivism take the viabilities of human practices, routines, and institutions as the starting point for discussing the successes or failures of constructions and methods, their usefulness or harmfulness, beauty or ugliness, adequacy or inadequacy as seen by observers, participants, and agents. The focus on practices helps to criticize strategies of closed discourses or ivory-tower speculations that attempt to immunize themselves against generous practical testing. Cultural practices as well as scientific and philosophical discourses are seen in interrelation and mutual reference. Many cultural practices have become possible through constructions and methods in the sciences and arts. On the other hand, the sciences and arts derive their concepts as well as frames of interpretation and methodological orientations and settings from larger cultural contexts. If we overemphasize the aspect of practices, we will readily end up in an uncritical sort of activism that accepts any view whatsoever as viable as long as it fits the prevailing order. If we underestimate the practical side, we may easily get lost in merely theoretical speculations and fictitious contentions with practically irrelevant adversaries.

In the 12 chapters of our book, we will introduce other and more specific core concepts of interactive constructivism along the way as we connect them with fundamental concepts of Deweyan pragmatism. With a specific focus in each chapter, we will show what the combination of pragmatist and constructivist perspectives can achieve for democracy and education in theory and practice with a special eye on the indispensability of philosophical reflection and criticism for both. We do so by addressing important constellations in social, cultural, political, and educational thought and practice that are often characterized by tensional relationships between forces, interests, developments, claims, and so on. For us these constellations and tensions represent crucial challenges for democracy and education in each chapter.

The architecture of this book and its 12 chapters is a construction that deserves a brief explanation. First, it is not our claim to cover the whole content and comprehensiveness of Dewey's book in all facets. His *Democracy and Education* contains 26 chapters while our book has only 12. What we do not address are the more specific questions and concerns connected with several fields of education and learning like specific subject matters inside and out of school. Unlike Dewey, we do not directly address teaching and learning in disciplines like geography, history, natural sciences, or vocational education (See MW 9: 16, 17, and 23). We think that in our times specialization has reached a degree that makes it presumptuous and even impossible to attempt such a comprehensive grasp in one book. To avoid overspecialization and narrow confinement of disciplines, however, we think it is necessary to rethink and reconstruct approaches in all of these fields from the perspective of a philosophy of education that reconsiders Dewey in and for our time.

What we address in this book are Dewey's philosophical core ideas about education from a democratic perspective. Roughly speaking, our text responds to the first 14 chapters of his book. Our procedure has a similar structure in every chapter. First, we expose a condensed portrait of Dewey's main concepts in the respective parts of *Democracy and Education*. Second, we supplement this portrait with arguments taken from other writings of Dewey's, especially from works published later. Third, we discuss what we think is a core challenge for education today in connection with the topics of each chapter. Here we attempt to reconsider and even reconstruct Dewey from a critical perspective that draws on constructivist assumptions and approaches of our time and responds to the changed constellations in education, society, culture, science, philosophy, and so on.

With this book we hope to provide a valuable companion to Dewey's *Democracy and Education* that could nonetheless stand on its own to inspire scholarship in the broad and challenging field of rethinking the implications of the text in all branches, fields, and disciplines of education.

Acknowledgement: The authors wish to acknowledge the helpful reading of the following students: Melissa Rose-McCully, Corey D. English, Lisa K. Penningtonn, Miranda L. Sigmon, Ren Harma, David Plaxco, Andrea Sharpe-Robinson, Veronica L. van Montfrans, Ayeshah Alazmi, Lisa B. Wever, Amanda B. Banks, Adrien DeLoach, and Rebecca Raine Raab.

Notes

1 We will also avail ourselves of the recovery of a manuscript believed lost in 1947 and recently published as "Unmodern Philosophy and Modern Philosophy," see Garrison (2014).
2 Cf. for example Neubert & Reich (2006, 2008, 2012); Reich (2007, 2008, 2009, 2012); Garrison (2008); Hickman, Neubert & Reich (2009); Green, Neubert & Reich (2012); Neubert (2012b).
3 See for instance, Larochelle, Bednarz & Garrison (1998) and Garrison (1995, 2008).
4 This is the way of radical constructivism, e.g., von Glasersfeld (1995); von Foerster (2003).

1

EDUCATION AS A NECESSITY OF LIFE

Every living creature is mortal and must perish. It is no different for human beings. We seldom pause to reflect on this fact of human existence, although every adult is more or less aware of it. Almost no one ever makes the connection to education, although it is perfectly evident and immensely important. It is why Dewey titles the opening section of his first chapter "Renewal of Life by Transmission." Humanity reproduces itself in two ways, biologically and culturally. Without biological reproduction, we would vanish as a species. Without cultural reproduction, all our cultural accomplishments upon which our biological preservation now depends, including all the meanings that live in language, the moral beliefs and values that help preserve our social group, the knowledge we have acquired across millennia, and much more, would likewise disappear. Education is the site of cultural reproduction. Dewey's Darwinism appears from the very beginning of the book and leads immediately to profound educational consequences.

In part, we may read *Democracy and Education* as an attempt to come to terms with Darwinism in the modern world; we are still struggling, which is one reason why Dewey's book remains so relevant. In his essay, "The Influence of Darwin on Philosophy," Dewey proclaims:

> In laying hands upon the sacred ark of absolute permanency, in treating the forms that had been regarded as types of fixity and perfection as originating and passing away, the *Origin of Species* introduced a mode of thinking that in the end was bound to transform the logic of knowledge, and hence the treatment of morals, politics and religion.

> (MW 4: 3)

He could have added education. Dewey strives to come to grips with a world in which everything evolves, in which there are no permanent identities for species, cultures or persons, no immutable epistemological or moral foundations, and in which there is no ultimate teleology, no perfect ideal ends or goals. All we may ever hope for are relatively enduring, stable, and reliable beliefs and values. In science, we may never expect to complete what Dewey calls "the quest for certainty" (LW 4). We may only secure well-warranted claims to knowledge. Dewey understands that Darwin's book "precipitated a crisis" (MW 4: 3). We might call it the crisis of the modern quest for order. This crisis is inevitable because the quest for order implies the expectation to cast out ambivalence by meta-narratives that present a world that is complete, transparent and comprehensively comprehended. The crisis appears throughout the history of modernity in many forms, some of which Dewey had already addressed in his philosophical criticisms.

The developments of sciences and technologies and the age of Enlightenment strongly influenced the crises of early modernity. In our own time—which Zygmunt Bauman (2000) calls "liquid modernity" to express the fluidity of a world in all its practices, institutions, concepts, and identities—we are still struggling with problems of modernity and ambivalence, tensions between order and uncertainty, conflicts of particular interests and equal opportunities and so on.

Dewey approaches education with biological and cultural insights that are remarkably clear and straightforward. However, because of their evolutionary depth, what initially appears quite unassuming and easily understood soon becomes intricate and complex as the ideas develop.[1] To survive and thrive, every species must successfully interact with its environment to meet its needs and desires; human beings (i.e., *Homo sapiens*) are no exception. Dewey reminds us: "Continuity of life means continual re-adaptation of the environment to the needs of living organisms" (MW4: 4). However, Dewey does not confine "life" just to the narrow biological sense. "Life," Dewey declares, "covers customs, institutions, beliefs, victories and defeats, recreations and occupations" (MW 4: 5). Human nature is a part of nature; hence, not its lord and master. The arts are an expression of human intelligence. Like opposable thumbs, our intelligence evolved according to Darwinian natural selection to enable survival and reproduction. It also enables aesthetic delight and reverent awe before the unfathomable mystery that there is something rather than nothing and, for a moment, we are among the actualized possibilities of the cosmos. Culture may approach the rest of nature as a gardener wishing to cultivate their garden. Dewey once wrote:

> We are led to conceive, not of the conflict between the garden and the gardener; between the natural process and the process of art dependent upon human consciousness and effort. Our attention is directed to the possibility of interpreting a narrow and limited environment in the light of a wider

and more complete one,—of reading the possibilities of a part through its place in the whole. Human intelligence and effort intervene, not as opposing forces but as making this connection . . . [M]an is an organ of the cosmic process in effecting its own progress.

(EW 5: 38)

In the lives of human beings, culture and biology are not completely separable; nature and nurture interact and may mutually modify each other.[2] Dewey famously used one word, "experience," to unify both, and to designate the entire range of human experience both individual and collective over enumerable generations.

In his essay "The Inclusive Philosophic Idea" (LW 3: 41–54), Dewey argues that the separation of natural and social/cultural often leads philosophical reflection astray and that the principle of continuity and interaction implies to start with the social in all its complexity, even when observing nature. From this perspective, philosophy and the sciences are constructions out of social-cultural and historical contexts and, as Dewey argues in "Context and Thought," "the most pervasive fallacy of philosophic thinking goes back to neglect of context" (LW 6: 5).

For Dewey, culture *emerges* from nature without breach of continuity. Therefore, human culture itself is a part of nature. It is the realization of some of nature's possibilities. We must avoid constructing a nature versus culture dualism. Although we may never reduce culture to physical or biological nature, we must never forget the dependence of the former on the latter. Nor should we forget that culture affects physical and biological nature. Deweyan pragmatism is consistent with ecological responsibility.[3]

Dewey identifies three plateaus of existence, each of which emerges from the matrix of the one below (see LW 1: Ch. 7). The distinction among them is "one of levels of increasing complexity and intimacy of interaction among natural events" (LW 1: 200). The first plateau is that of the "physico-chemical," whose distinctive properties are those depicted by the mathematical and mechanical systems of physics and chemistry. The second plateau is that of the "psycho-physical," which is the animate level of life involving carbon-based organic functioning studied by biology as well as the lower mental functioning of animals. The third is that of "body-minds." It involves "association, communication, participation" that "define mind as intellect: possession of and response to meanings" (LW 1: 209). This is the familiar level of culture and the social construction of cognition, of linguistic meaning, and logical essences. Dewey explains:

> But body-mind simply designates what actually takes place when a living body is implicated in situations of discourse, communication and participation. In the hyphenated phrase body-mind, "body" designates the continued and conserved, the registered and cumulative operation of factors

continuous with the rest of nature, inanimate as well as animate while
"mind" designates . . . a wider, more complex and interdependent situation.
(LW 1: 217)

Each plateau actualizes the potential of the plateau below much as water (H_2O)
extinguishes many kinds of combustion while hydrogen (H) is highly combustible
and oxygen (O) sustains combustion. You cannot reduce one level to the next
without losing essential properties.

The three plateaus accord well with Dewey's philosophical principles of
continuity and interaction. Dewey is *not* a reductive materialist. We cannot reduce
minds to brains and it is an even worse mistake to try to reduce minds to Turing
machines (i.e., computers). Pain and fear have a neuro-physiological biological
base, but the *meaning* of pain is not reducible to neurons firing any more than
the meaning of the color "red" is reducible to 7100 Angstroms (see LW 15: 113).
It is one thing to have an experience; it is another thing to have a meaningful
experience. When the same neurons are firing in two different people, one may
find it meaningless agony while another may find divine inspiration through
participating in the passion of Christ.

The distinction of the three plateaus is useful, but it is only an observer
perspective from a social and cultural standpoint and context and not reified
as a simple realistic account of existence in the sense of epistemological copy
theory. This is problematic because it reduces observer perspectives to a
simplified overview of connected fields for specific observation. This may reflect
established research divisions and habits in modern science, but according to
the philosophical principle of continuity we must insist that what happens
between such possible plateaus is as important as what happens within. Therefore,
we might equally distinguish a multitude of other fields of observation. This would
lead to the distinction of any number of possible plateaus—as sciences in all
their diversity show—and thus some philosophers even speak of a "thousand
plateaus" implying that the task of identifying plateaus is infinite (cf. Deleuze &
Guattari 1988).[4]

Dewey sometimes shows a tendency to over-universalize his interpretations
as an observer and fails to acknowledge distant observer perspectives—for instance,
when he rather unqualifiedly compares "civilization" and "savage tribes" with
regard to educational functions (see MW 9: 5, 6, 52). While Dewey's pluralism
implies he is usually ready and willing to change perspectives from the self- to
the distant-observer stance, his failure to do so in his "civilization" versus "savage
tribes" divide causes some to detect an occasional, subtle, and unintended racism
in Dewey's thought (see, e.g., Sullivan, 2006 and Fallace, 2011).[5] In these parts
of his text we can observe an influence of Western mainstream thought to portray
all cultures on one plateau or—as influenced by the historical experiences of
colonialism—on different plateaus that constitute a stairway from lower to higher
positions. This concept of a stairway to modernization downplays the diversity

and incommensurability of cultures that Dewey seems to become more aware of in his later writings (cf. MW 11: 41–54; LW 10).

The transmission of experience among individuals within a generation and collective experience across generations is a matter of communication. Dewey is a pioneer in anticipating the paramount import of communication for twentieth-century education. He observes:

> Society not only continues to exist *by* transmission, *by* communication, but it may fairly be said to exist *in* transmission, *in* communication. There is more than a verbal tie between the words common, community, and communication Men live in a community in virtue of the things which they have in common; and communication is the way in which they come to possess things in common. What they must have in common in order to form a community or society are aims, beliefs, aspirations, knowledge— a common understanding—like-mindedness as the sociologists say.
>
> (MW 9: 7, original italics)

Fundamentally, communication involves *creatively* working together to make something in common. Communion requires more than just cognitive verbal communication:

> This transmission occurs by means of communication of habits of doing, thinking, and feeling from the older to the younger. Without this communication of ideals, hopes, expectations, standards, opinions, from those members of society who are passing out of the group life to those who are coming into it, social life could not survive.
>
> (MW 9: 7)

Communication involves emotional and intellectual dispositions, and for Dewey both are equally important to healthy human functioning and development. We cannot think our world properly unless we can feel it appropriately and we cannot feel it appropriately unless we think it properly.

Dewey wishes to avoid the great vice of intellectualism. "By 'intellectualism' as an indictment," he writes, "is meant the theory that all experiencing is a mode of knowing" (LW 1: 28). We sustain many relations to existence, including doubt, joy, melancholy, despair, tragedy, reverence, amusement, fear, confusion, and hope. Further, we may communicate these relationships with the world and with each other unconsciously and below the level of cognition. Sympathy for others is as primordial as anger, and we often communicate our feeling in ways beyond words; indeed, such communication often betrays the emptiness of mere intellectual meaning and knowing as anyone that has ever loved surely knows.

Non-cognitive feelings and embodied habits of response that perform intelligent functions involving "know-how" instead of conscious propositional cognition (i.e., "knowing that") are dispositions to act that constitute the content of our character and the correctness of our actions as much as, and often more than, abstract principles and concepts. Very young children and the profoundly cognitively impaired may "read" their parents and teachers even when they cannot read a book.

Once we understand communication at depth, we may appreciate how communicative interactions among individuals reciprocally constitute everyone in the community that participates:

> Not only is social life identical with communication, but all communication (and hence all genuine social life) is educative. To be a recipient of a communication is to have an enlarged and changed experience. One shares in what another has thought and felt and in so far, meagerly or amply, has his own attitude modified. Nor is the one who communicates left unaffected. Try the experiment of communicating, with fullness and accuracy, some experience to another, especially if it be somewhat complicated, and you will find your own attitude toward your experience changing . . .
>
> (MW 9: 8)

Following these insights about the fundamental relation of education and communication, we must reject the confines of the conduit metaphor of communication and with it computer metaphors of the mind and self. We do not simply encode information and then send it down a pipe for a passive recipient to decode it at the other end.[6] Communication involves active interpretation, which includes misinterpretation, and the reciprocally transforming co-construction of meaning. Further, we communicate feelings as well as thoughts, and we cannot encode feeling in bits and bites of information. Dewey thought that except for "commonplaces and catch phrases [and bits of information] one has to assimilate, imaginatively, something of another's experience in order to tell him intelligently of one's own experience. All communication is like art" (MW 9: 9). In complete communication, we constructively *create* shared meanings together. It involves emotional perception, social awareness, and having a "feel" for the other person in a shared situation. Empathy must abound. In performing all these complex reticulated functions, we co-create (reciprocally transform) each other. Dewey has an emergent theory of communication. Communication involves information, but we must avoid reducing all communication to information processing. It is that, but much more than that. Dewey observes that communication has instrumental as well as consummatory (i.e., immediately fulfilling) aspects. With regard to the latter, he also uses the term "final":

> Communication is uniquely instrumental and uniquely final. It is instrumental as liberating us from the otherwise overwhelming pressure of

events and enabling us to live in a world of things that have meaning. It is final as a sharing in the objects and arts precious to a community, a sharing whereby meanings are enhanced, deepened and solidified . . . communication and its congenial objects . . . are worthy as means, because they are the only means that make life rich and varied in meanings. They are worthy as ends, because in such ends man is lifted from his immediate isolation and shares in a communion of meanings.

(LW 1: 159)

Meanings have an aesthetic as well as instrumental aspect. In Chapter 3, we will explore this further.

Because social life depends upon communication, "not only does social life demand teaching and learning for its own permanence, but the very process of living together educates" (MW 9: 9). Schooling is only a small part of education. Most of what we know, believe, and value we learned elsewhere by participating in social practices involving family, friends, public institutions, media, and more. Here we have the source of Dewey's now familiar distinction between formal and informal education (MW 9: 12).

Informal education is an incidental, even accidental, and often inadvertent hodgepodge of learning by living, working, and playing together that is, nonetheless, quite meaningful even if rather chaotic. However, institutions designed for specific practical purpose structure society. These purposes educate in a more structured way. To participate in an organized social practice, we must acquire the appropriate intellectual habits and emotional dispositions. Participating in organized religion is a good example; so too is economic participation.

At first, institutions achieve their purposes without conscious reflection upon their consequences beyond those explicitly intended:

While it may be said, without exaggeration, that the measure of the worth of any social institution, economic, domestic, political, legal, religious, is its effect in enlarging and improving experience; yet this effect is not a part of its original motive, which is limited and more immediately practical.

(MW 9: 9)

For instance, organized religion arose to "secure the favor of overruling powers" (MW 9: 9). What Dewey means is that initially any social institution simply serves as a means to securing some socially valued experience as its ideal end. At first, this is done unreflectively according to the established customs of a given culture. However, all human action has unintended as well as intended consequences. Among these are the effects of institutions on the lives and consciousness of people participating in them. It is one thing for an institution, or an individual participating in it, to do something for a purpose, it is another to become self-consciously aware of what pursuing, and perhaps securing, that purpose truly means. Eventually, we may become reflectively aware of "the quality and extent of conscious life," and eventually this awareness may be considered as "a directive factor in the conduct of the institution" (MW 9: 9–10).

The more humankind comes to recognize some of the consequences on them of any institution or form of life and not just the effects on the external world, the more they seek to regulate and direct it. For Dewey, institutions are not given by nature. Rather, they are contingent, falsifiable social constructions. Whatever we construct we create to satisfy our finite purposes. Hence, they are subject to deconstruction, reconstruction, and even complete destruction. However, in actual debates and attempts to understand changes in nature and culture, the embeddedness of social practices often goes unnoticed as compared to the immediately apparent and often rather material side of events. When this occurs, the contingency and falsifiability of cultural constructions are concealed. They are then reified as eternal and immutable essences that lie beyond critique and reconstruction.

Consider the idea of "intelligence." Stephen Jay Gould (1996), in the second and revised edition of his award-winning *The Mismeasure of Man*, challenges biological determinism, which he understands as the belief that "shared behavioral norms, and the social and economic differences between human groups—primarily races, classes, and sexes—arise from inherited, inborn distinctions and that society, in this sense, is an accurate reflection of biology" (1996: 52). He sees the problem as arising from the reification of the abstract idea of "intelligence":

> We recognize the importance of mentality in our lives and wish to characterize it, in part so we can make the divisions and distinctions among people that our cultural and political systems dictate. We therefore give the word "intelligence" to this wondrously complex and multifaceted set of human capabilities. This shorthand symbol is then reified and intelligence achieves its dubious status as a unitary thing.
>
> (Gould, 1996: 52)

From a Deweyan perspective, we must recognize that all abstractions are constructions carried out by someone or some community for some purpose or another. Once reified, such concepts as "intelligence" are taken as given in nature rather than as contingent and falsifiable social constructions. When Dewey speaks of "intelligence," he means the wondrously complex and multifaceted set of human capabilities.

The scientific and industrial age, like the ages before it, often forgets to comprehend its own practices in view of their social backgrounds and roots as well as effects and consequences:

> Even to-day, in our industrial life, apart from certain values of industriousness and thrift, the intellectual and emotional reaction of the forms

of human association under which the world's work is carried on receives little attention as compared with physical output.

(MW 9: 10)

Dewey believes that the emergence of institutions of formal education like schools is a response to growing complexity in social life. This applies to all modern societies. Today, 100 years after Dewey wrote *Democracy and Education*, formal education in all industrial and post-industrial nations gears into global economic competition with all its increasing complexities. The current trend to economize education and orient it towards powerful market interests produces various kinds of educational ideologies and practices driven by the notion that the young provide human capital for the global production function. Standardized test scores increasingly determine success in global competition. The effect of such standardized tests, paired with standardized curriculum and teaching methods is to refine human capital into standardized interchangeable parts in the global production function. But, from the perspective of democracy and education, the effect on our moral and aesthetic consciousness is devastating and it is not good to have education constrained solely to practical economic gain. We live by more than bread alone.

Dewey took it as a sign of moral progress that "humanity has made some headway in realizing that the ultimate value of every institution is its distinctively human effect—its effect upon conscious experience" (MW 9: 10). Once this realization dawns, society begins to take an interest in the kinds of consciousness formed by human association both structured and unstructured. When this occurs, it tends to introduce a new institution—formal education.

There is another impetus to the emergence of general formal education as its own distinct institution apart from other institutions. With the advance of technoscience, including social technoscience, society becomes increasingly specialized and complex and its storehouse of knowledge increasingly large: "the gap between the capacities of the young and the concerns of adults widens" (MW 9: 11). At this juncture, formal education (i.e., schooling) becomes fully instituted with specialists themselves inculcated in the practice: "Intentional agencies—schools—and explicit material—studies—are devised" (MW 9: 11). Still later, we arrive at professionals themselves formally taught to teach in schools of education.

While necessary, Dewey is wary of what occurs when formal instruction entirely separates itself from informal learning:

> But there are conspicuous dangers attendant upon the transition from indirect to formal education. Sharing in actual pursuit, whether directly or vicariously in play, is at least personal and vital . . . Formal instruction, on the contrary, easily becomes remote and dead—abstract and bookish, to use the ordinary words of depreciation.

(MW 9: 11)

Formal instruction too readily becomes detached from the practices unstructured as well as structured that initially gave learning its point and purpose. It becomes part of the deplorable compartmentalization of activities in modern life that Dewey repeatedly criticized throughout his work because it threatens the chances of continuity and interaction in human experience (see, e.g., LW 10).

Formal education relies primarily on abstract representative symbols, which is how technologically complex cultures store and transmit much of their knowledge. As Dewey observes: "It is far from translation into familiar acts and objects" (MW 9: 11). This distance provides useful contemplative perspectives, but becomes dangerous when there is little or no attempt to translate school knowledge back into the terms of everyday doings and makings. Schools turn into cloisters, or worse still, prisons of the mind and spirit. Any specialized institution risks severing from the larger society it seeks to serve. Schooling is no exception. School knowledge often cuts itself off from knowledge one can actually employ in practice. While the latter has direct use value, school knowledge often only has exchange value. That is, we may exchange it for success, power and privilege in a social order. But if learning generally and formal education in particular is confined to cash value in the marketplace, we denigrate the use value of learning and knowledge in the life of individuals and groups. From the perspective of democracy and education, this use value implies, e.g., that learning is a resource for acting constructively and cooperatively in a social world that depends on markets but is not only a marketplace. Dewey observes: "If democracy is possible it is because every individual has a degree of power to govern himself and be free in the ordinary concerns of life" (LW 6: 431). In Dewey's time as well as in ours, this divide largely goes hand in hand with power asymmetries between those who do and those who think. This social divide reflects the dualism of mind and body. This is disastrous for a pragmatist like Dewey, who believed that the essential aim of education in the broadest sense is to make individual, social, and collective practices more intelligent, critical, and constructive.

Dewey is deeply anxious that explicit, fully conscious, entirely symbolic formal cognitive learning will separate students from "what they unconsciously know because they have absorbed it in the formation of their characters by intercourse with others" (MW 9: 12). For him, we must never separate formal and informal education; we do harm to both sides if we, or the institutions in which we act as educators or learners, forget how deeply they are interwoven with each other. One danger in this context is "intellectualism" in the sense of taking the subjects of formal learning as substitutes of actual experiences. Schools as artificial learning environments always stand in danger of taking abstract symbolic forms for reality itself and of organizing learning processes solely through the lens and logic of formal theories. Dewey holds to the contrary: "An ounce of experience is better than a ton of theory simply because it is only in experience that any theory has vital and verifiable significance. An experience, a very humble experience, is capable of generating and carrying any amount of theory (or intellectual content), but a theory apart from an experience cannot be definitely grasped even as theory." (MW 9: 151). He worries that exclusively symbolic book learning will not entirely address "ordinary vital experience," by which he means the practical and emotional as well as intellectual dimensions of human experience. "Hence one of the weightiest problems with which the philosophy of education has to cope," Dewey contends, "is the method of keeping a proper balance between the informal and the formal, the incidental and the intentional, modes of education" (MW 9: 12).

Elsewhere, in *Art as Experience*, he explains: "The emotional phase binds parts together into a single whole; 'intellectual' simply names the fact that the experience has meaning; 'practical' indicates that the organism is interacting with events and objects which surround it" (LW 10: 61). This is at odds with behaviorism as it has influenced educational theories throughout the twentieth century. Reductionist behaviorism tends to focus on causal relations between stimulus and response as observable components of behavior thereby forgetting or even explicitly excluding as black-box emotional and cognitive aspects. Dewey himself, in his criticism of reductionist behaviorism, preferred the term conduct over behavior (cf. LW 5: 218–234) because he saw behavior always as part of action in the broader sense of doing and undergoing in experience. He anticipated that reductionist behaviorism would inevitably produce a host of behavior/emotion and behavior/cognition dualisms. Ironically, cognitive psychology often tends to do the same with action and emotion.

Today, with the constructivist turn that has taken place in recent decades in learning theories worldwide, it seems obvious that such reductionisms cannot do justice to learning processes in their complexity, diversity, and contextuality. Dewey strives throughout *Democracy and Education* to organically unify thought, feeling, and action as interdependent sub-functions of a single unified living function, thereby overcoming a host of false dualisms including those of mind versus body, thought versus feeling, self versus society among others.

Challenge for Today: Nature and Culture

If we consider the arguments given in this chapter from a broader perspective, we suggest that one of the main challenges of educational theory concerns the relation between nature and culture. This was true in Dewey's time as it is in ours. The position here taken throughout holds that we must see both sides as mutually connected and intertwined. Indeed, we can consider culture from a Darwinian standpoint as an emergent actualization of nature's potential. This claim stands against all tendencies to divide fields of inquiry and critical reflection into natural and cultural observations as reflected in the common split between the hard and soft sciences. As institutionalized to an advanced degree in our university systems today, the split actually becomes a gulf with regards to, e.g., administration, funding, influence, and social status. Although such hierarchies in the practices of science may never be completely avoidable, the current privilege of natural sciences seems problematic. Let us discuss this problematic from the standpoint of democracy and education.

First, we have to concede that part of the success of the natural sciences lies in their feasibility and practical efficiency in advancing technologies and increasing human welfare, prosperity, health, life-quality and so on. On the other hand, our generation—even more than in Dewey's lifetime—has come to experience technology as much more than a mere means by itself, but always a powerful cultural instrument with multiple environmental, social, economic, political, and other effects and side effects. If we pick up again the metaphor of the garden and the gardener mentioned above, we might say that the gardener not merely nurtures nature and natural growth, but constructs particular and specific "gardens" with unforeseen outgrowths that may even put at risk or destroy the plans of the gardener. The control of effects is itself a task we cannot accomplish without technologies, but often a narrow understanding of technological feasibility dominates over a more far-sighted sensitivity to social and cultural risks and costs.

Second, the Deweyan claim that the ultimate value of any (social, cultural, economic, political, education) institution lies in its contributions to making human life experiences more significant and valuable, gives us a clue for estimating the relative value of natural sciences and technologies in a democratic society. On the one hand, we should be critical with regard to the widespread tendency to adore and overestimate natural sciences and technologies while at the same time underestimating the social and cultural contexts in which they operate. We see this danger especially in the human sciences and education as appearing in all sorts of reductionism that function according to the nature/culture dualism, as when the mind is reduced to functions of the brain, when language is reduced to innate capacities, when social behavior is explained only by neurobiological processes, and so on. Contrary to the core convictions of Dewey's *Democracy and Education*, such reductionist tendencies seem to us to be currently increasing in influence and social reputation, because they apparently give human scientists and educators a clear "hard" and sustainable basis for formulating educational recipes that go with the reputation of natural science.

Third, in a capitalist society the privilege of natural sciences and technologies pays of itself as an exchange value on all markets. We must never neglect the power of markets in contemporary societies, even if we claim with Dewey that we must not confine education to the logic of markets. Against the background of these tensions, the capitalization and the economic narrowing of educational practices and institutions stands against a generous understanding of education as founded in experience in all its diversity and complexity. It leads to homogenization, standardization, generalized testing, will to measure, compartmentalization through selection, ranking, exclusion, and the suppression of difference and diversity. In this context, we think that Deweyan education today must consider the inevitable tension between necessary democratic claims to social and cultural diversity and capitalist competition.

Capitalism is a powerful context for interpreting nature and culture, and it has a tendency to reduce natural as well as social relations to forms of competition and to justify this tendency in terms of nature (see Hofstadter, 1944, 1992, especially Chapter 2). To some readers even the Deweyan claim to Darwinian naturalism may sound somewhat reductionist in this connection, because it seems to represent the notorious formula of "the survival of the fittest" that has been used in the nineteenth and twentieth centuries in Social Darwinist political ideologies and practices in brutal and very undemocratic ways as a program against diversity and the recognition of otherness. Social Darwinism attempted to apply the principle of the survival of the fittest and natural selection to social and political thought. Besides laissez faire capitalism, it has also been used to support eugenics and racism. In spite of the use of the word "Darwinism," the ideas of Social Darwinism are almost entirely due to Herbert Spencer. In his essay, "The Philosophical Work of Herbert Spencer," Dewey insists that we must strive "not only to understand the independence of Spencer's and Darwin's work in relation to each other, but the significance of this independence" (MW 3: 205). Dewey specifically mentions Spencer's false notion that evolution was teleological such that social progress is always assured, Spencer's emphasis on atomistic individualism (Darwinian evolution concerns populations), laissez faire theory, complete distrust of government, and Spencer's reading of social and political values back into nature as if they arose there. He might have added that Spencer was a Lamarckian; hence, not a Darwinian at all. Dewey does indicate that "whatever all this is, it is *not* evolution" (MW 3: 209). "Spencer is a monument," he concedes, "but, like all monuments, he commemorates the past" (MW 3: 208).

Following Dewey, we must recognize that we cannot realize democracy and education from scratch without taking the powerful contexts of modernity and capitalism seriously into account. This is a consequence of his philosophical anti-dualism. Dewey's life-long critical attitude towards laissez faire capitalism should be a reminder for us to question reductionist perspectives on nature like social Darwinist ideologies. While we may not simply overcome the dangers of reductionism to education, we must at least try to respond to it by construction and criticism (cf. LW 5: 125–144). We have dedicated our argumentation so far to the task of laying out some important theoretical frames and perspectives to criticize reductionism in education from the very start. Given Dewey's basic concepts of experience, habit, and communication in education, we may for example say that it is one pervasive trait of modernity that social life is often compartmentalized and social experience reduced to fixed categories. Such compartmentalization and reduction have become habitual and formed in institutional ways. The habits of reductionist compartmentalization influence our research and outlook on education. If, for instance, the classical behaviorists look on education, they see only stimulus and response around black boxes—the boxes implying the very issues that are at stake for education. When neuroscientists talk about education they often reduce learning processes to changes registered in scans of brains—the brains representing one isolated half of an unquestioned dualism. If neoliberal thinkers propagate education on a global scale as the formation of human capitals to increase economic welfare, they reduce experiences to market resources and life to a bargain counter—the market then apparently being the only place left for human interactions and communications. If educational specialists conceive of education in narrow ways like shortsighted measures of reform, one size (of teaching, evaluating, measuring, grading, and so on) for all, focusing on school or learners isolated from society, they forget about the necessary connections between education, individualism, citizenship, and democracy—taking a part of education for the whole.

Dewey's emergent continuity provides resources for criticizing these and other current reductionisms in education. From the perspective of interactive constructivism (see Garrison, Neubert & Reich, 2012, Chapter 4), the distinction between observer, participant, and agent positions can be helpful in explaining why reductionist positions seem to be seductive as well as effective while at the same time criticizing their dominance. The reductionist mainstream in education (as in other fields) is highly dangerous for democracy. Predominant perspectives on education are always constructions of observers within culture. There is no detached God's perspective or entirely decontextualized permanent neutral framework on education. There are only contingent and falsifiable cultural and individual interpretations. But we can distinguish between self- and distant-observer perspectives. The behaviorist, neuroscientist, neoliberal thinker, or educational specialist is a self-observer in the sense that they participate and act in the context of a specific discursive order with its selective interests, will to truth, and power games that constitute a discipline (see Foucault, 1981).

Unfortunately, we often neglect or underestimate these powerful contexts of subject positions that influence self-observer perspectives. Only if we take a larger view and turn from self-observer to distant-observer perspectives, we may find a meta-position from which we can by contrast reflect on the limits of our observations. Dewey's ideas about transactions in contexts remind us that there is always context involved in our self- and distant-observations, yet we still can take a narrower or broader view. If we consider the complexities of education, narrow ways of specification seem to be more responsive to powerful selective interests and they indeed produce important results in their limited fields. With regard to the complex contexts, however, they often tend to take the part for the whole. Against the background of precarious funding in education in almost all global societies, they often seem to combine efficiency with feasibility and provide tracks for successful careers. Therefore, it is hardly surprising that the current compartmentalization is so strong and omnipresent. All the more the challenge remains, if we conceive of education with Dewey in a broader sense, not only to combine the specialized results from different views, but even more importantly to overcome the very reductionism in order to save a generous understanding of democracy and education.

Even if it sounds utopian to overcome compartmentalization and reductionism altogether, it seems to us that on the profound level discussed in this first chapter, one advantage of connecting today with the Deweyan tradition lies in its capability to critically address the limits of specialization and division and their affirmative effects on social realities as given. As Bauman (2000) has argued, such affirmative perspectives conceive of criticism as giving hardly more than shortsighted and partial suggestions to fuel the machinery of light capitalism in the sense of making consumerism more smooth and pleasant. In education, we can observe a corresponding economization that depends on measuring small items, turning them into smooth components like credits, and employing them as resources in a game of cost and outcome.

For a discussion of Dewey's naturalism from a contemporary constructivist viewpoint, we suggest that it is possible for us today to distinguish between two perspectives on his statements about nature. As authors, we see the relevance and importance of both viewpoints and we think that it is useful for you, as our reader, to think about on which side you would prefer to position yourself.

Darwinian Naturalism

Dewey insists we must always see nature and culture in continuous, mutually modifying transaction with each other. Therefore,

> ways of interaction between human nature and cultural conditions are the first and the fundamental thing to be examined, and . . . the problem is to ascertain the effects of interactions between different components of different human beings and different customs, rules, traditions, institutions— the things called "social." A fallacy has controlled the traditional statement of the problem. It took results, good or bad—or both—of specific interactions as if they were original causes, on one side or the other, of what existed or else of what should exist.
>
> (LW 13: 286)

It is clear in this statement that Dewey conceives of certain images, or representations, ideas, and ideals of human nature as results of culture.

Actually, Dewey completely rejects the nature versus culture dualism. Instead he defended an "empirical naturalism or naturalistic empiricism" or "naturalistic humanism" in his version of pragmatism (LW 1: 10). For him, naturalistic, humanistic empiricism

> points to faith in experience when intelligently used as a means of disclosing the realities of nature. It finds that nature and experience are not enemies

or alien. Experience is not a veil that shuts man off from nature; it is a means of penetrating continually further into the heart of nature. There is in the character of human experience no index-hand pointing to agnostic conclusions, but rather a growing progressive self-disclosure of nature itself.

(LW 1: 4–5)

Evolving, ever-changing human nature is a *participant* in the evolution of the universe. Dewey is a Darwinian, which means that for him evolution is non-teleological. By progressive self-disclosure, he does not mean anything teleological. So what does he mean?

There are many ways to illustrate what Dewey proposes; here is only one. According to the best current cosmological theories, the original universe following the Big Bang was comprised of hydrogen that eventually condensed under the force of gravity into stars. Under continuing pressure, heavier elements began to fuse, which formed all the elements up to iron. When the first generation of stars began to collapse, the pressure led them to explode and disperse their contents as stardust throughout the expanding universe. Heavier elements emerged later with exploding nova and supernova that spread like dust across the expanding universe. Many of these elements comprise the human body. Indeed, since 93% of the mass human body is not hydrogen, we can say that we are primarily stardust. This is only one way to socially construct the meaning of nature. There are many others. We must distinguish existence from essence. Nature may exist before cultural meaning makers, but until beings capable of interpreting their world including their selves emerge as part of the self-disclosure of nature, nature itself is devoid of meaning and value.

Dewey titles the first chapter of *Art as Experience* "The Live Creature." There he claims

> Because experience is the fulfillment of an organism in its struggles and achievements in a world of things, it is art in germ. Even in its rudimentary forms, it contains the promise of that delightful perception which is esthetic experience.
>
> (LW 10: 25)

Other live creatures display a non-discursive, nonlinguistic intentionality. However, with human beings, language (meanings) provides the capacity to develop long-range purposes that we may, as creative agents, execute across a lifetime or a culture may develop over generations. Dewey titles the second chapter of *Art as Experience* "The Live Creatures and 'Ethereal Things'." He borrows the phrase "ethereal things" from the romantic poet Keats, who used it to designate those things that did not exist until human beings created them. Examples would be the rock garden of the Ryoanji Temple, the student drawings on the walls of a fourth grade classroom, and the currently heaviest element in the periodic table. *Ununoctium* did not exist in nature until nature progressively unfolded to actualize its potential to form human cultures and culture unfolded its potential to create

Ununoctium. We may say the same for the rock garden and the student drawings. Indeed, for the Deweyan naturalist, there are no meaning, knowing, and valuing until there are meaning, knowledge, and value makers. Such beings construct the meaning of nature, or even the very idea of nature. It is here we may perceive the greatest depths of constructivism; for many, it will appear an abyss.

For Dewey, there are no cosmic purposes fulfilling themselves in history. Although non-teleological, the disclosure is potentially infinite. Thus, we may take a mildly anthropocentric stance in saying that when nature contains the student drawings in a fourth grade classroom it has realized more of its possibilities than a universe that has only helium and non-human beings. Finally, we would like to remind the reader that natural science is only one way to understand the progressive unfolding of nature. There are the many other arts including music, architecture, sculpting, painting, and so on.[7] There are many different cultures and many different cultural interpretations of our personal and cultural origin. Science is one among many cultural symbolic representations constructed from an observer stance. We may view all the arts (including science) as simply different ways nature has evolved to understand itself. We would also like to remind the reader that there is nothing preventing the progressive destruction of any culture along with its artifacts as natural phenomena. Cultural constructions may be contingent and falsifiable, but we need them to maintain and exalt our lives, although we should be constantly willing to reconstruct them.

Cultural Constructivism

From the viewpoint of cultural constructivism, however, the question arises as what observer position Dewey himself takes when he makes his claims about Darwinian naturalism. If we consider his writings with that question in mind, we may distinguish two styles of argumentation that seem coherent with each other from the perspective of naturalism. Following Thomas S. Kuhn's (1962) theory of the structure of scientific revolutions, we may also speak of Darwinian naturalism as a paradigm. Paradigms provide observer positions for those who participate in them. The distinction between existence (say, events in nature) and essence (say, the meanings of events) is a fundamental observer position in naturalism and the whole point of our argumentation above in the foregoing section on Darwinian naturalism was to show that Dewey is consistent in building his pragmatist philosophy in accord with that important distinction. On this basis, there is the clear implication that Dewey positions himself as an observer, participant, and agent within a cultural context. When he does so, he may appeal to the natural sciences, but is not entirely dependent on them.

However, if we consider Darwinian naturalism itself as a construction in cultural history, we find a paradigm that is self-confident, sustainable, and largely viable in our culture for good reasons as shown in modernization, industrial, scientific, and technological growth. There can be no denying that cultural constructions in our time depend on empirical testing in ways that connect culture with nature.

But as participants in cultures with their diversity of traditions, paradigms, and controversial approaches to values and truth claims, we must admit that all observer theories depend on cultural contexts and selective interests, even if they appear as "natural", cohesive, and "indubitable" from within the paradigm itself. According to Kuhn, paradigms tend to exhaust those observations and results that do not fit into their frames of explanation. Considered as cultural constructions, we cannot exclude any scientific or philosophical approach from this meta-theoretical conclusion. Against this background, the very distinction between existence and essence gives a theoretical frame, while at the same time relying on specific observer positions. From the viewpoint of cultural constructivism the question is not, in the first place, whether the assumption behind the distinction is true or false, but to take the process of cultural construction into account. Deconstruction is a permanent challenge to take no paradigm as self-evident, not even constructivism. Naturalism is an evolvement in the history of Western philosophy and science. Among other things, it represents the reflection of important stages, e.g., in industrial, economical, scientific progresses that have changed conditions of living in almost all societies around the globe. As we see in contemporary contexts of globalization, progress has many faces. Postcolonial studies suggest in our time that with regard to global interdependencies there is a deep layer of power relations implied in Western narratives about progress. Darwinian naturalism is part of this larger context. If we consider it as a cultural construction, we may find that even the hypothesis of the "big bang" (although warranted to some extent by experimentation) is embedded in cultural narratives and not just a view into the heart of nature. Why is it so convincing in our culture? Given that there are only limited data, may we not ask whether the affinity of the "Big-Bang-hypothesis" with certain powerful religious narratives in Western culture, like the spark of creation by the hand of God, is purely incidental?

If we combine the foregoing reflections in regard to both Darwinian naturalism and cultural constructivism and draw a conclusion, we may say that the former is a paradigm that is still as viable in our time as it was in Dewey's. Cultural constructivism recognizes the viability and consistency of this paradigm while at the same time emphasizing its character as a cultural, historical, and contingent construction. Even if cultural constructivism, of course, admits that there is a world, or we may say nature, beyond our constructions and independent of our intentions as human beings, it insists that all descriptions and schemes of explanation about nature are constructions in the cultural contexts of their time. The challenge of deconstruction represents a kind of constructivist doubt with regard to the self-evidence of any paradigm. Dewey is very close to this constructivist conclusion, while his naturalism emphasizes the possibilities of growth and progress that characterize modern societies. The following quote shows his awareness of the complex relation between nature and culture, especially when he portraits nature as "an affair of affairs," because he leaves the interpretation of the meanings involved in such affairs completely to human cultures:

The genuine implications of natural ends may be brought out by considering beginnings instead of endings. To insist that nature is an affair of beginnings is . . . but another way of saying that nature is an affair of affairs, wherein each one, no matter how linked up it may be with others, has its own quality. It does not imply that every beginning marks an advance or improvement; as we sadly know accidents, diseases, wars, lies and errors, begin. Clearly the fact and idea of beginning is neutral, not eulogistic; temporal, not absolute. And since wherever one thing begins something else ends, what is true of beginnings is true of endings. Popular fiction and drama show the bias of human nature in favor of happy endings, but by being fiction and drama they show with even greater assurance that unhappy endings are natural events.

(LW 1: 83)

Darwinian naturalism as well as cultural constructivism must take "natural events" into account. Especially in education as a necessity of life, it is important to respond creatively and critically to the meanings attributed to natural events. What is the "nature" say of the child, of good learning, best education, just and fair relations, intelligence and so on? In all these and other respects, Dewey reminds us that nature purely as "existence" does not give us an answer to these questions. Rather, we have to find the meanings and "essences" by ourselves. In his manuscript published in 2012 under the title *Unmodern Philosophy and Modern Philosophy*, Dewey claims that philosophy is essentially a reflection of social beliefs and he has a clear understanding that such a task involves processes of construction as well as reconstruction and deconstruction—or what in the language of his time he called destruction. "For all philosophy as reflection upon existing beliefs operates both destructively and constructively" (Dewey, 2012: 20).

Dewey's Summary

It is the very nature of life to strive to continue in being. Since this continuance can be secured only by constant renewals, life is a self-renewing process. What nutrition and reproduction are to physiological life, education is to social life. This education consists primarily in transmission through communication. Communication is a process of sharing experience till it becomes a common possession. It modifies the disposition of both the parties who partake in it. That the ulterior significance of every mode of human association lies in the contribution it makes to the improvement of the quality of experience is a fact most easily recognized in dealing with the immature. That is to say, while every social arrangement is educative in effect, the educative effect first becomes an important part of the purpose of the association in connection with the association of the older with the younger. As societies become more complex in structure and resources, the need of formal or intentional teaching and learning increases. As formal teaching and training grow in extent, there is the danger of creating an undesirable split between the experience gained in more direct associations and what is acquired in school. This danger was never greater than at the present time, on account of the rapid growth in the last few centuries of knowledge and technical modes of skill.

(MW 9: 12–13)

Our Summary

Dewey's account of the necessity of education still holds today. We argued that his approach to understanding education in the tensional relations between culture and nature makes profound sense today. However, there is always the danger of preferring one side to the other. Although Dewey always saw the importance of culture, he sometimes tended, in accord with predominant opinions about science, to overestimate the side of nature. In his version of pragmatism as empirical naturalism (see LW 1), he did not consistently enough take into account that we only observe and construct nature as participants of a culture with specific versions of world-making and agents with selective interests. We have argued that there is no obvious and direct approach to nature and life. To speak of education as a necessity of life, as Dewey does in the first chapter of his book, should today be taken as a generous approach in the sense discussed above but not as a naturalistic claim that is unqualified by cultural contexts and insofar seems to be universal. This implies to be critical against reductionisms and to focus more on the long-term effects of educational policies and measures. In accord with Dewey's criticisms of compartmentalization of life, we suggest that more current perspectives on the reproduction of unfair and unequal opportunities through education, on diversity and power relations—not forgetting class, race, and gender, and on the economization and capitalization of educational fields and agents are necessary to continue Dewey's educational vision into our time.

Notes

1 Perhaps more than anything else, Dewey's Darwinism disturbs his detractors and rouses his admirers. Dewey's thinking was so advanced he is still referred to by prominent philosophers of biology and evolution. See Dennett (1995) and Kitcher (2005).
2 That nature is subject to nurture is now well established. For instance, phenotypic plasticity is the property of a given genotype to produce different phenotypes in response to distinct environmental conditions (see Pigliucci, 2001). Our genetic endowment alone does not necessarily determine our visible characteristics. Gene expression often depends on many other things including, but not limited to, environmental factors (from chemistry to parenting practices) during development. For an example of how parenting can control brain development (see Gregg, 2010).
3 Deweyan pragmatism is consistent with ecological responsibility (see Alexander, 2013).

4   For instance, Dewey assumes only human beings exist on the third plateau. However, as Steven Fesmire (2011) observes: "Dewey holds views that are today as empirically obsolete as Ptolemaic astronomy or Aristotelian biology. He echoes the prejudice of his contemporaries that all nonhuman animals act out of blind habit. . . His view that 'scientific men are under definite obligation to experiment upon animals' . . . was also typical of the 1920s, as was the still-common high/low evolutionary ladder metaphor" (p. 46). Fesmire also indicates: "The beauty of Dewey's naturalistic empiricism is that his own perspectives must be run through its threshing machine" (p. 47).

5   Nonetheless, Dewey played a minor role in establishing America's oldest and most influential civil rights organization, the National Association for the Advancement of Colored People (NAACP). He was an invited speaker at the inaugural meeting in 1909 and again in 1932.

6   To the open relation of processes of encoding and decoding, compare from a cultural studies perspective the influential essay of Hall (1973).

7   We say "other arts," because Dewey says that "science itself is but a central art auxiliary to the generation and utilization of other arts" (LW 10: 33). We will discuss Dewey's theory of intelligent inquiry in Chapter 8.

2

EDUCATION AS A SOCIAL FUNCTION

In every culture, both unintentional informal and deliberate formal education seek to socialize the young to become "robust trustees of its own resources and ideals" (MW 9: 14). Socialization is a necessary component of every culture. From the perspective of democracy and education, it is important to distinguish between education experienced as relatively narrow, unreflective adaptation to preexisting social conditions, expectations, practices, routines, institutions, on the one hand, and education experienced as encouraging and empowering for full, active, competent, critical, creative, and self-determined membership and participation in social processes on the other. It is especially important for educational theory and practice to consider the tensions and complex relations that exist between these two forms of socialization and their dependence on different historical, social, and cultural contexts.

Considered broadly, education as a social function is "concerned with the general features of the *way* in which a social group brings up its immature members into its own social form" (MW 9: 15).[1] Dewey does not approve of educational systems that indoctrinate the thoughts, habits, and feelings of the young to passively, obediently, and uncritically conform to the existing customs of a given culture. Every culture from the most self-reflectively democratic to the most mindlessly dogmatic strives to culturally reproduce its beliefs and values. However, the process is far more complex for the democrat than the dogmatist because unlike the latter the former believes that cultural reproduction involves continuous and necessary efforts to reflect and critically transform inherited customs, habits, beliefs, and values. Therefore, Dewey argues that one of the most important functions of philosophy and education lies in performing a "kind of intellectual disrobing" (LW 1: 40). Caught within the tension between education as uncritical and merely adaptive and education as creatively reflective, we "cannot permanently divest ourselves of the intellectual habits we take on and wear when we assimilate the culture of our own time and place. But intelligent furthering of culture demands that we take some of them off, that we inspect them critically to see what they are made of and what wearing them does to us" (LW 1: 40). For him, the self-critical fulfillment of this very task constitutes the difference between "individuals with minds"—i.e., socialized individuals in the narrow sense—and "individual minds"—i.e., more fully educated individuals as self-determined partakers in culture and society:

> I say individual minds, not just individuals with minds. The difference between the two ideas is radical . . . the whole history of science, art and morals proves that the mind that appears *in* individuals is not as such individual mind. The former is itself a system of belief, recognitions, and ignorances, of acceptances and rejections, of expectancies and appraisals of meanings which have been instituted under the influence of customs and tradition.
>
> (LW 1: 169–170)

Individuals with minds are the outgrowth of necessary processes of socialization involving the appropriation of conventional systems of knowledge in the contexts of prevailing social practices, institutions, and discourses—or what, according to Michel Foucault, we may call a set of socio-historical deposits and constellations that are connected with specific forms of power relations. The emergence of "individual minds"—as a result of education—constitutes the relative and always limited emancipation from such contexts—or, to put it differently, the relative and always contextual freedom of thought that is a necessary condition for genuine and self-determined democratic participation. Dewey believes that such freedom has more than just a negative side—i.e., the absence of constraints. Rather, it constitutes the critical, constructive, and reconstructive power of individuals in transaction with other individuals, groups, and societies to transform experience and culture:

> He knows little who supposes that freedom of thought is ensured by relaxation of conventions, censorships and intolerant dogmas. The relaxation supplies opportunity. But while it is a necessary it is not a sufficient condition. *Freedom* of thought denotes freedom of *thinking*; specific doubting, inquiring, suspense, creating and cultivating of tentative hypotheses, trials or experimentings that are unguaranteed and that involve risks of waste, loss, and error. Let us admit the case of the conservative; if we once start thinking no one can guarantee where we shall come out, except that many objects, ends and institutions are surely doomed. Every thinker puts some portion of an apparently stable world in peril and no one can wholly predict what will emerge in its place.
>
> (LW 1: 172)

Freedom involves risking our relationships and ourselves. Also, there are the paradoxes of freedom. Negative freedom, involves "freedom from" external constraint while positive freedom involves "freedom for" what requires self-discipline and constraint if we are to achieve our goals and purposes.

Culture has us before we have it. Becoming an individual with a mind of one's own is a lifelong endeavor of imaginative and reflective social self-creation. Otherwise, we are merely individuals with minds who think the thoughts prescribed to us by the customs of our culture. This becomes especially apparent in the consumer-driven popular media such as radio, television, the Web including social media such as Facebook, and the like. Merely doing what we unreflectively desire makes us a slave to our passions.

Let us now start to look more closely at different aspects of education as a social function. Dewey observes: "Beliefs and aspirations cannot be physically extracted and inserted" (MW 9: 14). So, he wonders, "How then are they communicated?" (MW 9: 14). Through the action of the environment is Dewey's answer. This leads to a stunning conclusion that is as undeniable as it is often ignored:

> We never educate directly, but indirectly by means of the environment. Whether we permit chance environments to do the work, or whether we design environments for the purpose makes a great difference. And any environment is a chance environment so far as its educative influence is concerned unless it has been deliberately regulated with reference to its educative effect.
>
> (MW 9: 23)

The metaphor of something being "food for thought" helps illustrate the point. "Others may present food or the conditions of education," Dewey declares, "but the individual alone can digest the food or educate himself" (MW 8: 342). Everything that lives has an aspect of autonomy. In many ways, we acquire and digest information much as we do food and drink. There is the truth in the old bromide, you can lead horses to water, but you cannot make them drink.

Etymologically, "instruction" derives from the Latin *instructus*, "arrange, inform, teach," literally "to build, erect," from *in-* "into." It is closely related to "inform" from Latin *informare* "to shape, form," figuratively "train, instruct, educate," from *in-* "into." This etymology suggests that instruction simply inserts learning "into" or "on" to the student to form them however we wish. This sense still dominates our thinking about teaching and learning. It inspires theories that the mind functions as an information processing machine (i.e., a computer) into which we may insert information. Genuine *education* is not like that. The problem is that a human being is a complex organism, which we can only comprehend as a living function.

Dewey approaches social and mental functioning as emerging from a matrix of biological functioning. Dewey's biological functionalism is familiar to any contemporary student of biology. We ourselves are biological beings. Let us follow Dewey's Darwinian functionalism from biological functioning to lower mental functioning involving the emergence of habits at the psycho-physical plateau to human social functioning and higher mental functioning that arises with the emergence of language in social groups. Habits are not merely biological adaptations of conduct, but involve contexts of culture and language. This opens the door for conduct and education to respond in constructive and creative ways to tensions, ambivalences, and contradictions that arise in and between cultures as well as between what appears as cultural and natural.

In *Democracy and Education*, Dewey only devotes two paragraphs to biological functionalism, so we supplement his remarks with his more extensive investigations elsewhere. What little he says here, however, is a good start:

> In brief, the environment consists of those conditions that promote or hinder, stimulate or inhibit, the *characteristic* activities of a living being. Water is the environment of a fish because it is necessary to the fish's activities—to its life . . . Just because life signifies not bare passive existence (supposing there is such a thing), but a way of acting, environment or medium signifies what enters into this activity as a sustaining or frustrating condition.
>
> (MW 9: 15)

We educate by stimulating or inhibiting the activities of learners as they interact with their environment. Learning, the formation of mental dispositions, occurs in the course of doing. The live creature is constantly striving to functionally coordinate its interactions with the environment upon which it depends. Dewey derived this way of thinking from William James' functionalist "biological conception of the psyche" (LW 5: 157). As Dewey observes, "Many philosophers have had much to say about the idea of organism; but they have taken it structurally and hence statically. It was reserved for James to think of life in terms of life in action" (LW 5: 158). Many educators still think statically and structurally. Pragmatists such as Dewey and James anticipated fluid "post-structuralism" long before the phrase became popular.

Dewey identifies "experience with a living function" (MW 13: 377). Elsewhere, he indicates:

> Life denotes a function, a comprehensive activity, in which organism and environment are included. Only upon reflective analysis does it break up into external conditions—air breathed, food taken, ground walked upon— and internal structures—lungs respiring, stomach digesting, legs walking.
>
> (LW 1: 19)

For instance, it is impossible to understand living creatures upon the planet earth without understanding the role of oxygenation of the blood with the concomitant removal of carbon dioxide (CO_2) and other metabolic wastes as a by-product of respiration (which also involves the heart and lungs in human beings). Similarly, we cannot understand the presence of oxygen (O_2) on earth until we understand that the flora of the planet break down CO_2 and water in photosynthesis and give off excess O_2 as a by-product. This is the oxygen cycle. In some ways, Dewey conceived what we might call the educational cycle in a similar way. Ultimately, the organism and environment are inseparable, and we may only understand either as a sub-function of an organic whole. The same holds for the individual and society.

Fundamentally, experience is an interaction between a sentient organism and the environment that emerges at the second plateau of existence; it partially defines the "psycho" in psycho-physical. We begin with some of the characteristics of any living function. Dewey claims: "Any process, sufficiently complex to involve an arrangement or coordination of minor processes, which fulfills a specific end in such a way as to conserve itself, is called a function" (MW 6: 466). Functions may consist of sub-functions themselves comprised of complex sub-functions internally and symbiotic with many other functions externally. Indeed, the very notion of external and internal collapses once we begin to think functionally: "Any operative function gets us behind the ordinary distinction of organism and environment. It presents us with their undifferentiated unity, not with their unification. It is primary; distinction is subsequent and derived" (MW 13: 377). Dewey believes "a living organism and its life processes involve a world or nature temporally and spatially 'external' to itself but 'internal' to its functions" (LW 1: 212). Indeed, so intimate is the unity of the organism and environment that they are really sub-functions of a single functional transaction, namely "the recurrent modes of interaction taking place between what we term organism, on one side, and environment, on the other. This interaction is the primary fact, and it constitutes a *trans-action*" (LW 5: 220). Dewey eventually came to prefer the transactional conception to that of interaction (see LW 16).

Oxygen, food, water, and a mate are external to our epidermis, but unless they sometimes become internal to our functioning, the Darwinian imperatives of survival and reproduction become impossible to satisfy. The same thing holds for the social interests, purposes, and ideas that comprise informal education and the formal school curriculum, both explicitly and implicitly. All of these have a history and different people actualize them in diverse ways, or perhaps, rebel against them. No organism, student, or teacher is simply located in space or time. Educators who realize the "ins" and "outs" in the interaction of organism and environment will also realize that the quality of education depends on the quality of the entire environment within which the student must function in school, at home, the local community, the nation, and the global community.

To survive and perhaps thrive, every living organism does not merely live in an environment, but "because of it, through interaction with it" (LW 10: 19). For Dewey, life is a dynamic equilibrium, or what contemporary biologists call a homeostasis, which allows the living being to maintain itself. Homeostasis is the ability of the body to maintain dynamic equilibrium within its internal environment (e.g., body temperature) when dealing with environmental changes. Heterostasis (sometimes called allostasis) involves preservation of relative biological stability in circumstances of environmental change through adaptation. Maintaining homeostasis or achieving heterostatic development and growth establishes an endless rhythm of need–demand–satisfaction of equilibrium–disequilibrium–restoration of equilibrium. Disequilibrium is as important as equilibrium. The restoration of harmonious heterostatic functioning establishes a form that completes a cycle of expansive growth.

In any atemporal cross-section, Dewey insists, "there is no basis of distinguishing organism and environment" (MW 13: 378). The element operating to maintain functioning during any temporal phase is the organism, while what first intervenes to disturb and later restore equilibrium is the environment. This rhythm sets up a constantly repeating need–demand–satisfaction cycle. It is the fundamental rhythm of life. It is also the fundamental rhythm of learning. We learn as obstacles that entail a situation of disrupted functioning disturb our dynamic equilibrium. We inquire to overcome obstacles and restore equilibrium. The results of successful inquiry become the acquired dispositions in thought, feeling, and action that serve as the basis of restoring equilibrium in similar situations in the future. For Dewey, the art of teaching revolved around designing environments that disrupt a student's experience such that the students may use their preexisting emotional and cognitive dispositions to act effectively to resolve the disrupted situation and thereby acquire new or more refined dispositions. Such teaching involves a dynamic, and ideally creative, relation between teacher, student, subject matter, and the social contexts of learning in a diverse society (which include social class, gender, race, ethnicity, sexual orientation, learning style, and such).

The foregoing properties are sufficient to allow Dewey to identify several critical aspects of any experience, which educators should remember when designing educational environments. First, "experience as such, is neither subjective nor objective but, being a function that is a temporal process, includes all that is differentiated and labeled subjective and objective" (MW 13: 379). Experience distributes itself; it is just not inside the organism. Second, we must also recognize experience is "a rhythm of doing and modification . . . acting and undergoing in consequence of the doing; with the need of adapting or using the undergoing— or 'suffering'—so as to restore functional unity" (MW 13: 379). Third, the organism–environment transaction always involves reciprocal transformation. In Darwinian terms, the organism must constantly adapt to an environment that it is constantly transforming. The co-evolution of hummingbirds and flowers is an example. The flowers have nectar suited to the birds' diet, their color suits the birds' vision, and their shape fits that of the birds' bills; the hummingbirds help pollinate the flowers that help feed them. It is a transactional relationship.

Teachers and students also often co-evolve in classroom situations. Each has something the other needs and wants. For Dewey, the distinction of subject and object is a functional construction within experience:

> The self, subject, individual, like organism, refers to just those factors in a moving and re-organizing function which at any point in the process immediately and directly determine the going on of the process. The object, world, other or external, designates those factors which as influenced by these immediate factors tend to prevent their onward movement and which must be converted into meanings of its on-going—an on-going no longer direct but a consequence.
>
> (MW 13: 379)

Fourth, functional integration initiates and terminates one cycle in the rhythm of life. The terminus of action constitutes an immediate qualitative consummatory experience (i.e., satisfaction or restoration of equilibrium). The consummatory unity is the product of the processes, the series of activities that produce it including any learned dispositions of thought or feeling. Further, many aspects of the process must remain to constitute the consummatory product, and the organism must repeat much of the process to reproduce the satisfying consequence. The result is a "vital experience" that is an intellectually meaningful, emotionally unified practical experience (*op. cit.*) Such experience characterizes a fully educational experience. The fifth insight is that while we may isolate an organism (physiology, anatomy, etc.) or subject (mind, knower, etc.) from its surroundings as a useful methodological simplification, we must never forget that "at every point the connection with environment—or a prior unity of function is presupposed and implied" (MW 13: 381). We may study lungs, heart, and blood circulation apart from the chemical properties of the surrounding air, but we cannot hope for an adequate understanding without reference to the oxygen and carbon dioxide cycle involving the fauna and flora of the planet. Likewise, we cannot understand our students unless we can understand the physical, biological, and social environment in which they live.

Let us pause to consider the foregoing aspects of functional experience with regard to essential insights about educational experience. We must fully recognize unity of thought and affect in *action*. Whenever one becomes confused about Dewey's theory of education, it is often best to think about the live creature striving to functionally coordinate transactions with its environment. This approach yields two principles of pragmatic pedagogy: First, we should not give students something to learn, we should give them something to do that prompts the formation of cognitive and emotional dispositions as they transact with it. Explicit teaching is never the primary thing, although in practice teachers must often aid the students as they strive to coordinate with their environment. Second, what surrounds the students is not necessarily their environment. Dewey notes: "The words 'environment,' 'medium' denote something more than sur-roundings which encompass an individual. They denote the specific *continuity* of the surroundings with his own active tendencies" (MW 9: 15). Something is part of an organism's environment only if it somehow enters the functioning of the organism in the organism–environment transaction. It is a common pedagogical mistake to assume that what surrounds a student is part of their environment simply because it is a part of the parent or teacher's environment. "On the other hand," Dewey insists, "some things which are remote in space and time from a living creature, especially a human creature, may form his environment even more truly than some of the things close to him" (MW 9: 15). Student-centered teaching must recognize that the students' environment is not simply located in the school or classroom, nor is it just what surrounds them.

Dewey declares: "Continuity and interaction in their active union with each other provide the measure of the educative significance and value of an experi-ence" (LW 13: 26). "The principle of continuity in its educational application means," according to Dewey, "that the future has to be taken into account at every stage of the educational process" (LW 13: 26). That is, "every experience should do something to prepare a person for later experiences of a deeper and more expansive quality" (LW 13: 26). It is a functional transaction. Since we only educate indirectly through the environment, the design of the environment and the obstacles and affordances it contains in conjunction with the innate and learned dispositions of the students is critical to what the students learn. The problem with dogmatic education is that these kinds of oppressive interactions disrupt the continuity of growth by directing it in ways that contribute to narrow, preordained, and unreflective adaptations.

Dewey observes that the social "interaction of human beings, namely, association, is not different in origin from other modes of interaction" (LW 1: 138). The result is uniquely human experience:

> And in distinctively human experience, life is of the *social* kind. It is equally fallacious to ignore the biological aspect and to use it to determine subject-matter as the narrower form of behaviorism does. By *social* is denoted such things as communication, participation, sharing, communion.
>
> (MW 13: 382)

Social experience has all the characteristics already discussed, plus the emergent properties that occur at the plateau of body-mind functioning. Dewey lists some of the distinct features of social functioning that supervene on biological functioning. "When tools and language enter in, these interdependences are transformed; they get a meaning" (MW 13: 283). Both tools and language operate as mediating means. Dewey is thinking of language (as he elsewhere thinks about logic and technology) in terms of its *mediating* instrumental function in human experience. However, every experience also has an *immediate* consummatory function. We may distinguish between the functions much as we may distinguish organism and environment, but we must not construct a misleading dualism from the distinction. For instance, finding aesthetic pleasure in the use of a tool enhances its utility while we may use the tool to secure the aesthetic pleasure in contemplating something we have created. There is a beauty in grammar that helps us make and shape linguistic meaning.

Dewey distinguishes between "referential" or significant meanings that mediate experience and immediate consummatory experiences, which Dewey calls "sense," or sometimes, "immanent meanings . . . The former present in consciousness the significance of things as means," while "the latter of consummations" (MW 13: 388). We will examine this distinction in the next chapter. It leads directly to the second emergent property, which is that "community-life introduces new functions: Fine Art and Reflective behavior—thinking, inference" (MW 13: 382). As we saw in the previous chapter, language and the use of signs involve communicative transaction and the possession of and response to meanings. Logic is but ordered language, an extension of grammar, and capable of beauty in form and function. Many species facilitate social transaction by communicating using nonlinguistic signals. So do we. Fleeing fire at the smell of smoke is an example. What is distinct is our ability to engage in abstract, arbitrary linguistic transactions. Linguistic communication makes use of animal behaviors in a novel way. We will identify the role of language in social functioning here, but will not take it up in detail until the next chapter.

Dewey begins his discussion of the social environment in *Democracy and Education* with the following observation:

> A being whose activities are associated with others has a social environment. What he does and what he can do depend upon the expectations, demands, approvals, and condemnations of others. A being connected with other beings cannot perform his own activities without taking the activities of others into account.
>
> (MW 9: 15–16)

The success of our efforts to coordinate our activities in thought, feeling, and action with our social environment depends on the thoughts, feelings, and actions of others. Therefore, Dewey reminds us: "Thinking and feeling that have to do with action in association with others is as much a social mode of behavior as is the most overt cooperative or hostile act" (MW 9: 16). Indirect education involves designing the right kind of social transactions including proper expectations, demands, approvals, condemnations, and such, but that is barely a start. There is something more.

Dewey draws on the Darwinian continuity uniting *Homo sapiens* with other species. The body of our body-minds acquires its habits and emotions of action much as do other animals with neurological systems. Habits are the biological basis of learning, but in the case of humans, they always involve transactions within a cultural environment. Dewey observes that in human conduct the cultural context is of primary importance. Native impulses and activities, "although first in time are never primary in fact; they are secondary and dependent" (MW 14: 65). In order to be sustainable and effective, human activities rely on opportunities to express themselves "in ways which have meaning" (MW 14: 65). And "the *meaning* of native activities is not native; it is acquired. It depends upon interaction with a matured social medium" (MW 14: 65).

Let us say something about the role of habits in learning. We are born with innate reflexes and impulses. Such characteristic dispositions of all human functioning are not learned. Dewey recovers the distinction between first nature and acquired habits as second nature, which is as old as the philosopher Aristotle. "Habit is second nature," Dewey reminds us, and second nature is "under ordinary circumstances as potent and urgent as first nature" (LW 13: 108). First nature involves whatever species-typical (i.e., innate) impulses such as the knee jerk or grasping reflexes that exist at birth. Second nature emerges and supervenes upon first nature to alter and transform it in such a way that novel properties emerge. Foremost among these novel properties is the acquisition of meanings both significant and immanent.

Everything said earlier about any living function applies equally well to acquired functions. Dewey proclaims: "Habits may be profitably compared to physiological functions like breathing, digesting. The latter are, to be sure, involuntary, while habits are acquired" (MW 14: 15). But "habits are like functions in many respects, and especially in requiring the cooperation of organism and environment" (MW 14: 15). For instance, "the functions of breathing and digesting are not complete within the human body . . .[F]unctions and habits are ways of using and incorporating the environment in which the latter has its say as surely as the former" (MW 14: 15). He further remarks that "habits endure, because these habits incorporate objective conditions in themselves" (MW 14: 19).

Dewey suggests that we think of "habits as technical abilities" (MW 14: 21). This is to say, "habits are arts" involving "skill of sensory and motor organs, cunning or craft, and objective materials. They assimilate objective energies, and eventuate in command of environment" (MW 14: 15–16). We may be said "to *know how* by means of our habits" (MW 14: 124). Embodied habits perform so large an array of culturally informed and meaningful activities and operations that Dewey concludes:

> Concrete habits do all the perceiving, recognizing, imagining, recalling, judging, conceiving and reasoning that is done. "Consciousness," whether as a stream or as special sensations and images, expresses functions of habits, phenomena of their formation, operation, their interruption and reorganization.
>
> (MW 14: 124)

However, if we pursue habits as precursors of cognitive method and knowing just a bit further, we see where they fail: "Yet habit does not, of itself, know, for it does not of itself stop to think, observe or remember . . . Habits by themselves are too organized, too insistent and determinate to need to indulge in inquiry or imagination" (MW 14: 124). The distinction is between "knowing how" and "knowing that". Habit embodies, enacts, affirms, or ignores meanings and objects, but it does not know them. "A certain delicate combination of habit and impulse is requisite for observation, memory and judgment. Knowledge which is not projected against the black unknown lives in the muscles"—i.e., knowing *how*— but "not in consciousness"—i.e., knowing *that* (MW 14: 124). Learning, in short, consists for Dewey not simply in the acquisition of habits, but much more in the intelligent and meaningful reconstruction of habits in response to concrete problematic or tensional situations. We will further discuss the contribution and place of habits in the next two chapters. For the moment, we continue by focusing in more detail on the educational implications of saying that habits involve embodied or incorporated immanent meanings.

When we train a rat in a maze, the creature does not share the ideas and the emotions of the trainer: "Human beings control animals by controlling the natural stimuli which influence them . . . operating steadily to call out certain acts, habits are formed which function with the same uniformity as the original stimuli" (MW 9: 16). Dewey bemoans the fact that the same so often holds for human beings and interactions (e.g., the teacher–student relation):

> Now in many cases—too many cases—the activity of the immature human being is simply played upon to secure habits which are useful. He is trained like an animal rather than educated like a human being. His instincts remain attached to their original objects of pain or pleasure. But to get happiness or to avoid the pain of failure he has to act in a way agreeable to others.
> (MW 9: 17)

Under such circumstances, we may train individual human beings using demands, approvals, and condemnations as social behavioral reinforcers and punishments that function much the same as food, bits, and bridles. Dewey identifies the problem: "So far, however, we are dealing with what may be called *training* in distinction from educative teaching. The changes considered are in outer action rather than in mental and emotional dispositions of behavior" (MW 9: 16). So, what is the difference between training and education?

In mere socialization or training, the learner "is not a partner in a shared activity"; hence, does not have "the same interest in its accomplishments which others have"; therefore, does not "share their ideas and emotions" (MW 9: 17). When a learner "really shares or participates in the common activity," his or her activity is modified so that everyone "not merely acts in a way agreeing with the actions of others, but, in so acting, the same ideas and emotions are aroused in him that animate the others" (MW 9: 17). When this occurs, the learner may share the needs, desires, interests, ideas, and ideals of the group. That is, they passionately share the *meaning* of the experience.

Using and responding to meanings marks the difference between mere training and genuinely educative experiences. "The bare fact that language consists of sounds which are *mutually intelligible,*" Dewey observes, "is enough of itself to show that its meaning depends upon connection with a shared experience" (MW 9: 19). Gestures—including vocal gestures (i.e., sounds)—gain meaning by "being used in a given way" (MW 9: 19). Educationally, it involves employing a sound to coordinate "a *joint* activity, as a means of setting up an active connection between the child and a grown-up" (MW 9: 19). In general: "Understanding one another means that objects, including sounds, have the same value for both with respect to carrying on a common pursuit" (MW 9: 19). Rather than an immediate response to a stimulus-object, linguistic beings respond to abstract representative signs that refer to objects perhaps entirely absent from the immediate situation but available for them in imagination and symbolization. Dewey concludes: "After sounds have got meaning through connection with other things employed in a joint undertaking, they can be used in connection with other like sounds to develop new meanings, precisely as the things for which they stand are combined" (MW 9: 19). Once this occurs, we may even enter the realm of abstract, arbitrary symbol systems detached from any particular context of use other than their reference to each other. We may operate on them any way we like. At this level of abstraction, it is easy to lose sight of the origin of language in socially shared transactions. Dewey points to one possible path in which words lose their meaning altogether:

> When words do not enter as factors into a shared situation, either overtly or imaginatively, they operate as pure physical stimuli, not as having a meaning or intellectual value. They set activity running in a given groove, but there is no accompanying conscious purpose or meaning. Thus, for example, the plus sign may be a stimulus to perform the act of writing one number under another and adding the numbers, but the person forming the act will operate much as an automaton would unless he realizes the meaning of what he does.
>
> (MW 9: 20)

In formal school education, students frequently learn to manipulate symbols to satisfy their teachers and pass tests like an automaton (e.g., a computer perhaps), but they fail to consciously grasp the larger purpose or meaning of what they are doing. They merely comprehend the school meaning.

We will explore the development of language and its role in the social construction of individual minds and selves in terms of both their mental (beliefs, forms of knowing, imagination, and such) and emotional (desires, interests, and such) dispositions in the next chapter. There, we will consider the tensions between the self and society, the role of social reflection in the creation of unique individuality, creative expression, imagination, and more.

For now, let us simply follow Dewey's remarks on the differences between informal versus formal learning. "Our net result thus far," Dewey sums up, "is that social environment forms the mental and emotional disposition of behavior in individuals by engaging them in activities that arouse and strengthen certain impulses, that have certain purposes and entail certain consequences" (MW 9: 20). By participating in joint social transactions involving mutual interests and purposes mediated by shared linguistic meanings that transform the environment (including other human beings), we modify spontaneous traits (like impulses or tendencies) and acquire emergent and enduring emotional and mental dispositions. There is no other way to educate.

Dewey recognizes that informal education is the primordial and permanently most influential form of education, which formal education may only hope to modify. Such modification often requires immense effort and frequently fails:

> [O]ur powers of observation, recollection, and imagination do not work spontaneously, but are set in motion by the demands set up by current social occupations. The main texture of disposition is formed, independently of schooling, by such influences. What conscious, deliberate teaching can do is at most to free the capacities thus formed for fuller exercise, to purge them of some of their grossness, and to furnish objects which make their activity more productive of meaning.
>
> (MW 9: 21)

The family, peer groups, social networks, and, often, public media remain the primary educators. This is a fact formal educators should never forget. Because "this 'unconscious influence of the environment' is so subtle and pervasive that it affects every fibre of character and mind," Dewey observes, "it may be worthwhile [sic] to specify a few directions in which its effect is most marked" (MW 9: 21). Dewey discusses four directions, which, while important, are still only a start. The first is "the habits of language" that are "formed in ordinary intercourse of life." Dewey here thinks of the fundamental "modes of speech" and the "bulk of the vocabulary" that constitute our main linguistic resources for experiencing the world in meaningful ways (MW 9: 21). Second are manners. Initially, this seems trivial, but Dewey reminds us that "manners are but minor morals," and example "is notoriously more potent than precept." Manners are important because they are the basis of more formal moral instruction: "Moreover in major morals, conscious instruction is likely to be efficacious only in the degree in which it falls in with the general 'walk and conversation' of those who constitute the child's social environment" (MW 9: 22). A third direction is the aesthetic dimension. Dewey does not confine aesthetics only to the appreciation of beauty, much less art theory, although that is important. For him, aesthetics involves human beings creatively making and immediately enjoying meanings. The last direction is really a crossroad for all directions taken. It concerns the standards of value we use to judge the worth of any ethical, aesthetic, and cognitive good we may wish to pursue:

> To say that the deeper standards of judgments of value are framed by the situations into which a person habitually enters is not so much to mention a fourth point, as it is to point out a fusion of those already mentioned . . . our conscious estimates of what is worth while [sic] and what is not, are due to standards of which we are not conscious at all.
>
> (MW 9: 22)

The things "we take for granted without inquiry or reflection are just the things which determine our conscious thinking and decide our conclusions." Further, "these habitudes which lie below the level of reflection are just those which have been formed in the constant give and take of relationship with others" (MW 9: 22). Formal education can teach us to critically and creatively examine just those habits and customs that possess us until we become conscious of them.

When we allow informal environments to educate, we are trusting entirely to custom and chance. Schools and other formal educational structures are deliberate, intentionally designed environments. We have seen that they rely extensively on written symbols (i.e., book learning) to convey knowledge. It is a unique institution with many benefits and risks. Dewey identifies three functions distinct to institutionalized education. First, since "a complex civilization is too complex to be assimilated *in toto*. It has to be broken up into portions, as it were, and assimilated piecemeal, in a gradual and graded way" (MW 9: 24). Therefore,

> The first office of the social organ we call the school is to provide a *simplified* environment. It selects the features which are fairly fundamental and capable of being responded to by the young. Then it establishes a progressive order, using the factors first acquired as means of gaining insight into what is more complicated.
>
> (MW 9: 24)

Here we have the notion of the curriculum; that is, a course of studies. Second, to determine a curriculum requires educators to make value judgments of what forms of knowledge, moral attitudes, and aesthetic dispositions are of most worth. Therefore, "[s]election aims not only at simplifying but at weeding out what is undesirable" (MW 9: 24). Of course, the quality of the curriculum depends on the quality of the society. Third,

> [I]t is the office of the school environment to balance the various elements in the social environment, and to see to it that each individual gets an

opportunity to escape from the limitations of the social group in which he was born, and to come into living contact with a broader environment.

(MW 9: 24–25)

Here, Dewey goes beyond the bounds of formal socialization to make a substantive claim for democratic pluralism.

Challenge for Today: Education and Social Context

With his characteristic sensitivity to the necessity of context, Dewey responds to a general challenge of educational philosophy that deserves special attention in our time—at least as much as in his. This second challenge intimately connects in many ways with the first one—the challenge to resist reductionism that we discussed at the end of Chapter 1. We first approach the importance of contextualism in some more systematic ways by using one of Dewey's later philosophical writings—the essay "Context and Thought"—before we come to specify some of the ways in which both challenges are related.

Dewey believes we should take the idea of context more seriously than philosophers have in the past. He presented his ideas about contextualism in a lecture delivered in Berkeley in 1931 that was a theoretical outgrowth of his 1925/29 major philosophical work *Experience and Nature*. In this lecture, published under the title "Context and Thought" (LW 6: 3–21), Dewey draws a connection between the necessity of context and the preference for experience (see more comprehensively Neubert, 2008). Among other things, he concludes: "The significance of 'experience' for philosophic method is, after all, but the acknowledgement of the indispensability of context in thinking when that recognition is carried to its full term" (LW 6: 20). Carrying it to its full term means acknowledging the importance of context for all our observations and interpretations, even if we can never completely reflect all relevant contexts at any given moment. In our everyday experience, context is largely just taken for granted: "We do not think about it unless some part of it becomes problematic because we are confronted with a new and unexpected situation. As humans we inhabit our world by means of habits formed in the intercourse with a natural and cultural environment" (Neubert, 2008: 93). Habit implies that our experiences are pervaded by what Dewey calls "background" that is "both temporal and spatial" namely, the diachronic and synchronic contexts of history and culture that are implicit in our experiences, actions, observations, and interpretations (see LW 6: 12). Dewey addresses some of the most important components of such cultural contexts. For instance, he explains that language and the use of symbols are powerful contextual conditions that inform our every thought (see LW 6: 4f). He addresses the role of traditions: "Traditions are ways of interpretation and of observation, of valuation, of everything explicitly thought of. They are the circumambient atmosphere which thought must breathe; no one ever had an idea except as he inhaled some of this atmosphere" (LW 6: 12). While traditions are examples of "temporal background," we must not forget the actual environment in which reflection takes place:

> Spatial background covers all the contemporary setting within which a course of thinking emerges . . . The spatial context is the ground through which the road [of thinking] runs and for the sake of which the road exists. It is this setting which gives import to the road and to its consecutive illuminations.
>
> (LW 6: 13–14)

Moreover, Dewey reminds us that we must also consider the more "subjective" phases of context. All our experiences, observations, interpretations, and valuations imply what he calls "selective interests" (LW 6: 14 f.). This phrase represents attitudes informed by desires, motives, and predilections. Selective interests make us choose and distinguish, e.g., the relevant from the irrelevant. "Every particular case of thinking is what it is because of some attitude, some bias if you will" (LW 6: 14). Even the effort of being "objective" in thinking is an attitude in this sense and presupposes a certain form of subjectivity. Without these phases of subjectivity, there would be neither individuality nor originality in thought.

The cultural, temporal, spatial, and individual contexts of experiences informed by language, traditions, customs, habits, selective attention, etc., provide resources as well as limitations. They offer us the necessary instruments for acting and thinking. At the same time, they hold us captives insofar as we often become oblivious about contexts and simply take them for granted. In everyday life, this forgetfulness is for the most part unproblematic and even unavoidable. But Dewey thinks that for philosophy there are specific dangers that spring from neglect or ignorance of context. "I should venture to assert that the most pervasive fallacy of philosophic thinking goes back to neglect of context" (LW 6: 5). More specifically, he mentions two "counterpart" fallacies in this connection. He speaks of an "analytic fallacy" whenever the tendency prevails to dissolve reality into distinct and isolated units and to treat these elements not as results constructed within the contexts of inquiry, but as something final and independent, e.g., as the original constituents out of which reality supposedly is made up (LW 6: 6 ff.). The "fallacy of unlimited universalization," on the other hand, is found "when it is asserted . . . that the goal of thinking, particularly of philosophic thought, is to bring all things whatsoever into a single coherent and all inclusive whole" (LW 6: 8). In both of these two cases, neglect or denial of context is harmful "because it involves forgetfulness of the limiting conditions of philosophic inquiry. It therefore violates an important principle of every pluralist approach—the relatedness of specific perspectives to specific contexts and thus the limited-ness and incompleteness of any perspective that we take" (Neubert, 2008: 94). Although context can never be fully illuminated and made explicit by reflection, Dewey suggests that critical acknowledgement of the limits of context can teach us philosophic "humility" and prevent us from "a too unlimited and dogmatic universalization" of our conclusions (LW 6: 13).

We believe that this second challenge—the "necessity of context"—has implications for education that are as important today as those discussed in the first chapter with regard to the challenge of "nature and culture." Indeed, both challenges are deeply intertwined. Remember, as argued throughout Chapter 1 of this book, culture and nature are mutually necessary contexts we cannot separate or isolate from each other. Human beings inhabit nature through culture; hence, culture provides the environment of meaning for our interpretations of our natural environment. More specifically, we may also observe that the dangers of reductionism in and for education discussed earlier in this connection clearly illustrate the link between both challenges. To take the necessity of context seriously involves being cautious and critical against all sorts of compartmentalization in education and the human sciences. If we think of specialized approaches in education, psychology, sociology, economics, neurosciences, and so on, we must always consider the conditions of context that pervade and delimit them: "Within the limits of context found in any valid inquiry, 'reality' thus means the confirmed outcome, actual or potential, of the inquiry that is undertaken" (LW 6: 8 f.). When, however, context is forgotten and "'reality' is sought for at large, it is without intellectual import" (LW 6: 9).

Following Dewey, we have entitled this second chapter of our book "Education as a Social Function" to indicate that the most comprehensive context of education is the world of the "Social" as it was explained in Chapter 1. Dewey himself always saw education and "the Social" in intimate and inseparable connection, as becomes evident already from the titles of some of his most important educational writings like *The School and Society* or *Democracy and Education*. We may find an example of his own limited outlook on the social contexts of education in his time (1916) from today's perspective through a critical observation of his comments on race and diversity in Chapter 2 of *Democracy and Education*. Among other things, he observes that in a country like the United States there are a "variety of races, religious affiliations, economic divisions . . . different groups with different traditional customs" that have "forced the demand for an educational institution which shall provide something like a homogeneous and balanced environment for the young" (MW 9: 25). He praises that the "assimilative force of the American public school is eloquent testimony to the efficacy of the common and balanced appeal" (MW 9: 26).

Here, we begin to run into a tension in Dewey's, or any other, democratic pluralism. It is the tension of unity in diversity. If we assimilate, to what do we assimilate? What are the norms that everyone, regardless of their differences, must agree? Commentators have observed, in this connection, that Dewey sometimes seems to disregard or underestimate the menaces of racism, sexism, and other forms of oppressive discrimination against groups and individuals that put the democratic project of "common and balanced appeal" at risk (compare Fraser, 1998; Seigfried, 2002: 55; Sullivan, 2003; Fallace, 2011; Neubert, 2012a). This is an especially serious challenge today in an era dominated by the global mobility and immigration of labor. Nel Noddings, drawing on the thought of Jane Addams, asserts: "Assimilation to American culture, attachment to an original culture, and a move toward universal culture need not be mutually exclusive" (Noddings, 2013: 136). Dewey, who knew Addams well and was influenced by her, draws on Addams' work to make pluralistic claims similar to Noddings' (see MW 2: 85–86). Pluralism is one of democracy's highest ideals, but difficult to realize in practice. From today's perspectives (like cultural and postcolonial studies), we may even add that all three alternatives mentioned by Noddings—namely assimilation, tradition, and universalization—do not cover the increasingly important phenomena of transcultural experiences and developments that have been addressed by authors like Stuart Hall and Homi Bhabha as "translation" (see Hall, 1992), "third space" (see Bhabha, 1994), or "culture's in between" (see Bhabha, 1996).

Dewey's Summary

The development within the young of the attitudes and dispositions necessary to the continuous and progressive life of a society cannot take place by direct conveyance of beliefs, emotions, and knowledge. It takes place through the intermediary of the environment. The environment consists of the sum total of conditions which are concerned in the execution of the activity characteristic of a living being. The social environment consists of all the activities of fellow beings that are bound up in the carrying on of the activities of any one of its members. It is truly educative in its effect in the degree in which an individual shares or participates in some conjoint activity. By doing his share in the associated activity, the individual appropriates the purpose which actuates it, becomes familiar with its methods and subject matters, acquires needed skill, and is saturated with its emotional spirit. The deeper and more intimate educative formation of disposition comes, without conscious intent, as the young gradually partake of the activities of the various groups to which they may belong. As a society becomes more complex, however, it is found necessary to provide a special social environment which shall especially look after nurturing the capacities of the immature. Three of the more important functions of this special environment are: simplifying and ordering the factors of the disposition it is wished to develop; purifying and idealizing the existing social customs; and creating a wider and better balanced environment than that by which the young would be likely, if left to themselves, to be influenced.

(MW 9: 26–27)

Our Summary

Education and socialization can hardly be separated from each other if we want to avoid two extremes of one-sided misunderstanding: on the one hand, education seen as merely individualistic and, on the other hand, socialization seen as deterministic. The first position intends to educate children independently of social contexts and constraints, i.e., to construe an educational counterworld to existing social conditions. Because only the rich can afford to profit from the construction of such detached educational counterworlds in private institutions, this usually ends up in confining education to highly exclusive gated communities. The other extreme often leads to educational pessimism conceiving of the social world as fixed and fully established, including its hierarchies and compartmentalizations into high and low status, winners and losers, those who profit and those whose lives are wasted. Seen from a Deweyan perspective as applied to today's educational challenges, both extremes fundamentally misconceive what is at stake in connecting democracy and education. If we believe that democracy is the necessary context of education, and at least there is no proponent of democracy who would officially deny that necessity, then neither egoistic interests of particular groups nor claims to deterministic adaptation can give key orientation to what education is as a function for society. The project of reconsidering Dewey's *Democracy and Education* today insists on taking these fundamental insights about the connection of democracy and education seriously.

Note

1   All italics in Dewey quotes are original throughout this book.

3
EDUCATION AS INTERACTION AND COMMUNICATION

Communication is part of interaction, namely the part that constitutes social life. Today it seems self-evident that communication is a core element in education. Surprisingly, Dewey was the first influential philosopher of education in the early twentieth century that gave communication a central role in cultural and educational theory. In Chapter 2, we saw that, for Dewey, education in its indirect and direct forms is more than intentionally controlled, directed, or guided interaction. Yet, we must not ignore the influence of control, direction, and guidance in social life. Let us start with Dewey's account of that influence.

The phrase "social control" was so widely used in Dewey's day that he felt the need to address the question of individuality and social cohesion using such language. While the phrase is now antiquated, the conundrum remains. Dewey thinks we fundamentally misconceive the issue as forcible coercion rather than social cooperation. To comprehend the difficulty correctly, we must recognize that human beings are social creatures that depend on social as well as biological functions to sustain themselves. Dewey was particularly anxious to address the dangers of atomistic individualism, which assumes that "an individual's tendencies are naturally purely individualistic or egoistic, and thus anti-social" (MW 9: 28). Supposing such a concept of an individual, "[c]ontrol then denotes the process by which he is brought to subordinate his natural impulses to public or common ends" (MW 9: 28). Dewey disparages the commonly preferred solution for the misconceived problem of the individual and society:

> Since, by conception, his own nature is quite alien to this process [socialization and social control] and opposes it rather than helps it, control has in this view a flavor of coercion or compulsion about it. Systems of government and theories of the state have been built upon this notion, and

it has seriously affected educational ideas and practices. But there is no ground for any such view.

(MW 9: 28)

The coercive solution tends toward crude training to secure conformity of outer action rather than an education effecting emotional and intellectual opportunities. Trained, second-nature responses might meet with social approval while remaining dangerously mechanical:

> But in the merely blind response, direction is also blind. There may be training, but there is no education. Repeated responses to recurrent stimuli may fix a habit of acting in a certain way. All of us have many habits of whose import we are quite unaware, since they were formed without our knowing what we were about. Consequently they possess us, rather than we them. They move us; they control us. Unless we become aware of what they accomplish, and pass judgment upon the worth of the result, we do not control them.

(MW 9: 34–35)

When Dewey speaks of habits that possess us, probably the first thing that comes to mind is the abuse of drugs and alcohol, but we should also think of ways of categorizing the world—e.g., dividing the world into gendered or racialized stereotypes or other ways of binary thinking.

To control ourselves—against the background forces of control by social customs and expectations—we must learn to consciously reflect on our habits in critical and creative ways and to develop a balance between those moments of experience where we cannot help depending on acquired habits that insofar control us and those aspects of experience where we need to achieve deliberate control of situations to find new and viable solutions for growth as individuals and groups. Further, since we may only educate and be educated through the environment, we must alter our environments and relationships to control and transform our selves. Because we are social beings, we need others to achieve self-creation.

For Dewey, mere training alone is not educative because it does not involve response to meanings on a relevant scale: "The difference between an adjustment to a physical stimulus and a *mental* act is that the latter involves response to a thing in its *meaning*; the former does not" (MW 9: 34). His example is useful: "A noise may make me jump without my mind being implicated. When I hear a noise and run and get water and put out a blaze, I respond intelligently; the sound meant fire, and fire meant need of being extinguished" (MW 9: 34). "When things have a meaning for us," Dewey notes, "we *mean* (intend, propose, purpose) what we do: when they do not, we act blindly, unconsciously, unintelligently" (MW 9: 34). We may respond because we grasp the meaning of the elements within a given situation: we literally have an idea of what needs doing; therefore, we may act intentionally and with purpose:

To have an *idea* of a thing is thus not just to get certain sensations from it. It is to be able to respond to the thing in view of its place in an inclusive scheme of action; it is to foresee the drift and probable consequence of the action of the thing upon us and of our action upon it.

(MW 9: 35)

Against the background of Dewey's distinction between training and education, it is alarming to see how much of present education remains on the level of mere training. Insofar as it does, it violates the principle of shared activities that is a core component of the necessary connection between education and democracy. Shared activities are a precondition of shared ideas, social relationships, and necessary frames for every community: "To have the same ideas about things which others have, to be like-minded with them, and thus to be really members of a social group, is therefore to attach the same meanings to things and to acts which others attach. Otherwise, there is no common understanding, and no community life" (MW 9: 35). Like-mindedness and social coordination are necessary to the social construction of minds and selves. It is usually good for everyone to obey traffic signs and signals.

However, two points should receive some brief commentaries in this connection. First, like-mindedness is an ambivalent construct. Depending on the context, it may or may not be good for the individual and the community. It is certainly true that without some extent of like-minded orientation, we could not construct meaning, and communities could not exist and develop. It is important for democracy to combine such like-mindedness of orientation with openness for diversity, although such combination will always be a precarious balance. Like-mindedness readily degenerates into *Gleichschaltung* (i.e., the Nazi term for forcible coordination) of minds and practices. This danger is why democratic education is so important to Dewey.

Second, the distinction between training and education, although clear in Dewey's text, appears in a somewhat different light in view of today's mostly constructivist learning theories. In human resource management, there is often still a narrow understanding of training, while in contexts of systemic coaching, counseling, and supervision, training is often conceived of as constructive and critical learning with active participation and joint problem solving. We then no longer see education and training in sharp contrast; rather the emphasis is on the constructive dimension of learning either way. Today's educational training or counseling by coaches is often an innovative field of practice containing new methods of communication and work in positive relationships. Only narrow skill training for tests still has the bad reputation that worries Dewey. On the other hand, education, in all its forms of application, always stands in danger of narrowing the horizons of experience and supporting affable and affirmative practices, too. Research on institutional socialization and the effects of the hidden curriculum have, since the 1970s, shown with an abundance of examples how education as well as training are influenced by covert forces and interests that manifest themselves in educational practices, routines, and institutions and that lead to dominating forms of social control by ideas like learning to the test (not for life), competition (and not growth), narrow gender roles (and not diversity), and other forms of discrimination and exclusion (and not inclusion).

Coercive control provides the very worst example of narrow socialization wherein the conflict between an individual's autonomy and her or his adaptation to the demands of society is resolved entirely in favor of the latter. From a democratic standpoint, like-minded socialization is of necessity ambivalent. It is necessary for the constitution of shared values, norms, and orientations, but it also always implies the dangers of dogmatic indoctrination into the customs and dominant ideals and ideas of a culture. Dewey thinks that "the control afforded by the customs and regulations of others may be short-sighted. It may accomplish its immediate effect, but at the expense of throwing the subsequent action of the person out of balance" (MW 9: 30–31). Perceptive teachers will approve Dewey's assertion that with coercion "instincts of cunning and slyness may be aroused, so that things henceforth appeal to him on the side of evasion and trickery more than would otherwise have been the case" (MW 9: 31). Even the most agreeable form of socialization may suppress individual creativity, freedom, and expression, or else channel it into directions involving educational interactions lacking developmental continuity and leading to youthful deceit and outright criminal evasion later in life. What makes affable as well as coercive socialization so attractive is modernity's deep commitment to egoistic, and thus anti-social, atomistic individuality.

In this chapter, we concentrate primarily on the social construction of meanings whence our minds emerge. Along the way, we will also learn how Dewey reconstructs freedom and rationality. For him, the very idea of an ahistorical, socially detached individual born with a mind, free will, and rationality who only pursues his or her selfish interests is simply a colossal mistake his philosophy of education seeks to correct. He acknowledges his work "may be conceived as an attempt to contribute to what has come to be called an 'emergent' theory of mind" (LW 1: 207). Therefore, he proclaims: "Personality, selfhood . . . are eventual functions that emerge with complexly organized interactions, organic and social. Personal individuality has its basis and conditions in simpler events" (LW 1: 162). Our minds and selves emerge when socio-linguistic functions supervene upon biological functions. Let us see how.

For Dewey, to have a mind is to have meanings and to have meanings involves the use of language. Furthermore, he explains free will with an ideal of "intelligence," which takes account of how culture educates our feelings and habits of action. It is also part of culture that our emotional, practical, and intellectual dispositions respond to cultural situations including customs, rules, and norms of conduct. "Intelligence," he concludes, "is the key to freedom in act" (MW 14: 210). Intelligence discerns the environmental constructions that condition our conduct and then strives to re-create the self by re-creating the environment. In later chapters, we will find that intelligence for Dewey is embodied, passionate, and imaginative. A cold, detached rationality is for him not the average instance of intelligence. Additionally, intelligence itself emerges and evolves, so it requires constant revision. Once we understand how Dewey reconstructs intelligence, we will comprehend how he reconstructs freedom. In this chapter, we will emphasize his reconstruction of mind as emerging from social interactions. He was a social constructivist long before the term was popular (see Garrison, 1998).

We develop our minds by acquiring meanings in interaction with others, and we develop a sense of selfhood by taking the attitude of others toward our own actions. The latter emerges along with the former through *activity* coordinated by language. Dewey's most complete account of the role of language and communication occurs in Chapter 5 of *Experience and Nature*, to which we will soon turn. Nonetheless, the following summary of social control from Chapter 3 of *Democracy and Education* clearly points the way:

> The net outcome of the discussion is that the fundamental means of control is not personal but intellectual. It is not "moral" in the sense that a person is moved by direct personal appeal from others, important as is this method at critical junctures. It consists in the habits of *understanding*, which are set up in using objects in correspondence with others, whether by way of cooperation and assistance or rivalry and competition. *Mind* as a concrete thing is precisely the power to understand things in terms of the use made of them; a socialized mind is the power to understand them in terms of the use to which they are turned in joint or shared situations. *And mind in this sense is the method of social control.*
>
> (MW 9: 38)

Any linguistic interaction has reciprocal social control built into it; it is unavoidable. What is avoidable—at least from an ideal-typical perspective—is unjust coercion and improper application of power. While Dewey was well aware of the former, he was not as attentive to the latter as we are today. We will come back to questions of power extensively in Chapter 7. For the moment, it may suffice to mention that, upon the whole, Dewey was rather optimistic with regard to the potentials of individual and collective intelligence to solve social problems on the basis of common interests. He believed that, given goodwill and basic consent, individuals and groups could reach relevant and warranted assertions about knowledge and truth claims through cooperative inquiry. What he tended to underestimate was the conflict and sometimes even the clash of interests in modern societies and the hindrance that opposing and antagonistic interests often put to goodwill and consent. We should at least consider three aspects in this connection:

First, diversity in all modern societies implies distinctions as well as hierarchies in fields like class, race, gender, and also ethnicity, religion, age, disability and so on. Second, research on intersectionality shows that in all of these fields, diversity of opportunities connects with multiple forms of exclusion and discrimination. Participation and equity are necessary claims and a precondition for a democratic way of life, but they are put at risk by unfair and inequitable power asymmetries. Participation needs empowerment—not all potential participants already have the capacity to articulate themselves and act successfully on behalf of their own evolving interests. Third, diversity of interests is today a general condition of life and has even grown through processes of migration, emancipation, empowerment, as well as the general globalization of capitalism. This makes ideas about social control even more controversial and problematic than in former times. Capitalism in itself is a form of social control and has developed many different forms of shaping the social world. Fordism was an example in Dewey's day. Today, capitalism, following Bauman (2000), has developed much lighter forms of social control through networks, financial markets, and the capitalization of human capacities including education and learning. Dewey was aware of the dark sides of Fordism and laissez faire liberalism. Today, we must take account of the dark sides of liberalism (cf. Hollinger, 1996) and neoliberalism (cf. Crouch, 2004, 2011) as expressions of contemporary tendencies of capitalism. We will return to this point extensively in Chapter 10.

We now turn to the socio-linguistic emergence of meaning. Dewey titles Chapter 5 of *Experience and Nature*, "Nature, Communication and Meaning." Language emerges when two or more agents can co-designate an object that allows them to functionally coordinate their social interactions to achieve some shared goal. The two agents and the object emerge simultaneously. The later Dewey used the term transaction to distinguish this dynamic and evolving understanding of interaction from interaction in the more trivial sense of an exchange, say of information or money, between given and stable agents and objects. In this chapter we use the term interaction consistently to avoid confusion. It is always meant in the wider dynamic sense.

Remember Dewey's observation already referred to in our Chapter 1: "Try the experiment of communicating, with fullness and accuracy, some experience to another, especially if it be somewhat complicated, and you will find your own attitude toward your experience changing" (MW 9: 8). It does not matter where you start in the interpretive hermeneutic circle of agents and objects. The result is a three-term schema depicting the social emergence of linguistic meaning.

When two beings as partaker in culture succeed in functionally coordinating their interactions in conjunction with some object using abstract signs (i.e., symbols), linguistic meaning emerges:

> Language is specifically a mode of interaction of at least two beings, a speaker and a hearer; it presupposes an organized group to which these creatures belong . . . It is therefore a relationship, not a particularity . . . The meaning of signs moreover always includes something common as between persons

and an object. When we attribute meaning to the speaker as *his* intent, we take for granted another person who is to share in the execution of the intent, and also something, independent of the persons concerned, through which the intent is to be realized. Persons and thing must alike serve as means in a common, shared consequence. This community of partaking is meaning.

(LW 1: 145)

Dewey's ideas about interaction, communication, and control in education have been developed on the background of the theoretical model given by his friend and colleague George Herbert Mead, who presented a classical and very influential concept of socialization, self, and society. Compared with George Herbert Mead's approach, however, Dewey's discussion of communication and symbolic interaction remains rather short and superficial. In a remembrance of his friend, Dewey himself said of Mead:

His mind was germinative and seminal. One would have to go far to find a teacher of our own day who started in others so many fruitful lines of thought; I dislike to think what my own thinking might have been were it not for the seminal ideas which I derived from him. For his ideas were always genuinely original; they started one thinking in directions where it had never occurred to one that it was worth while even to look.

(LW 6: 24)

It seems helpful, therefore, to introduce the core ideas of Mead's concept. Mead is especially strong in explaining the *self* as a social construct that implies a necessary tensional relationship as a result of the tension between individuality and society. He captures this tension by his famous distinction between the "I" and "me" as parts of the self. In this tension, the "I" represents the pole of the individual's interests, desires, emotions, imaginations, free will, spontaneous impulses, and such, while the "me" stands for the internalized social expectations, habits, conventions, generalized norms, values, and so on. When the self encounters others in interactions, the "me" is generated as a result of the individual's experiences of taking the role of the other, i.e., imaginatively positioning itself into the perspectives of others. There is always a "generalized other" included in this process, by which Mead means the necessary commonalities and forms of like-mindedness as in shared norms, values, rules, laws, practices, routines, institutions. In the frame of this theoretical model, we can identify two aspects of educational importance can be emphasized: First, educators should never underestimate the power of the "I." If the self were only "me," education would degenerate into indoctrination, heteronomy, and mere adaptation to given social realities. The original and creative capacities and powers of individuality would be neglected and practically destroyed. Second, educators would be naïve if they underestimated the power of the "me." If the self was only "I," that "I" would be ineffective and have no social resources for articulating its interests, desires, imaginations, etc., on a common field with social consequences.

This interactive model of the self and socialization applies to the acquisition of language as both Mead and Dewey have argued. There is considerable empirical research confirming that the acquisition of language is a social interaction involving at least two communicants capable of taking the attitude of the other toward a third thing. Neuro-scientific research even suggests that so-called mirror neurons greatly facilitate taking the attitude of the other in many animals and humans (see Provine, 2005). However, the human experience of mirroring others is a cultural experience conditioned by relationships and contexts of inter-action for which no mirror neurons can account—as little as a person's heartbeat or breathing rhythm. If we did not address others, we would never address our-selves. Even the contemplative hermit continues to depend on others living and dead: "If we had not talked with others and they with us, we should never talk to and with ourselves" (LW 1: 135). For Dewey, there are no private languages; the creation of meaning and knowing is always a social co-creation. Meaning, for him, is primarily a property of social behavior and only secondarily of socially constructed objects:

> The heart of language . . . is communication; the establishment of coopera-tion in an activity in which there are partners, and in which the activity of each is modified and regulated by partnership . . . Meaning is not indeed a psychic existence; it is primarily a property of behavior, and secondarily of objects. But the behavior of which it is a quality is a distinctive behavior; cooperative in that response to another's act involves contemporaneous response to a thing as entering into the other's behavior, and this on both sides.
>
> (LW 1: 141)

This is precisely the kind of joint or shared situations that yield social control. Literally, we cannot acquire linguistic meanings unless we can regularly allow others to partially control our behavior. It is a reciprocal interaction.

To a certain degree, Dewey anticipated the linguistic turn that was important in the twentieth-century development of philosophy, considerably influenced by Wittgenstein (1953) and his *Philosophical Investigations*, which showed how lin-guistic means and cultural understandings are interwoven and construct each other in the process of their deployment.[1] Even if individuals can produce new linguistic expressions and metaphors, the meaning of these new constructions only emerges in social deployment.

Dewey argues that minds emerge in the social activities of making mean-ing. "Through speech a person dramatically identifies himself with potential acts and deeds; he plays many roles, not in successive stages of life but in a contemporaneously enacted drama. Thus mind emerges" (LW 1: 135). For Dewey, the mind was at home in the world that it sought to understand and act upon: "If . . . language . . . is recognized as the instrument of social cooperation and mutual participation, continuity is established between natural events (animal sounds, cries, etc.) and the origin and development of meanings. Mind is seen to be a function of social interactions and to be a genuine character of natural events" (LW 1: 6; see Segerdahl, Fields & Savage-Rumbaugh 2005). He concludes:

> Mind denotes the whole system of meanings as they are embodied in the working of organic life; consciousness in a being with language denotes awareness or perception of meanings; it is the perception of actual events, whether past, contemporary or future, *in* their meanings . . . The field of mind—of operative meanings—is enormously wider than that of consciousness . . . Mind is constant . . . consciousness intermittent . . .
> (LW 1: 230)

Within the field of mind, consciousness emerges as a transient focus in response to a concrete situation. The totality of situatedness is elusive and ineffable because it is an immediately given, intuitive experience of existence. Initially, we intuit the quality of a situation; conception only comes later. In his essay, "Qualitative Thought," Dewey states that, temporally, "intuition precedes conception and goes deeper" (LW 5: 249). Such intuition is part of the background context of any cognitive problem. "Intuition, in short," writes Dewey, "signifies the realization of a pervasive quality such that it regulates the determination of relevant distinctions or of whatever, whether in the way of terms or relations, becomes the accepted object of thought" (LW 5: 249). Dewey felt that our intuitions of any given situation were important, as are the operations of unconscious selective attention within those situations. We only respond to that to which we attend.

Dewey emphasizes what we might call the primacy of aesthetic experience, as long as we do not understand "aesthetic" narrowly as referring only to the beautiful: "If we take advantage of the word esthetic in a wider sense than that of application to the beautiful and ugly, esthetic quality, immediate, final or self-enclosed, indubitably characterizes natural situations as they empirically occur" (LW 1: 82; Johnson, 1993, 2007). Shusterman helps clarify Dewey's thinking about the relation between nature and culture:

> [L]anguage enables the organism's feelings and movements to be named, and thus objectified and given a determinate meaning that can be reidentified and deployed in communication. Mind remains in the realm of natural events, but Dewey's linguistic requirement for mind also places it squarely in the realm of culture. No inconsistency is involved in this double

status. Just as mind is not opposed to but is rather an emergent expression of the human body, so culture is not the contradiction of nature but rather its fulfillment and reshaping.

(Shusterman, 2008: 186)

Shusterman might have derived the foregoing from the following: "The qualities never were 'in' the organism; they always were qualities of interactions in which both extra-organic things and organisms partake. When named, they enable identification and discrimination of things to take place as means in a further course of inclusive interaction" (LW 1: 198–199). The qualities are not in nature either. They arise in interactions involving sentient beings and other natural events. Further, until named by members of socio-linguistic communities (i.e., cultures), they have no meaning: "[D]ifference in qualities (feelings) of act when employed as indications of act performed and to be performed and as signs of their consequence, *mean* something . . . Without language, the qualities of organic action that are feelings are pains, pleasures, odors, colors, noises, tones, only potentially and proleptically" (LW 1: 198).

Meaning emerges in nature when socio-linguistic practices (i.e., culture) emerge in nature. If we reconsider our previous distinction between Darwinian naturalism and cultural constructivism (see Chapter 1), we may say that the Deweyan perspective on nature and culture is an elaborated approach in the wake of Darwinian naturalism and at the same time itself a cultural construction.

For Dewey, "[a]ny quality as such is final; it is at once initial and terminal; just what it is as it exists. It may be referred to other things, it may be treated as an effect or as a sign. But this involves an extraneous extension and use" (LW 1: 82). Signs mediate among immediate experiences. It is common to use the term "symbols" to designate abstract, arbitrary linguistic signs. Dewey calls them "instrumental" or more frequently "significant" meanings.

In Chapter 2, we mentioned that gestures, including vocal gestures, gain meaning when used in a certain way. Indeed, natural signs even allow human beings to communicate with other animals such as dogs (see Pongrácz, Miklósi, Molnár & Csányi, 2005). We now understand that what is crucial to sharing linguistic signs is taking the attitude of another toward a third thing. Dewey calls the social use of natural signs "signaling." Linguistic communication extends social and semi-otic psycho-physical activities: "It is also an obvious empirical fact that animals are connected with each other in inclusive schemes of behavior by means of signaling acts, in consequence of which certain acts and consequences are deferred until a joint action made possible by the signaling occurs. In the human being, this function becomes language, communication"(LW 1: 213; see Tomasello, 2008).

This is the basis of cultural interaction and experience as significant and re-flective.[2] For Dewey, a fundamental criterion of experience is interaction ("transaction" in his later writings). Human individuals interact with their environments, which can be natural as well as social. Therefore, Dewey saw the concepts of experience, life, nature, and culture as corresponding to each other, and we can only make correct distinctions if we, at the same time, recognize the necessary interconnections. For example, we can say that experience is lived culture, we can speak of life-experiences, we can understand culture as an emergence from nature, and we can talk about nature only through the perspectives of experience. But for Dewey, experience is no confused mixture of nature and culture in general but a very specific term that can and must be broken down to concrete implications and actions with regard to their contexts. For this purpose, he distinguishes between primary and secondary experience:

Primary experience happens, for instance, when we reach with our fingers into a flame for the first time, unprepared, simply as part of our pre-reflective interactions with a given situation. It hurts. Here, we take our experience as simply given: we act, do and undergo, enjoy and suffer, and so on. Although such action seems to be immediate, innocent, naïve, and "natural," a closer observation shows that it is already laden with meanings from cultural contexts that we have learned so far for granted through our acquisition of habits. For example, even the child who reaches for the first time into a flame already has the habit of reaching in order to learn about objects. But on the level of primary experience, the behavior is not yet reflective. It becomes so if we ourselves define or perceive the situation as problematic, i.e., as a situation that demands intellectual response.

Secondary experience is Dewey's term for the process of intellectual response to problematic situations. For example, we learn that fire is dangerous and that we have to approach it in ways different to other objects. Since we live in a culture, we do not even have to have this experience ourselves firsthand but can learn from what others tell us. The reflective experience helps us to avoid undesirable consequences of primary experience. However, if we rely too exclusively on secondary experience, especially that of others, we run the risk of losing vital contact to our world through primary encounters. We then easily become oblivious of the actual conditions and challenges of our actions. Dewey often criticizes one-sided forms of intellectualism because, caught in this trap, they forget about the realities of life.

In Chapter 1, we noted that meanings are consummatory as well as instrumental. In Chapter 2, we discussed the role of habit and feeling in experience and learning. With regard to language, we may now observe that, at first, habits, emotions, and linguistic resources and abilities mutually involve and inform each other. Dewey says that signification "involves the use of a quality as a sign or index of something else, as when the red of a light signifies danger" (LW 1: 200). This is the instrumental "use" of language. By contrast, "The sense of a thing . . . is an immediate and immanent meaning; it is meaning which is itself felt or directly had" (LW 1: 200). Abstract, representational, instrumental meanings, or what Dewey more often calls "signification," have a *reference*; that is, an object (person, place, thing, and so on). However, once we secure the reference of significant meaning, the habits and emotions involved impart an immanent, consummatory, aesthetic meaning to the reference. We express such immanent meanings, e.g., as "ahh, I understand now." You may grasp the meaning of a situation and the intent of the actors in it without being able to fully articulate all you comprehend. Likewise, children barely able to read a text may yet "read" a teacher's mood and intention perfectly. Indeed, much of this ability is sub-linguistic. To fully grasp the meaning of a word, we must grasp its "immanent meaning" (or "sense" as Dewey more often calls it) in a given context of action. Similar remarks hold for any aesthetic experience. Considered from today's perspective, we can see Dewey's understanding of the intense interplay of habit, emotion, meaning, and sense as an anticipation of later research and developments in communication theories as well as more recent neuro-scientific approaches regarding the role of emotions. For example, such research shows that we have long underestimated the role of emotions as an important factor in information processing and communication.

Dewey's example of experience involving immanent meaning is that of an experienced versus an inexperienced sailor who hears a loud snap in the sails during a ferocious storm. The inexperienced sailor must consciously, deliberately, and slowly "infer—use the noise as a symbol—and do something to find the signified"; that is, to find the referent and perhaps repair it (LW 3: 89). For the experienced sailor, having made many such referential inferences, "the noise will be, to him, a sail blown out of its bolt ropes" (LW 3: 89). The experienced sailor has the habitual know-how and intuitive feeling for what binds him/her together with the nautical functions and environmental conditions into a single whole such that he/she may quickly restore dynamic functional unity to the disrupted situation without conscious reflection. Dewey concludes, the latter "sort of thing is what is intended by the phrase 'immanent meaning'" (LW 3: 89). Immanent meaning, or sense, is the fulfilling meaning of a reference. He asserts, "Whenever a situation has this double function of meaning, namely signification and sense, mind, intellect is definitely present" (LW 1: 200). Instrumental meanings lead to and emerge from immediate consummatory meanings that are the fulfillment of instrumental signification. Few educators or philosophers ever seem to notice that embodied, affective immanent sense meanings are as important to mental functioning as instrumental meanings.

Educationally, the almost exclusive emphasis in formal education on abstract symbolic instrumental meanings harms mental development. As shown in the example of the sailors, immanent meaning is the supreme mode of social control. Recall that habits are social functions for Dewey. "Customs persist," wrote Dewey, "because individuals form their personal habits under conditions set by prior customs. An individual usually acquires the morality as he inherits the speech of his social group" (LW 1: 43). The questions of customs, conduct, and habits are not in themselves moral ones. Dewey concluded, "Conduct is always shared[;] this is the difference between it and a physiological process. It is not an ethical 'ought' that conduct *should* be social. It *is* social, whether bad or good" (MW

14: 16). To acknowledge oneself as controlled by habits and conditioned by social customs is simply to recognize that one's values, beliefs, interests, perceptions, and so on are largely predetermined by the reinforcement schedules that comprise the social context, including dominant cultural texts, of a given historical epoch. We cannot eliminate that a certain amount of social conditioning is involved in education. This implies the possibility of acquiring prejudices from social customs. We should not deceive ourselves into believing that we can entirely prevent such influences. That does not mean we cannot reconstruct ourselves if we can become aware of the contingencies that originally conditioned and continue to shape our behavioral habits.

The power of cultural customs is so prevalent that it creates profound questions concerning individuality and freedom. As powerfully as social customs condition the habits that constitute the content of our character, free choice and individuality remain possible. Beyond the endowments of the biologic individual, though, freedom and moral individuality are achievements, consequences of deliberate conscious reflection. In *The Public and Its Problems*, Dewey proclaims: "Freedom or individuality is not an original possession or gift. It is something to be achieved, to be wrought out" (LW 2: 61). Recall that our unconscious, unreflective habits possess us; perhaps more accurately, we should say, we are captured by our own unreflective habits and passions. Freedom is first the work of individuals' reflective and social intelligence. This includes investigating how culture has trained and educated us. On this basis, the work of creative intelligence is to re-create ourselves in relation to others. Formal education in Dewey's sense, would teach us to appropriately possess, critically inspect, and creatively reconstruct those habits and customs acquired through former education and socialization.

Why is it, in spite of the fact that teaching by pouring in, learning by a passive absorption, is universally condemned, that they are still so entrenched in practice? That education is not an affair of "telling" and being told, but an active and constructive process, is a principle almost as generally violated in practice as conceded in theory. Is not this deplorable situation due to the fact that the doctrine is itself merely told? It is preached; it is lectured; it is written about. But its enactment into practice requires that the school environment be equipped with agencies for doing, with tools and physical materials, to an extent rarely attained. It requires that methods of instruction and administration be modified to allow and to secure direct and continuous occupations with things (MW 9: 43–44).

Challenge For Today: Educational Interaction and the Chances and Limits of Communication

Although meaningful experience always presupposes language in our symbolic and discursive undertakings, this is not to say that it is completely exhausted or swallowed up in language. As Dewey observes:

> A universe of experience is the precondition of a universe of discourse. Without its controlling presence, there is no way to determine the relevancy, weight or coherence of any designated distinction or relation. The universe of experience surrounds and regulates the universe of discourse but never appears as such within the latter.
>
> (LW 12: 74)

There is a great deal of pre-cognitive experience that may matter immensely to us, although we are unable to articulate what we feel: "Immediacy of existence is ineffable. But there is nothing mystical about such ineffability; it expresses the fact that of direct existence it is futile to say anything to one's self and impossible to say anything to another" (LW 1: 74). The incommunicable aspect of personal experience—our fleetingly unique subjectivity—contributes to what we will call below, following Mead, the "I" as opposed to the "me." We construct meanings to engage in socially shared practices. To have a mind is to have such meanings, which we may then use to organize our individual lives. Those who do so critically and creatively become individual minds and not just individuals *with* minds. However, if we remember that experience includes many other relations with existence than those that are cognitive, that is, if we avoid the vice of intellectualism discussed in Chapter 1, we may readily acknowledge that much of reality overflows the limits of our linguistic containers. Even the best love poem may only point to what we may only hope to show, but may never say.

Philosophy after Wittgenstein as reconstructed by Rorty (1979)—drawing on the works of, for example, Putnam, Davidson, and followed by Brandom and others—has taken the unavoidable linguistic turn that has posted language into a predominant position.[3] From this point of view, experience is always already mediated through language. For some of these thinkers, it has completely lost the existential grounding that Dewey tried to establish. But even this linguistic discourse finds its surprising supplement in Derrida's *différance*, which denotes the reappearance of displacement and omission even within the symbolic and points beyond (see Garrison, 2002). Language itself is an important phase of a developing experience, but limited in its scope. If we call this limit "the real"—as the Cologne program of interactive constructivism does (cf. Neubert & Reich 2006)—then what we get is a void signifier, which gives us the chance to relativize the new dominance of language. Let us take a closer look at the concept of "the real" in combination with experience as discussed above.

In experience, what matters most often only appears in our imaginations as desire or wishes not yet refined through language or reflection. And, experience always implies the possibility that we encounter something real that we can linguistically reconstruct only after the event. The real as a phenomenon is a very open-ended construct. What is experienced as real is largely up to the observer in his or her cultural contexts of participation and acting. Think, for example, of situations that had been unexpected and in which a new symbolic meaning suddenly strikes your mind. You heard a lot about cancer, but for you it makes a considerable difference if you learn that you yourself are suffering from it. On the other hand, there are situations in which we experience the real as a symbolic effect. For example, you have been confident to fully understand the implications of some symbolic representation, say the concept of democracy, and you find yourself surprised to find that in a different situation, a different time, or for a different group of people, the term seems to represent a different meaning with implications that render you speechless.

After all, symbolic systems are part of experience and experiencing. Although constructed in culture, they affect experience as a social reality in their use by humans. What is more, even imagined situations can appear as a reality that matters, such as schizophrenic delusions. Symbolically, I may swear that my marriage will last; I can imaginatively trust that it will, but only future real events will show if it does. People who continually reject the real to put an emphasis on the symbolic may appear to others as rationalizing; people who reject it to primarily retain for themselves the imaginative may appear as daydreamers or deranged; but people who tend to excessively exhaust the real appear as fatalists. Here, it is important for us to see through the tactics of changing observer perspectives between the symbolic, the imaginative, and real events. Therefore, we think that it is essential to establish a constructivist observer theory to avoid the traps of playing language off against experience. After all, only observers' perspectives can help us to situate ourselves as observers in our participations and actions in the world. The real warns us not to overestimate ourselves.

Communication is more than discussion; it always implies a context of interaction. Dewey gives a classical explanation:

> A requests B to bring him something, to which A points, say a flower. There is an original mechanism by which B may react to A's movement in pointing. But natively such a reaction is to the movement, not to the pointing, not to the object pointed out. But B learns that the movement is a pointing; he responds to it not in itself, but as an index of something else. His response is transferred from A's direct movement to the object to which A points. Thus he does not merely execute the natural acts of looking or grasping which the movement might instigate on its own account. The motion of A attracts his gaze to the thing pointed to; then, instead of just transferring his response from A's movement to the native reaction he might make to the thing as stimulus, he responds in a way which is a function of A's relationship, actual and potential, to the thing. The characteristic thing about B's understanding of A's movement and sounds is that he responds to the thing from the standpoint of A. He perceives the thing as it may function in A's experience, instead of just ego-centrically. Similarly, A in making the request conceives the thing not only in its direct relation-ship to himself, but as a thing capable of being grasped and handled by B.

> He sees the thing as it may function in B's experience. Such is the essence and import of communication, signs and meaning. Something is literally made common in at least two different centres of behavior. To understand is to anticipate together, it is to make a cross-reference which, when acted upon, brings about a partaking in a common, inclusive, undertaking.
>
> (LW 1: 140 ff.)

Here, Dewey could as well have referred to Mead (1934), especially what has later been called symbolic interaction. Mead argued that communication between two or more persons always presupposes and is regulated by what he called the "generalized other," i.e., the values, norms, and symbolic orders shared by a group and internalized by its members. Dewey has a similar insight as to the importance of group expectations and orientations for individual and personal encounters: "Language is specifically a mode of interaction of at least two beings, a speaker and a hearer; it presupposes an organized group to which these creatures belong, and from whom they have acquired their habits of speech" (LW 1:145).

Mead's work has been very influential, among other things, for Jürgen Habermas' development of the theory of communicative action (see Habermas, 1984, 1987). In a different way than Dewey, Habermas tries to consider the possibilities of delimiting relations of domination with regard to democratic communication. In this connection, interactive constructivism takes a position that partly picks up the threads of both Mead and Habermas and combines them with a critical reconsideration of Dewey's approach. In Mead, the dimension of interaction between self and others finds a path-breaking elaboration. Figure 3.1 summarizes the core points.

The position of the "I" refers to what we feel as subjects, what we perceive for ourselves from a position in which we can be spontaneous, creative, selfish, egoistic. But our culture does not allow us to remain this way. It brings us together with others. Through behavioral feedback—or what Mead calls "taking the role of the other"—we learn bit by bit what is proper in this culture and what is considered unacceptable. All these experiences produce within us the position of the "me." This includes the various social roles we play as well as the various social roles played by others. We may play many roles in our lives such as parent, teacher, child, and student. We also have some understanding of how to play the roles of others we interact with in person or via public media such as police officer, rock star, politician, janitor, and postal clerk. The conduct of the various roles played by the multiple instances of "me" is socially controlled by the approving or disapproving responses of others (e.g., parents, teachers, and others that we look to for approval). Thus, there is a tensional relationship between the poles of "I" and "me." A self, an identity, is integrated, although we have to concede that over the years this self undergoes changes also. In what ways and how much it changes is entirely dependent on the balancing of the "I" and "me" parts.

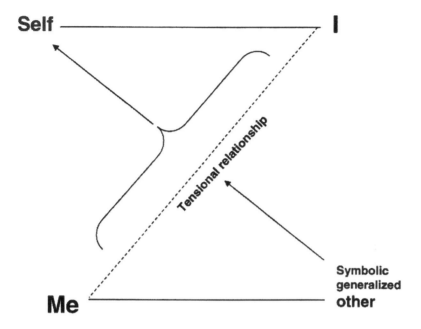

FIGURE 3.1 Interaction in Mead

Figure 3.1 expresses the fact that, for Mead, there can be no direct access from one self to another, albeit a certain pressure of the other upon the self, which is transmitted via the tensional relationship between "I" and "me." Communication as interaction between subjects only occurs via this tensional relationship. But Mead certainly places the emphasis on the symbolic, generalized other. The socialized pressure on the self occurs solely through the generalization of the behavior of others, and through the socialized pressure to conform, which appears to be crucial for finding one's role and shaping one's identity in a culture. As a pragmatist, Mead is aware of the fact that a person has to undergo some extent of behavioral conformism if he/she is going to be socialized. In this way, the multitude of possibilities and ideas of the "I" are curbed and disciplined via the internalized looks of third persons in the "me." When we come into this world as children, we must make claims on all the possibilities from the position of our "I," but all educators in the world will predominantly rely on the development of a "me" to sneak into this important part of the self with its socially controlling norms, values, and meanings. Thereby, they take part in shaping the self. This procedure is commonly called socialization and stands for the entrance of the subject into the symbolic systems of culture.

As a challenge for education, we may say that we need symbolic systems because they give us the necessary orientation and control in our culture and make communication possible. However, the cultural history of the symbolic shows that the possession of sufficient symbolic certainties or an ultimately stable foundation for all observers, participants, and agents is impossible. Symbolic systems themselves are contingent and undergo change. Seen in a larger perspective, they only achieve particular views. They emerge in the process of civilization because they help us as observers in marking the opportunities and boundaries of our intentional standpoints. Symbolic communication is essential for every culture, but it is not the only dimension or access to communicating with others. The imaginative is another way of access. It is part of the educational challenge to observe the necessary and unavoidable ambivalence that characterizes the relationship between the two dimensions in communication. In *Art as Experience*, Dewey writes: "works of art are the only media of complete and unhindered communication between man and man that can occur in a world full of gulfs and walls that limit community of experience" (LW 10: 110). The actualizing of artful imaginative possibilities may achieve relatively unhindered communication by creating a community of shared aesthetic communion. Interactive constructivism has developed a comprehensive theory of mirror-experiences in interaction with others that will allow us to expand Dewey's insight about artistic communication. It is the imaginative desire of the other in mutual mirrorings that allows for an abundance of lively and multifaceted relationships.

This opens new perspectives on intersubjectivity. We will briefly give an example for this concept of interaction: A couple in love thinks that the other can understand everything, that they know how to interpret every gesture and read every wish from one's lips. The imaginative seems like a mutual river that is rejoiced together. But is there not always also some doubt as to how long such joy may last? The lovers may indulge in navigating the mutual river. But ultimately they will have to learn that they cannot take the other prisoner in their own imaginative wishes and mirror cabinets. The pleasure will last only temporarily. If the lover counts on what love is or could be, then she or he soon begins to cry out for symbolic clarities: faithfulness, marriage, renouncement of further possibilities, work on everyday realities, the first annoyances. In brief: symbolic demands, expectations, and constraints move in to embed the imaginative river according to cultural contexts, social conventions, and individual expectations. Or, to quote Rilke: "Look at these lovers, tormented by love, when first they begin confessing, how soon they lie!" (Rilke, 1990: 212). The imaginative stands for those impulses and images that we initially only experience and feel, but whose tracks are still so open that we end up being closer to the emotions than to the intellect, closer to intuition than to rationality, and closer to experience than to a symbolic account of experiences. In imaginative mirror-experiences, there are wishes and desires not yet refined or transformed by symbolic work.

Dewey has a sense of the importance of the imaginative in experience and communication, and he at times observes the level of mirror-experiences:

Two men meet; one is the applicant for a position, while the other has the disposition of the matter in his hands. The interview may be mechanical, consisting of set questions, the replies to which perfunctorily settle the matter. There is no experience in which the two men meet, nothing that is not a repetition, by way of acceptance or dismissal, of something which has happened a score of times . . . But an interplay may take place in which a new experience develops . . . The experience is of material fraught with suspense and moving toward its own consummation through a connected series of varied incidents. The primary emotions on the part of the applicant may be at the beginning hope or despair, and elation or disappointment at the close. These emotions qualify the experience as a unity. But as the interview proceeds, secondary emotions are evolved as variations of the primary underlying one. It is even possible for each attitude and gesture, each sentence, almost every word, to produce more than a fluctuation in the intensity of the basic emotion; to produce, that is, a change of shade and tint in its quality. The employer sees by means of his own emotional reactions the character of the one applying. He projects him imaginatively into the work to be done and judges his fitness by the way in which the elements of the scene assemble and either clash or fit together. The presence and behavior of the applicant either harmonize with his own attitudes and desires or they conflict and jar. Such factors as these, inherently esthetic in quality, are the forces that carry the varied elements of the interview to a decisive issue. They enter into the settlement of every situation, whatever its dominant nature, in which there are uncertainty and suspense.

(LW 10: 49 f.)

This is a very good example of how the symbolic and the imaginative are related in communication. What happens when we take a closer look at this relation? You can feel a difference between the gestures, sentences, and symbolic statements, the multitude of words and linguistic utterances on the one hand and internal moods, impulses, wishes, and desires on the other. Sometimes it's difficult for us to tell whether what affects us comes from inside or outside. Then we maybe ask ourselves: "Why do I feel this or that way in this moment?" But already thinking about it changes the emotion, which subsequently becomes refined and rationalized. If we try to symbolically express our imaginations, we may associate words like the following: visionary freedom, imaginative power, fantasy, emotions, intuition, qualitative experience, magic, mood, atmosphere, and images.

In interactive constructivism, the imaginative and the symbolic are two observer perspectives on communication that we may take. While we can distinguish between these two perspectives it's important not to separate them too far. For example, as learners, we cannot entirely learn on the symbolic level outside imaginative possibility. Neither can we remain entirely on the imaginative level, since we need the symbolic to curb and discipline our dreams and impulses.

The symbolic always introduces a reality principle on which we must rely in our culture. As constructivists, we pay particular attention to the imaginative dimension of all communication. In addition to pragmatist communication theories like the ones developed by Mead and Dewey, we here also draw on other approaches within the linguistic turn. Especially, Jacques Lacan has launched a tradition of thinking about communication that opens a different focus on the symbolic and imaginative.[4] For him, there is a language barrier between the subject and the other. In symbolic interaction between self and other we cannot directly capture the imaginative. There remains something unspoken in every linguistic exchange, because in the imaginative, we are speechless. Let us take a further look at Figure 3.2.

One subject stands in a communicative relationship to another. Yet—and this is the crucial difference from previous models—this subject has no direct access to the other via symbols or language. A language barrier bars this passage. Instead of a direct symbolic access to the other (the symbolic generalized other), Figure 3.2 suggests that communication occurs via an imaginative axis (o to o'). The subject (S) needs his or her imagination of the other in the encounter as it is subjectively experienced and intuitively constructed. This involves a process of

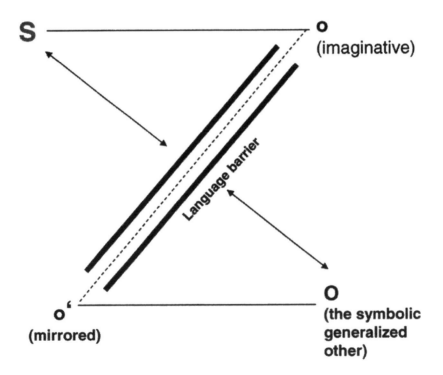

FIGURE 3.2 Imaginative Interaction in Interactive Constructionism

mediating one's own desire (o) through the mirrored effects of imaginative encounter with the other (o'). The positions o and o' are partly comparable to those of "I" and "me" from Figure 3.1. What has been laid out for symbolic interaction above reappears here for the imaginative, too.

Let us remember once again the image of the lovers. Even that partner in communication who is closest to me in my life remains in this sense a stranger: she has her own imaginative, and we can only discuss about our imaginations in the symbolic. We cannot develop a direct linguistic access to the imagined other, which we here call "small o." We have intuitions, sympathies or antipathies, moods, and feelings that point to this observer dimension. However, if we try to communicate about these intuitions, etc., with each other, we must unavoidably change our perspective. The imaginative in all its particularity first needs to be symbolically articulated and refined so that we may achieve understanding.

From the perspective of the imaginative, the lovers develop an idealized image of their own desires (o) as well as of the felt expectations towards the other (o'). Only in their actions will the lovers experience real effects in the symbolic encounter with the other. Given the vicissitudes of human interaction (the source of both comedy and tragedy), we may often misinterpret others or find them acting out of character. These effects may either confirm or disappoint their imaginations. Here we need to think of the symbolic and the imaginative as being part of an ongoing tensional relationship. This tension may be illustrated in recourse to Mead. Without ever wanting to exclude emotions and sensations, Mead already saw the "I" as that part which situates the self in the world as relatively spontaneous and open, as creative and event-oriented. Our theory of imaginative mirror-experiences gives an extended background to this position. It links the "I" to an imaginative desire (o). But this "I" in the position of (o) would remain in hallucinations and unrealistic dreams if it could not build on the tensional relationship through which it is mirrored by others (o'). From childhood on we learn through the look of the other, e.g., as represented by mother and father, to delimit our own imaginative desires through these related mirror-experiences. The process of identity formation involves the presence of a self, which depends on the imaginative process of being mirrored by others.

The language barrier illustrated in Figure 3.2 can be described from two perspectives. On the "subjective" side of this barrier, the imaginative is individual, singular, unknown to another, and even largely unconscious to ourselves. This is the ineffable domain of private experience. On the "objective" side of the language barrier, the imaginative is expressed in a process of symbolic articulation and thereby publically transformed. Part of any freedom project involves learning how to articulate the previously inarticulable. The context of this transformation is experience in culture where we construct symbolic commonalities driven by imaginations that then circulate among and within us and, further on, develop or delimit our imaginative horizons. This is how the imaginative merges with the symbolic even as it overflows the limits of language and the bounds of any system of categories and concepts.

Earlier, we saw that Dewey made a distinction between the personal and intellectual as factors in social control and that his approach somewhat favored the importance of the latter over the former. If we think of imaginative mirror experiences and the effect of the language barrier, however, we find that the contrast is rather artificial or at least ideal-typical. The personal appears in the intellectual, and the imagined other appears in the generalized other. This is why the interplay between the imaginative and the symbolic (between desire and intellect) is so important. Dewey has a clear anticipation of that importance but theories like Lacan's or the approach of interactive constructivism help us better to specify its complex implications for communication and human interaction.

The challenge for education connected with the tension between the symbolic, the imaginative, and the real starts with the need to distinguish between different observer positions. From an inner perspective on communication, the self-observer may construct a highly subjective world. But in communicating through mirrored experiences with others, she/he will not be able to realize her/his merely subjective intentions, but has to rely on a reality principle that includes the world of interaction and, thus, delimits her/his privacy. Delimitations through mirrorings are necessary for living together and communicating with each other, and culture takes pains to secure such delimitations through symbolic systems. Whenever the imaginative is articulated in the varied forms of language, the symbolic appears— then a generalized other steps onto the scene. This is where we have Mead's "me" position, which already implies generalizations in the discourse of others. And, for all of us, these symbolic generalizations in culture are very powerful contexts.

In education, we find the dominance of the symbolic whenever educational experience and practice is primarily ordered and structured according to generalized rules, expectations, standards, and so on. Think, for example, of the current tendencies of standardized testing, measuring, and credentialism. As children, we have almost no chance of defending ourselves against the symbolic expectations of others. Thus, we tend to overestimate the symbolic and to neglect the importance of imaginative interaction. For us, it seems clear that this touches on the borders of the unconscious—whether or not one thinks of the unconscious in Freudian terms. Connecting with Dewey, we recall his credo that imagination is (as Shelley taught us) "the chief instrument of the good" (LW 10: 350), because only "imaginative vision elicits the possibilities that are interwoven within the texture of the actual" (LW 10: 348).

On the other hand, the challenge consists of finding a sustainable balance between the necessary claims of symbolic orientation and openness for imaginative visions and mirrorings in relationships with others. We think it is a strength of Dewey's philosophy of communication that he so much appreciates the role of imagination in culture. His instrumentalism and theory of inquiry help us to find symbolic solutions and delimit unrealistic speculations, but he was never blind to the fact that imagination stretches beyond our symbolic realities. And, recognizing the importance of education, he would even today emphasize the indispensability of the imaginative in all dimensions of communicating and learning, especially with regard to emotional learning.

Reconsidering *Democracy and Education* today, we suggest that it is necessary to connect Dewey's account with more recent discussions on experience and language. Here, the work of Richard Rorty has been very influential. As we have already mentioned above, Rorty argues for a conceptual shift from experience to language. We partly agree with Rorty in this attempt insofar as his intention is to avoid foundationalism and naturalistic essentialism. This seems to be a crucial task for the development of pragmatism and constructivism. But we must see this strategy itself as an observer perspective we construct as a viable interpretation for the development and application of language games in the symbolic dimension. If we give the symbolic perspective a home in language alone and make this perspective predominant, then we get, on the one side, a necessary linguistic approach that, on the other side, cannot fully measure up to the multitude of phenomena in observation, participation, and action. The imaginative, as we see it, provides a good example here. Although it can only be articulated and discussed in language, it shows at the same time also the limits of language and the language barrier. It is not sufficient to look on poetic vocabularies or sensitive narrations, like Rorty does, that long for the imaginative. It makes more sense, we think, to see the imaginative in its tensional relationships with the symbolic and the real as discussed above.

Insofar, we can share the objections raised against Rorty, for example, by Richard Shusterman (1999), who tries to remind us of the dimension of a non-discursive experience, which, for him, resides especially in the human body. He takes this non-discursive experience from Dewey, even if he critically observes against Dewey: "He was wrong to think that an unconscious, non-discursive immediate quality was the necessary grounding guide or regulatory criterion of all our thinking, though he was right to insist that non-discursive background experience influences our conscious thought" (Shusterman, 1999: 207). But the main target of Shusterman's criticism is Rorty, against whom he insists on the somatic dimension of experience.

> Before burying the body, we need to assess more critically philosophy's resistance to non-discursive experience. Such resistance is based not only on arguments but on deeply entrenched biases and agendas which work, most effectively, beneath the level of conscious thought.
>
> (Shusterman, 1999: 208)

In this turn to the somatic dimension we see another observer perspective, but one must be careful not to fall back behind the linguistic turn. This is only possible if we recognize that reflection on the limits of discursive realities is bound to the symbolic dimension. For interactive constructivism, this is itself always a symbolically constructed observer position. And we think it's wiser not to delimit our perspectives about the non-discursive to the somatical. In principle, both discursive and non-discursive experiences can only be articulated and discussed in the symbolic. This is a dimension where the linguistic turn cannot be denied. But in the symbolic, we also have to be aware of the limits of symbolization.

Interactive constructivism, to conclude, claims two main perspectives for reflecting on the limits of the symbolic and, in this sense, reaching beyond it. One perspective is the imaginative; the other is the real. Both can only be understood as observer perspectives that we construct to overcome a narrow linguistic understanding. But, we need language to discuss them. So, it is possible to have nonlinguistic experiences in the imaginative and the real, but to recognize them, we have to change into the symbolic, and to communicate them in a full sense we have to change into language games.

Dewey's Summary

The natural or native impulses of the young do not agree with the life-customs of the group into which they are born. Consequently they have to be directed or guided. This control is not the same thing as physical compulsion; it consists in centering the impulses acting at any one time upon some specific end and in introducing an order of continuity into the sequence of acts. The action of others is always influenced by deciding what stimuli shall call out their actions. But in some cases as in commands, prohibitions, approvals, and disapprovals, the stimuli proceed from persons with a direct view to influencing action. Since in such cases we are most conscious of controlling the action of others, we are likely to exaggerate the importance of this sort of control at the expense of a more permanent and effective method. The basic control resides in the nature of the situations in which the young take part. In social situations the young have to refer their way of acting to what others are doing and make it fit in. This directs their action to a common result, and gives an understanding common to the participants. For all *mean* the same thing, even when performing different acts. This common understanding of the means and ends of action is the essence of social control. It is indirect, or emotional and intellectual, not direct or personal. Moreover it is intrinsic to the disposition of the person, not external and coercive. To achieve this internal control through identity of interest and understanding is the business of education. While books and conversation can do much, these agencies are usually relied upon too exclusively. Schools require for their full efficiency more opportunity for conjoint activities in which those instructed take part, so that they may acquire a *social* sense of their own powers and of the materials and appliances used.

(MW 9: 44–45)

Our Summary

Education as interaction, continuity, and communication is a process that emerges from complex tensions of culture and nature. Today, we can see interaction, communication, and culture as interwoven fields with complex and diverse implications for education. There are at least four main aspects to take into account. First, the importance of experience is as relevant as it was in Dewey's time, and his overall approach to connect education and experience still applies in our time. The advantages of the concept of experience are among other things to connect education with actions (learning by doing and undergoing), lived relationships, cultural diversity, and social growth. The dangers for democracy and education, in Dewey's time as well as ours, lie in the often powerful tendencies to confine actions to routines (learning not by doing but by being institutionalized), reducing others to symbolic expectations in often artificial and virtual relationships, performing monocultural habits, introducing barriers for exchange through social compartmentalization (especially by capitalist structures). Second, we need observer theories that do justice to the complexities of interaction, communication, and culture in pluralist societies. The chances in this connection are to increase our abilities to understand and address complex contexts of education, interaction, and communication. The limits are set by a culture that stresses the needs of reproduction, standardization, measurement, and feasibility of perspectives and learning in the contexts of market expectations. Third, we must learn to appreciate the importance of the imaginative in education more generously and develop cultures of communication and learning that do justice to the diversity of imagination and allow for encounters with otherness. Opportunities exist to cooperate creatively across differences and to understand diversity as a means to enrich experience. The limits lie in the counter-imaginative powers of a commercialized, serialized, and virtualized culture that tends to reduce experiences to superficial effects of consumerism. Fourth, educative communication can only be co-developed by participants who have opportunities to use their capacities and social intelligence in interaction with others. The chances are to create communities with sufficient openness for diversity in observing, acting, and partaking. The limits are, for instance, set by failing to understand each other (the language barrier), failing to reach common understanding (conflict of values), neglecting or underestimating power effects within communities (hidden or open exclusions), and idealizing consent over dissent (neglect of pluralism). Generally speaking, the challenge of education in all these respects lies in empowering the opportunities and critically addressing the limits.

Notes

1   See Rorty (1979). Quine (1969) even argues that Dewey was ahead of Wittgenstein.
2   The following passage on experience draws on our book Garrison, Neubert & Reich (2012: 11), where readers may find a more comprehensive account of Dewey's cultural turn in philosophy.
3   The following paragraphs on experience and communication draw largely on Neubert & Reich (2006).
4   For an introduction to Lacan's thinking, cf. Lacan (2006).

4

EDUCATION AS GROWTH

The Deweyan concept of growth is related to the Darwinian idea of evolution in nature, but he uses it primarily in a cultural sense when he defines education as "that reconstruction or reorganization of experience which adds to the meaning of experience, and which increases ability to direct the course of subsequent experience" (MW 9: 82). Reductionists often ignore culture and cultural constraints on student learning such as poverty, neighborhood crime, and a parent's level of education. They may also ignore how culture, including the economic system, spirituality, and social security may enable growth.

Properly understood, education as growth is physical, social, and cultural, since each influences the other. For example, a culture that cares can provide for those who are physically handicapped as well as those biologically sick, socially marginalized, or hungry. However, even when we take a cultural perspective on growth, we also find possible misunderstandings or at least a multitude of interpretations. This is why Nel Noddings (2012: 26) observes that growth is a sometimes problematic and very open term in Dewey. In this chapter, we try to show that—from the perspective of education and democracy—growth is at the same time a necessary as well as an ambivalent and potentially even dangerous term. To define and reconstruct its meanings is itself an inherent part of the democratic process and its educative effects. Let us take a closer look at Dewey's views before we discuss educational challenges in connection with the idea of growth for today.

Chapter 4 ("Education as Growth") and Chapter 5 ("Preparation, Unfolding, and Formal Discipline") of *Democracy and Education* conclude the formal investigations of Part I of Dewey's book. Chapter 5 criticizes the three foremost theories of education—preparation, unfolding, and formal discipline—with which Dewey disagrees. All three make the same fundamental mistake of assuming a preexisting, fixed, and final aim of growth. In one guise or another, all three still have considerable influence. Therefore, while we concentrate on Chapter 4, we will briefly discuss Dewey's criticisms from Chapter 5.

Dewey claims: "The primary condition of growth is immaturity" (MW 9: 46). At first, this seems an empty truism until we realize that he entirely rejects preestablished potentials. We may think of potentiality or capacity negatively as "mere receptivity," a "merely dormant or quiescent state" (MW 9: 46). Here is why:

> Our tendency to take immaturity as mere lack, and growth as something which fills up the gap between the immature and the mature is due to regarding childhood *comparatively*, instead of intrinsically. We treat it simply as a privation because we are measuring it by adulthood as a fixed standard.
> (MW 9: 46)

Such a static comparative standard assumes a fixed society and fixed ideals of "adulthood" that itself has no more potential for growth:

> The fulfillment of growing is taken to mean an *accomplished* growth: that is to say, an Ungrowth, something which is no longer growing. The futility of the assumption is seen in the fact that every adult resents the imputation of having no further possibilities of growth; and so far as he finds that they are closed to him mourns the fact as evidence of loss.
> (MW 9: 47)

In an ever-evolving world there are no ultimate, perfect ends; ungrowth means eventual extinction. "Taken absolutely, instead of comparatively," Dewey maintains, "immaturity designates a positive force or ability,—the *power* to grow" (MW 9: 47). It is "the *ability* to develop" (MW 9: 46). Dewey's sense of immaturity as a power is an instance of evolutionary thinking: "Where there is life, there are already eager and impassioned activities. Growth is not something done to them; it is something they do. The positive and constructive aspect of possibility gives the key to understanding the two chief traits of immaturity, dependence and plasticity" (MW 9: 47).

By dependence Dewey means "need for others" with whom we transact (MW 9: 57). Such growth in ability exemplifies that social dependence is as important as personal freedom, since it permits the social construction of meaning among the young and old alike. By plasticity, Dewey means potential to grow. The idea of potential is an essential component of the concept of development, including human development. Most theories of growth, educational or otherwise, assume latent potentials unfolding into predetermined, fixed, and final ends. The idea of little acorns becoming mighty oak trees is a common example. It is a mistake. Acorns become whatever their environmental transactions make of them. If the acorn does not transact with an environment with adequate rainfall, sunlight, and nutrient soil, the acorn will not grow. Even under ideal conditions, most acorns become food for squirrels rather than mature oak trees, nor do the squirrels think it an unnatural result. What any living thing becomes depends upon intricate reciprocally transforming organism–environment transactions producing continuity of development. The aim of any kind of growth depends upon coordinating a complex transactional ecology. Similar remarks hold when the environment is a cultural construct. It takes more than a village to educate a child.

Dewey notes that we never appeal to the term potential "except where there *is* change or a process of becoming" (MW 8: 11). Dewey holds an evolutionary concept of potentiality. Influenced by the consequences of Darwinism for philosophy, Dewey reconstructs the idea of potential in such a way that transaction and interdependence become intrinsic to the concept. For him, "there is no isolated occurrence in nature" (LW 1: 207). Existence is comprised of events in actual or potential interaction. Furthermore, everything is a mixture of the actual and the potential. The actual event "A" (person, place, thing, etc.) actualizes the potential in another event "B" and, conversely, the actual in "B" actualizes the potential in "A." Student–teacher interactions provide a fine example.

Dewey holds that we live in a pluralistic universe in which difference is essential to development:

> When the idea that development is due to some indwelling end which tends to control the series of changes passed through is abandoned, potentialities must be thought of in terms of consequences of interactions with other things. Hence potentialities cannot be *known* till *after* the interactions have occurred. There are at a given time unactualized potentialities in an individual because and in as far as there are in existence other things with which it has not as yet interacted.
>
> (LW 14: 109)

Dewey draws the following pluralistic conclusion: "Potentiality thus implies not merely diversity, but a progressively increasing diversification of a specific thing in a particular direction" (MW 8: 11). Dewey thinks every individual has unique potential, but it is only possible to actualize it through transaction with otherness and difference:

> Individuality itself is originally a potentiality and is realized only in interaction with surrounding conditions. In this process of intercourse, native capacities, which contain an element of uniqueness, are transformed and become a self. Moreover, through resistances encountered, the nature of the self is discovered. The self is both formed and brought to consciousness through interaction with environment.
>
> (LW 10: 286–287)

Note that individuality is primordially a potential concretely actualized through transactions with already actualized surrounding conditions and, especially, cultural social conditions, as we saw in our discussion of Mead in Chapter 3. The influence of one side of the transaction actualizes the potential of the other side, and conversely. With each transaction, the unique potentials of the self undergo ever-evolving transformations as they creatively transform themselves by transforming the environment:

> To cooperate by giving differences a chance to show themselves because of the belief that the expression of difference is not only a right of the other persons but is a means of enriching one's own life-experience, is inherent in the democratic personal way of life.
>
> (LW 14: 228)

Dewey's notion of human potential rejects concepts of atomistic individualism. Think about it. If we were born with the same innate rationality and innate free will, then if everyone exercises their rationality and disciplines their will appropriately, every individual would do the same thing in the same situation, which makes a mockery of the very idea of individuality. Dewey's notion of a mutually dependent, plastic individual provides, however, an ideal of individuality as a unique capacity. In *Individualism, Old and New*, Dewey indicates: "Individuality is at first spontaneous and unshaped; it is a potentiality, a capacity of development. Even so, it is a unique manner of acting in and with a world of objects and persons" (LW 5: 121). Individuals need others as unique as themselves to develop their distinctive potentials as well as their collective and democratic norms and values.

Educational growth, therefore, implies the developmental formation of an individual's unique potential so she or he can make her or his unique contribution to society. In an authorized report of a talk Dewey gave, he is reputed to have said: "Self is thus something wrought out of original tendencies in the course of social intercourse" (MW 7: 404). As we showed in Chapter 3, Mead was able to work out such a stance in greater detail. Dewey's ideal of a pluralistic, communicative democracy discussed in Chapter 5 below depends on his transactional theory of individual unique potential (see Cunningham, 1994).

Plasticity includes the capacity to acquire culture. Unlike other creatures, newborn human beings take many years to maturate before they are able to care for themselves. They must acquire habits of adjusting to the environment since they are not born with the requisite structures:

> The specific adaptability of an immature creature for growth constitutes his *plasticity* . . . It is essentially the ability to learn from experience; the power to retain from one experience something which is of avail in coping with the difficulties of a later situation. This means power to modify actions

on the basis of the results of prior experiences, the power to *develop dispositions*. Without it, the acquisition of habits is impossible.

(MW 9: 49)

Once again, we return to the importance of embodied habits. Human beings actualize their potential by developing skillful habits of action in their transactions with others, including language and communication. What Dewey says about habits in his chapter on education as growth (Chapter 4) extends what we have already learned. First, he points out that habits provide a form of executive skill in doing things. Further,

A habit means an ability to use natural conditions as means to ends. It is an active control of the environment through control of the organs of action. We are perhaps apt to emphasize the control of the body at the expense of control of the environment.

(MW 9: 51)

Reductionist approaches like Skinnerian behaviorism usually think of habits as conditioned (or trained) responses to environmental stimuli. What these accounts neglect is, from a Deweyan perspective, that habits are not merely passive adaptations to an existing environment but, at the same time, active powers by which individuals in transactions with others influence, change, transform, and reconstruct their environments as well as themselves.

As we become educated, we acquire linguistic meanings and can form complex discursive intentions, purposes, ideas, and ideals of action. As agents, our habits allow us to execute intelligent plans of action. Dewey, therefore, distinguishes between relatively passive habituation and active habits, a distinction that is of fundamental importance for educational growth:

Habit as habituation is indeed something relatively passive; we get used to our surroundings—to our clothing, our shoes, and gloves; to the atmosphere as long as it is fairly equable; to our daily associates, etc. Conformity to the environment, a change wrought in the organism without reference to ability to modify surroundings, is a marked trait of such habituations.

(MW 9: 51–52)

Such habituations constitute the necessary background of experience, but they do not explain the capacities of individuals to respond creatively and constructively to their environments and situations. Dewey gives the following example:

Consider getting used to a strange city. At first, there is excessive stimulation and excessive and ill-adapted response. Gradually certain stimuli are selected because of their relevancy, and others are degraded. We can say either that we do not respond to them any longer, or more truly that we have effected a persistent response to them—an equilibrium of adjustment. This means, in the second place, that this enduring adjustment supplies the background upon which are made specific adjustments, as occasion arises. We are never interested in changing the whole environment; there is much that we take for granted and accept just as it already is. Upon this background our activities focus at certain points in an endeavor to introduce needed changes. Habituation is thus our adjustment to an environment which at the time we are not concerned with modifying, and which supplies a leverage to our active habits.

(MW 9: 52)

To a certain extent, habituation consists of fixed habits and routines. "Routine habits, and habits that possess us instead of our possessing them," Dewey proclaims, "are habits which put an end to plasticity" (MW 9: 54). Active habits, on the contrary, consist—in this case as well as others—of capacities like observing, recollecting, imagining, judging, reasoning, inquiring, communicating, and criticizing. Like all habits they imply selective interests, emotions, and desires to sustain action. Habits help to create and execute plans by focusing our energies. The necessary connection between habituation as background and active habits as focus of action explains why not only intentional meanings but also immanent meanings are indispensable in all sorts of actions in culture.

Dewey preferred the word "conduct" to behavior because it better captured the continuity of action including the complex sequence of acts as well as the notion of cultural context (cf. LW 5: 221–222). Against this background, Dewey acknowledges the value of the stimulus–response (S-R) paradigm, but strongly disagrees with how it is usually understood: "It seems to me that there is considerable behavioristic and semi-behavioristic theory in psychology at present that is content merely to subsume the phenomena in question under the rubric of *S-R* as if they were ready-made and self-evident things" (LW 5: 223, original italics). For Dewey, stimulus and response emerge simultaneously in a circle of coordinated action involving equilibrium, disequilibrium, and restoration of equilibrium. One problem with traditional behaviorist theories is that they fail to acknowledge that living organisms are always already acting, and that a stimulus can only redirect action: "No stimulus is a stimulus to action as such but only to a change in the *direction* or intensity of action. A response is not action or behavior but marks a change in behavior" (LW 5: 224). It is a mistake to think it is necessary to prod any living creature into action; they act by virtue of being alive. The always already active organism determines the stimuli it responds to by first selectively attending to them rather than to the infinite other possible stimuli in its environment. Much as we create the self in the transactional creation of objects, "it is the motor response or attention which constitutes that, which finally becomes the stimulus to another act" (EW 5: 101–102). What we have is a continuously moving organic circle of coordination and not a reflex-arc. Habits are far more complicated than behaviorists realize.

Dewey's understanding of habits allows us to better comprehend intelligent, reflective action than behaviorism. As we have seen, to have a mind is to have meaning (e.g., ideas, intent, purposes, and such). "The chief objection, it seems to me, to the narrower forms of behaviorism is that their obsession against the mental, because of previous false theories about it, shuts the door to even entering upon the inquiry" (LW 5: 227). Once language supervenes, the organism begins to act using meanings that allow it to formulate plans that are not restricted to the local context in space and time. Dewey reminds us: "A habit also marks an intellectual disposition" (MW 9: 53). He means that "there are habits of judging and reasoning as truly as of handling a tool, painting a picture, or conducting an experiment" (MW 9: 53). Summing up, Dewey points to an important paradigm shift for education:

> When it is said that education is development, everything depends upon *how* development is conceived. Our net conclusion is that life is development, and that developing, growing, is life. Translated into its educational equivalents, this means (*i*) that the educational process has no end beyond itself; it is its own end; and that (*ii*) the educational process is one of continual reorganizing, reconstructing, transforming.
>
> (MW 9: 54)

Just as there is no ultimate teleology, no absolute, static, fully actualized, fixed, and final goal to Darwinian evolution, there is no absolute goal to individual or social development. Dewey thinks that the answer to the existential question "What is the meaning of life?" is: The meaning of life is to make more meaning. Educationally, this signifies that the aim of education is more education. Dewey is saying that life and education are necessary goods, but not fixed and final ones. He also answers the existential question "How should I live my life?" thusly: I should live my life in a way that makes more meaning. Because there are no private languages, making meaning is always a social activity. Educationally, we should educate so that our students and our teachers make more meaning together. In this connection, the concept of growth in all its openness and vagueness is a powerful tool for educational theory in a democratic perspective, because it leaves the definition and reconstruction of its very own meaning open to all who participate in the process of educating and being educated.

Regarding the statement that education has no end beyond itself, Dewey acknowledges that, in comparative terms, directing the child's potential to the formation of habits "involving executive skill, definiteness of interest, and specific objects of observation and thought" of an adult is appropriate to a point (MW 9: 55). However, we must remember that the "adult uses his powers to transform his environment, thereby occasioning new stimuli which redirect his powers and keep them developing" (MW 9: 55). Likewise, "The child has specific powers [unique potential]; to ignore that fact is to stunt or distort the organs upon which his growth depends" (MW 9: 55). Dewey draws the obvious conclusion. Both the adult and child "are engaged in growing" (MW 9: 55). While children should be growing so as to become sufficiently socialized into the practices and institutions of the culture, they should never lose their unique capacity to make original contributions. Conversely, "With respect to sympathetic curiosity, unbiased responsiveness, and openness of mind, we may say that the adult should be growing in childlikeness" (MW 9: 55). Being childlike while not being childish allows us to respond to a changing world with playfulness, passion, and agility. Emotionally and intellectually, we should remain forever young.

With regard to the idea that the educational process is one of continual reconstruction, Dewey makes a further observation: "Since in reality there is nothing to which growth is relative save more growth, there is nothing to which education is subordinate save more education. Since life means growth." Dewey continues, "a living creature lives as truly and positively at one stage as at another, with the same intrinsic fullness and the same absolute claims" (MW 9: 56). The best preparation for life is to draw from it the most we may from moment to moment. Then life and learning become a delight, and we are as prepared as we can be for what may come in a contingent, ever-changing world.

This leads to one more insight: "The inclination to learn from life itself and to make the conditions of life such that all will learn in the process of living is the finest product of schooling" (MW 9: 55). We should learn as much as we can from all the circumstances of life, formal and informal. Too often, formal schooling actually fails to prepare us for the everyday informality of affairs. Small wonder educators worry constantly about learning transfer.

To conclude, we may say that Dewey's concept of growth is a very helpful and even necessary conceptual tool for education. We may see its very openness as a strength, especially because it allows for democratic negotiations and reconstructions in response to changing social needs and constellations. However, growth in its vagueness and openness can also become a dangerous orientation if not provided with sufficient options for participation and mutual negotiation. There is the standing danger that social elites of powerful interests define for all what are the best forms of growth for them. We should not forget that even a narrow neoliberal policy that concentrates on the formation of what is called "human capital" has at least an implicit ideal of growth, even if it is certainly not a Deweyan one. So the concept of growth taken by itself and isolated from fundamental democratic needs and principals, like claims for participation, diversity, and inclusion, easily becomes hallowed or even a shelter of justification for hidden forms of exploitation and undemocratic oppression.

Dewey begins Chapter 5, "Education as Preparation, Unfolding, and Formal Discipline," by reminding us that "the educative process is a continuous process of growth, having as its aim at every stage an added capacity of growth" (MW

9: 59). He notes that this stance contrasts sharply with more prevalent ideas. These ideas still dominate educational discourse, so they are worth our brief consideration.

Education as preparation for life assumes the privation or deficit model where comparison to the current adult world is taken as the only measure for education. He has four major criticisms of this concept of preparation. First, such a view fails to realize that children "live in the present"; for them, "the future lacks urgency" (MW 9: 59). Instead of finding motivation in what is present and engaging to the student, we must constantly tell them their studies will be useful later, which is usually too vague and remote to sustain them. Second, students feel they can procrastinate, since, to the young, the future is far away, so why hurry (see MW 9: 58–59). A third undesirable result "is the substitution of a conventional average standard of expectation and requirement for a standard which concerns the specific powers of the individual under instruction" (MW 9: 60). In the face of an increasing will toward standardized testing and credentialism, one can hardly overestimate how appropriate Dewey's criticism is today.

In his essay, "Individuality, Equality and Superiority," Dewey acknowledges individuals are not equal cognitively and physically, but he insists on their moral equality:

> Moral equality means incommensurability, the inapplicability of common and quantitative standards. It means intrinsic qualities which require unique opportunities and differential manifestation; superiority in finding a specific work to do, not in power for attaining ends common to a class of competitors, which is bound to result in putting a premium on mastery over others.
>
> (MW 13: 299)

Dewey decried passive conformity to predetermined standards (cf. MW 9: 55). He remarks that there are "as many modes of superiority and inferiority as there are consequences to be attained and works to be accomplished" (MW 13: 226). He felt that the most "severe standards" involved personal responsibility for actions performed (cf. MW 9: 186). If we educate every individual's unique potential to make their unique contribution, we will find modes of superiority previously unknown to us, including functions for those labeled "disabled." Therefore, Dewey opposed the very idea of one-size-fits-all standards and standardized tests. Today, global human capital theory where each unit of human capital is simply a standardized interchangeable part in the global production largely determines the adult standard. Dewey thought such thinking not only disgraceful, but dangerous for democracy (see Garrison, 2012a).

Dewey's fourth, and last, criticism is that "the principle of preparation makes necessary recourse on a large scale to the use of adventitious motives of pleasure and pain. The future having no stimulating and directing power when severed from the possibilities of the present, something must be hitched on to it to make it work" (MW 9: 60). The preparation theory offers little in the present to internally motivate students, so we must use external sources of motivation.

Since *education as unfolding* "is only a variant of the preparation theory" (MW 9: 61), it need not detain us for long. Dewey describes the slight difference:

> Practically the two differ in that the adherents of the latter make much of the practical and professional duties for which one is preparing, while the developmental doctrine speaks of the ideal and spiritual qualities of the principle which is unfolding.
>
> (MW 9: 61)

Each stage of development is merely a movement "toward a completed being, the final ideal is immobile. An abstract and indefinite future is in control with all which that connotes in depreciation of present power and opportunity" (MW 9: 61). Here, the ultimate, fixed, and final telos controls the present. Everything we do is done for it. So, for example, if we are referring to ultimate salvation in God or the dictatorship of the proletariat, in both cases the ultimate telos determines present experiences and reduces our opportunities of growth.

Education as formal discipline or mere isolated training of faculties is a holdover from pre-developmental, pre-evolutionary thinking (cf. MW 9: 65). It depends on the old notion of psychological faculties: "The forms of powers in question are such things as the faculties of perceiving, retaining, recalling, associating, attending, willing, feeling, imagining, thinking, etc., which are then shaped by exercise upon material presented" (MW 9: 66). It is the antiquated idea that the mind is like a muscle that becomes stronger by being exercised. Although totally refuted by functionalist psychology, it remains entrenched in popular thought, especially today in talks about human capital (cf. Chapter 10).

Challenge for Today: Educational growth and social justice

We have suggested throughout this chapter that Dewey's concept of growth is a strong as well as a problematic tool for educational theory. Its strength consists in its openness for democratic participation in the processes of defining and reconstructing the meanings of social practices. In this connection, "growth" represents an attitude of democratic and educational hope, the belief in the power of individuals, groups, communities, and societies to develop the necessary capacities, skills, resources, and conditions to make their lives meaningful and rewarding. The problematic side arises as soon as we recognize that there is always a multitude of perspectives and interpretations about what individuals, groups, communities, and societies conceive of growth, or welfare, or progress. We must not forget that while Dewey's notion of growth is non-teleological, the understanding of growth in any social context is always historically embedded in the ideals and goals that provide the individual and collective ends of a given culture. When we look back at industrial progress in Western societies over the twentieth century, we have learned to speak not only of increased wealth but also of the emergence of the greenhouse effect, exhaustion of resources, ecological catastrophes like Chernobyl and Fukushima, and other limits or ambivalences of "growth." Dewey was already aware of the problem in his time:

> Education would then become an instrument of perpetuating unchanged the existing industrial order of society, instead of operating as a means of its transformation. The desired transformation is not difficult to define in a formal way. It signifies a society in which every person shall be occupied in something which makes the lives of others better worth living, and which accordingly makes the ties which bind persons together more perceptible— which breaks down the barriers of distance between them.
>
> (MW 9: 326)

The problem with Dewey's notion of growth is that often the term is interpreted against the background of taken-for-granted contexts, norms, and values that are themselves not sufficiently in accord with democratic principles and practices. But even under democratic conditions, growth remains an ambivalent construct because it is always connected with our wishes, expectations, selective interests, and self-confident omissions. In times of global capitalism, today, even more than in Dewey's age, the competing definitions of the meaning of growth no longer depend on inherited class interests, but more and more on liquefied market mechanisms and surplus values strategies. We must expect that there is not only a diversity of perspectives but antagonistic struggles between interests that concern the very definition of growth.

Colin Crouch (2004, 2011) argues that the development of liquefied markets supported by neoliberal ideologies of growth, and made possible by unrestrained economies and monetary systems, even takes us down the road towards a post-democratic society in which politics is more and more displaced by economy. Following the Deweyan tradition, education and educators must take a stance in this struggle and develop clear democratic visions about what growth may mean in concrete ways. For them growth must include individual as well as social norms and values. On the side of individuality, education must provide opportunities and resources for all learners to develop individual interests, achievements, skills, knowledge, capacities, and so on, that help them to make their experience more meaningful *de facto*. On the side of society, educational and welfare politics have to provide sufficient opportunities to increase equity of chances for participation and growth for all.

Today, some educational and democratic approaches draw on social and political experiences of the twentieth and early twenty-first century and provide relevant orientation. Among these is the so-called capabilities approach that has its roots in global struggles about human rights. Among contemporary economists and political philosophers, Amartya Sen (1985, 1992, 1993) and Martha Nussbaum (2000, 2006) in particular discuss capabilities with a perspective on questions of equality of opportunities. Dewey's view of potentiality accords well with the capabilities approach, which emphasizes not only how human beings may function presently, but also what they might be capable of being and doing, provided the right resources. These resources may range from food, safety, and health care to opportunities for higher education. For instance, we may understand poverty as capacity deprivation due to a society's misdistribution of wealth. Capabilities are not just potentials the individual alone must develop. Often he or she lacks the possibilities. Rather, democratic institutions must provide resources for the development of these potentials; they must be offered structurally by society to ensure the possibility of individual and social life in dignity. We may view capabilities as all the possible alternative combinations of functioning that an individual or an entire society might conceivably achieve. A democratic society is responsible for providing physical, biological, social, economic, and cultural environments that can help to actualize them.

Dewey thinks it is society's obligation to actualize the unique potential of each of its members so that they could make their unique contribution to the greater good of the society. In "Creative Democracy—The Task Before Us," Dewey states:

> The democratic faith in human equality is belief that every human being, independent of the quantity or range of his personal endowment, has the right to equal opportunity with every other person for development of whatever gifts he has. The democratic belief in the principle of leadership is a generous one. It is universal.
>
> (LW 14: 226–227)

Dewey does not suggest every individual has an equal opportunity to take his or her place in the existing social order or be treated according to exactly the same standards. Rather, if they have the opportunity to release and develop their capacities, we may find that individuals alone, or in concert, can do things that alter the existing social order (see Garrison 2009).

In our times, the capabilities approach is a reaction to challenges that have emerged in the first place with concern to human rights issues. There has for some time been a hesitation to include questions of economic inequality in human rights debates. This is an actual challenge in the development of capabilities approaches. Any capabilities approach that does not pay sufficient regard to economic conditions remains too limited. In its diagnosis of the difficulties lurking along the path to greater justice, it would put the finger mainly on rights and not sufficiently on structures. When in theory and practice we come up against structural conditions—such as are especially evident as a result of the underfunding, in particular, of education—we are always reminded of a key imperative: to work out with greater clarity the dimensions of education, democracy, and economy. It is not enough to determine only the communicative, social, cultural, or educational aspects of a life in diversity and the associated opportunities for inclusion and educational justice. Rather, we also have to examine the foundations of the mounting capitalization of all spheres of life that generate for our efforts a frame, a background, and, often enough, structural prerequisites as well. We will come back extensively to these questions later in Chapter 10.

We can only respond educationally to the multitude of perspectives involved in the social construction of growth, in a Deweyan sense, by communication and transactions across differences that strive to take diversity and participation into account. In some of the following chapters, we will connect this issue with more concrete educational challenges of our time.

It remains here for us to introduce three more general theoretical and educational perspectives that have become explicit and influential in more recent constructivist approaches, but which connect well with Dewey's overall approach to educational growth. They help to make the general idea of growth more specific with regard to learning. Let's have a closer look at these three perspectives (see Garrison/Neubert/Reich 2012).

Construction

In educational theory and psychology today, it is widely acknowledged that constructive learning is key to successful learning. It helps to achieve growth for the learner. If we look into a typical introduction into the field, we find statements like the following:

> One of the most important principles of educational psychology is that teachers cannot simply give students knowledge. Students must construct knowledge in their own minds. The teacher can facilitate this process by teaching in ways that make information meaningful and relevant to students, by giving students opportunities to discover or apply ideas themselves, and by teaching students to be aware of and consciously use their own strategies for learning. Teachers can give students ladders that lead to higher understanding, yet the students themselves must climb these ladders.
>
> (Slavin 2006: 243)

If one reads a passage like this it seems astonishing that in our time, authors in educational psychology very often do not even explicitly mention Dewey, although their theories clearly stand in the line of his educational and psychological approach. Proponents of constructivist education and psychology can, among other things, learn from Dewey that construction implies a broad field of creative and productive activities that are necessary components in the self-organization of learning in every learner. "I have used the word construction," Dewey says, to denote "the creative mind,"

> that is the mind that is genuinely productive in its operations. We are given to associating creative mind with persons regarded as rare and unique, like geniuses. But every individual is in his own way unique. Each one experiences life from a different angle than anybody else, and consequently has something distinctive to give others if he can turn his experiences into ideas and pass them on to others.
>
> (LW 5: 127)

Dewey uses the terms "to construct" or "construction" in many of his works. These terms point not only to the construction of material complexes like buildings or walls but also to the construction of ideas and meanings. In this sense, Dewey suggests that one constructs ideas, concepts, theories, values, etc. These constructions differ from person to person and from culture to culture to a certain extent. Constructions, therefore, are necessary processes in the development of experience. "We use our past experiences to construct new and better ones in the future" (MW 12: 134). Constructions are not arbitrary as Dewey explains with regard to the construction of theories and knowledge in social and moral matters:

> When it is realized that in these fields as in the physical, we know what we intentionally construct, that everything depends upon determination of methods of operation and upon observation of the consequences which test them, the progress of knowledge in these affairs may also become secure and constant.
>
> (LW 4: 149)

In this connection, there are many debates about the role of subjectivity in processes of construction that always imply a certain degree of necessary objectivity if they are to be viable in a culture. But what degrees of subjectivity can culture concede to individuals and how far must we delimit arbitrariness to avoid unqualified relativism? Both ways are connected with growth.

According to Deweyan pragmatism, in every process of inquiry, there are subjects at work in communities with other subjects. All of them bring their own experience with their cultural as well as individual backgrounds to the process. Their subjectivity and diversity of standpoints and original perspectives are essential for growth in scientific research as well as in all areas of social life. For, if subjects were only copies of their environment, nothing new could ever emerge. With his fundamental and path-breaking insights into the connections between growth, action, and construction and the relevance of cultural contexts, Dewey clears the ground for a constructive pragmatism or even a pragmatic constructivism, as we may call this position today. Constructions often give us the sense of order, regularity, and security. But Dewey forcefully reminds us that in culture and nature our constructions will always be limited and selective. In such a world, constructions can always have positive and desirable as well as negative and undesirable consequences. Therefore, Dewey insists that construction must always be accompanied by criticism. Dewey describes a necessary interaction: "Production that is not followed by criticism becomes a mere gush of impulse; criticism that is not a step to further creation deadens impulse and ends in sterility" (LW 5: 140).

Against the background of Dewey's radical democratic thought, such criticism has to respond to social conditions as well as cultural tradition, practices, and institutions. If we see only the side of construction and forget about social criticism we run the risk that our constructivism becomes naïve to the power of vested interests in societies that are largely characterized by social and economic inequalities as discussed above.

Reconstruction

From the perspective of individual learners, each of them has to construct their own reality. But without further qualifications this statement invites misunderstandings. In the process of construction, every individual uses resources that are not individual, but cultural, like symbols, languages, meanings, rules, ideas, knowledge, etc. They have to discover the world of culture in the very process of inventing their own learning through construction. Further growth depends on the growth that has already taken place. A central problem of teaching is to connect construction with reconstruction on the basis of necessary cultural contexts. This implies that there will be a certain amount of reproduction of learning contents. But, as Dewey's concept of experience and growth suggests for learning theories in his time, it is crucial for learning that the learners have sufficient opportunities to actively use cultural resources and learning materials to construct their own learning processes in cooperation with other learners.

We find the terms "to reconstruct" and "reconstruction" in many of Dewey's writings. Reconstruction for him always has to do with making things over or reinventing them. Construction and reconstruction are companions for him in any learning experience. With regard to the necessary reproductive side of learning, Dewey's account of learning as problem solving is very instructive. As learners we always start with an emotional response to a concrete situation before we begin to assimilate and appropriate cultural contents, events, or situations. If teachers insist too much on the side of reproduction, however, the danger is that learning will become boring and oppressive.

Deconstruction

The words "to deconstruct" or "deconstruction" were not part of the vocabulary of Dewey's time. But the sense of these terms is not alien to him. There are many places in his work where he discusses the value and the limits of deconstruction in the sense of criticism. Criticism is discovering the self-consistency of arguments and scientific theories; with criticism, one can analyze the backgrounds and viabilities of these theories in their contexts. In our time, the need for and emphasis on deconstruction as a form of criticism has increased to an extent that the term has become an explicit label for a broad field of social and cultural criticism. Speaking on a rather general level, we can say that the sensitivity to discontinuity, contingency, indeterminacy, omissions, fallacies, contradictions, paradoxes, and ambivalences is important for deconstructive criticism. Such criticism is not fault-finding, it "is judgment engaged in discriminating among values" (LW 5: 133). Therefore, it is a necessary supplement to creativity and construction. And, Dewey already suggests an insight that has become widespread today among all sorts of deconstructionists:

> Thus we may say that the business of philosophy is criticism of belief; that is, of beliefs that are so widely current socially as to be dominant factors in culture. Methods of critical inquiry into beliefs mark him [the philosopher] off as a philosopher, but the subject matter with which he deals is not his own. The beliefs themselves are social products, social facts and social forces.
> (LW 5: 164)

At the same time, Dewey warns us against a criticism that contents itself with deconstructing everything whatsoever and does not sufficiently combine deconstruction with constructive and reconstructive efforts.

Dewey's Summary

> Power to grow depends upon need for others and plasticity. Both of these conditions are at their height in childhood and youth. Plasticity or the power to learn from experience means the formation of habits. Habits give control over the environment, power to utilize it for human purposes. Habits take the form both of habituation, or a general and persistent balance of organic activities with the surroundings, and of active capacities to readjust activity to meet new conditions. The former furnishes the background of growth; the latter constitute growing. Active habits involve thought, invention, and initiative in applying capacities to new aims. They are opposed to routine which marks an arrest of growth. Since growth is the characteristic of life, education is all one with growing; it has no end beyond itself. The criterion

of the value of school education is the extent in which it creates a desire for continued growth and supplies means for making.

(MW 9: 57–58)

Our Summary

Growth is a genuinely constructivist idea. We have suggested that to make the general idea of growth applicable to concrete cases of learning, the perspectives of construction, reconstruction, and deconstruction are helpful, because they illuminate important aspects of any growth experience. The idea of growth requires translation into more concrete descriptions of learning experiences. On the other hand, specification of what growth means is also important with regard to questions of social justice and equity of opportunities. In this respect, we have argued that growth in a democratic context is of necessity an ambivalent construct that needs specification regarding claims to participation, diversity, and inclusion lest it become an instrument of undemocratic forms of particular interests, exclusion, and exploitation.

5

THE DEMOCRATIC CONCEPTION
IN EDUCATION

Given that the title of Dewey's book is *Democracy and Education*, it should come as no surprise that Chapter 7, "The Democratic Conception in Education," is pivotal. It is the first chapter of the book that explicitly refers to the concept of democracy. Like Dewey, we believe that an explicit elaboration about the necessary connections between education and democracy is essential not only in the development of the argumentation in our book, but also for educational theory and philosophy in general. We share his conviction and belief in pluralistic, participatory, deliberative, and communicative democracy, although we think his work requires considerable reconstruction after 100 years.

We have learned so far that social life is an extension of biological existence. From Dewey's Darwinian perspective, social structures and institutions are contingent historical constructions that arise out of human practices. Philosophy itself is for him a reflection and critical assessment of cultural practices, beliefs, structures, and institutions. It recognizes that social life is a continuously evolving, complex coordination of practices that conserve and reconstruct the social. We cannot sharply demarcate social institutions from their surrounding contexts because social practices consist in continual transactions with their environments such as ecological and natural habitats. This is constitutive for every human culture. From this ecological perspective, we can observe with Dewey that social institutions (like schools) are always located within an environment and actually represent in themselves a human response to this environment. They must at least maintain a minimum of equilibrium in their dynamic relations with the environment. We can only comprehend practices and environments as a transactional whole.

In the language that Dewey sometimes uses to explain his transactional understanding of experience (e.g., EW 5: 96–109), we may say that a social institution is itself a function or sub-function of a larger coordination of life activities we cannot fully understand in isolation or abstracted from this functional context. For example, political institutions and actions always interconnect with education as part of social life. It depends on which observer perspective we take whether we see education as a sub-function of the political or politics as a sub-function of education. It is a basic error to think of the political while ignoring education. At the same time, educators cannot be neutral to the political without becoming naïve regarding the opportunities and risks of education. Dewey was one of the few influential educational reformers in the early twentieth century to understand the full implications of this necessary connection. As we saw above, he introduced very early in the first chapter of his 1916 book the concept and theory of communication as an indispensable approach to education. This move already anticipates his later explicit elaboration on the connection between democracy and education in his Chapter 7. Communication, especially linguistic communication, is essential to socialization, including socialization into a given political or economic context. In a democracy, we must scrutinize any institutional practice as to how it contributes to the socialization of its members.

The aim of any democratic society is growth for both itself and its citizens. Dewey explains his understanding of the relation between democracy and education by contrasting it with ideas from three historically influential epochs in the development of Western political thought and action: first, the ancient Greek theory of the polis (especially Plato); second, the eighteenth-century Enlightenment movement, with its claims to individualism (e.g., Rousseau); and, third, the nineteenth-century idealistic philosophies of social, political, and national institutions (e.g., Kant, Fichte, Hegel). With respect to the first, Dewey observes that it had "an ideal formally quite similar to that stated" by himself, "but which was compromised in its working out by making a class rather than an individual the social unit" (MW 9: 105). With regard to the second, he argues that the

> so-called individualism of the eighteenth-century enlightenment was found to involve the notion of a society as broad as humanity, of whose progress the individual was to be the organ. But it lacked any agency for securing the development of its ideal as was evidenced in its falling back upon Nature.
> (MW 9: 105)

The third tradition and its insistence on the necessary role of the nation and bourgeois state politics partially compensates for this deficiency. However, in making the national state the primary agency of educational politics, it "narrowed the conception of the social aim to those who were members of the same political unit, and reintroduced the idea of the subordination of the individual to the institution" (MW 9: 106).

Dewey develops the idea of the social as a coordination of functions and sub-functions out of a historical perspective that highlights the contingency and openness of human practices and life in culture. "To say that education is a social function . . . is to say in effect that education will vary with the quality of life which prevails in a group" (MW 9: 87). In the context of this perspective, he argues that the ideal of democracy is a necessary construction in response to the openness of human experiences. He observes that in face of the changeability of education and social life, we need "a measure for the worth of any given mode of social life" (MW 9: 87). He eschews both abstract ideals completely detached from actual experience and docile conformity to actual conditions:

> In seeking this measure, we have to avoid two extremes. We cannot set up, out of our heads, something we regard as an ideal society. We must base our conception upon societies which actually exist, in order to have any assurance that our ideal is a practicable one. But, as we have just seen, the ideal cannot simply repeat the traits which are actually found.
>
> (MW 9: 88)

Dewey distinguishes between real and merely imaginary possibility. A real possibility is a potential for which there is something actually existing that can help realize it. An entirely imaginary possibility has no such grounding in existence. It is more like an escapist fantasy. On the other hand, Dewey decries passive conformity to the actual that lacks any sense of moral and aesthetic possibility. Trusting in experience, therefore, Dewey believes we cannot develop a political ideal, like democracy, as an *a priori* conception. Every such conception "must be arbitrary" (MW 9: 63). It lacks grounding in experiences and practices shared by a multitude of partakers in political life and social living together. He criticizes that, historically, the most influential political ideas are either arbitrary *a priori* ideals or ideals arising from docile compliance with the world as it currently exists in some time and place, or both. Neither extreme nor some compromise between them suffices in a world where social-political functions resemble organic functions in that they become extinct if they do not evolve.

"Any education given by a group tends to socialize its members," Dewey remarks, "but the quality and value of the socialization depends upon the habits and aims of the group" (MW 9: 88). Dewey seeks a standard for the evaluation of the democratic quality of a given group, community, or society. From what we have already said, it follows that this standard must connect with its ability to enlarge and improve the quality of experience. Such a standard must prove "a practicable one" given actual conditions, but must not "simply repeat the traits which are actually found" (MW 9: 88). He notes two characteristics always found in any actual society: "Now in any social group whatever . . . we find some interest held in common, and we find a certain amount of interactions and cooperative intercourse with other groups" (MW 9: 89). He constructs his democratic standards in connection with these very general characteristics (cf. Reich, 2008).

His first criterion is an internal one. It asks: "How numerous and varied are the interests which are consciously shared?" (MW 9: 89). The crucial point here lies in the diversity and mutual communication of interests allowed for and encouraged within a social group. This criterion stands against uniformity as well as separation of experiences and exclusion of or discrimination against members of the group who are being prevented from full participation and sharing. Dewey also observes its creative and constructive implications: "Diversity of stimulation means novelty, and novelty means challenge to thought" (MW 9: 90). Diversity cannot develop when there are "rigid class lines preventing adequate interplay of experiences" (MW 9: 90). Democracy needs "reciprocity of interest" (MW 9: 91). Its prosperity rests on recognition and understanding of different interests within the framework of social control. We can say that a plurality of interests shared within a community is a necessary precondition of education for democracy.

The second criterion is an external one. It asks: "How full and free is the interplay with other forms of association?" (MW 9: 89). The key point here is that for the development of its democratic relations and experiences, a given group, community, or society needs generous and unhindered exchanges taking place with other groups, communities, or societies. Democracy can grow (in families as in nations) more efficiently if interaction takes place not only between social groups of one common interest, one nation, or one special society, but also when people continually create and constantly readjust new challenges within the frame of social changes by means of different interactions with different interpretive communities, families, nations, or societies. This criterion stands against isolation, unilateral politics, colonialism, imperialism, and all forms of one-sided dominance and oppression of all kinds of groups. Closed, oppressive, and authoritarian societies narrow and close off experience thereby shrinking the scope and quality of human existence and exchange.

Dewey applies the first criterion in terms of a despotic state and order. He points out: "It is not true there is no common interest in such an organization between governed and governors" (MW 9: 89). Further, "the bond of union is not merely one of coercive force" (MW 9: 89). At one level, the problem is that "the activities appealed to are themselves unworthy and degrading—that such a government calls into functioning activity simply capacity for fear" (MW 9: 89). Nonetheless, even "fear need not be an undesirable factor in experience," because there is much to fear in a Darwinian world. "The real difficulty," Dewey surmises, "is that the appeal to fear is *isolated*" (MW 9: 90). The result is human potential left either unused or perverted if called upon. "Instead of operating on their own account" in seeking fulfillment in social interaction with others, capacities are "reduced to mere servants of attaining pleasure and avoiding pain" (MW 9: 90). This is a waste of human potential.

In such a society "there is no extensive number of common interests; there is no free play back and forth among the members of the social group. Stimulation and response are exceedingly one-sided" (MW 9: 90). Without a large diversity of shared interests, "the influences which educate some into masters, educate other into slaves" (MW 9: 90). Slavery is sometimes a subtler concept than it seems and may operate even in societies supposedly democratic.

A society may have a democratic constitution, but that alone does not make it a democracy. For instance, in the current global economy, many are slaves to their jobs. Dewey acknowledged that efficiency of production demands division of labor, but concludes: "It is reduced to a mechanical routine unless workers see the technical, intellectual, and social relationships involved in what they do, and engage in their work because of the motivation furnished by such perceptions" (MW 9: 91). We may substitute "students" for "workers" in this passage without changing the meaning.

In this connection, it is helpful to distinguish between skilled training, or education for passive like-mindedness and social control on the one hand, and a critical, constructive, and creative education on the other hand that enables all citizens—whether students, workers, or executives—to achieve autonomy and control of their own destiny. So, in *Democracy and Education*, Dewey declares: "An occupation is a continuous activity having a purpose. Education *through* occupations consequently combines within itself more of the factors conducive to learning than any other method" (MW 9: 319). Nonetheless, he observes that an often prevalent reductionism under capitalist conditions is to reduce work to mere utility, with fatal consequences for vocational education:

> I object to regarding as vocational education any training which does not have as its supreme regard the development of such intelligent initiative, ingenuity and executive capacity as shall make workers, as far as may be, the masters of their own industrial fate.
>
> (MW 8: 411)

Rather he urged an "industrial intelligence based on science and a knowledge of social problems and conditions" (MW 8: 411). In "Democracy and Educational Administration," Dewey asserts that "all those who are affected by social institutions must have a share in producing and managing them" (LW 11: 218). We will not live in a democracy until all social institutions and all forms of social control, including especially schools, exhibit democratic participation.

The Darwinian knows that genetic diversity is decisive for adaptation to changing environments (see Lankau and Strauss, 2007). Dewey, the democrat pluralist, thinks the same thing holds for social diversity. "Lack of the free and equitable intercourse which springs from a variety of shared interests makes intellectual stimulation unbalanced" (MW 9: 91). Remember, individuality is originally only a potentiality. We need others different from ourselves if we are to grow and develop our unique potentiality. Societies also need diversity to develop.

Dewey remarks that "isolation makes for rigidity and formal institutionalizing of life, for static and selfish ideals within the group" (MW 9: 92). He acknowledges that for societies devoted to static ways of life "it is wholly logical to fear intercourse with others, for such contact might dissolve custom. It would certainly occasion reconstruction" (MW 9: 92). Static societies are especially at risk of extinction in an evolving world. Dewey asserts that "alert and expanding mental life depends upon an enlarging range of contact with the physical environment. But the principle applies even more significantly to the field where we are apt to ignore it—the sphere of social contacts" (MW 9: 92). He concludes:

> Travel, economic and commercial tendencies, have at present gone far to break down external barriers; to bring peoples and classes into closer and more perceptible connection with one another. It remains for the most part to secure the intellectual and emotional significance of this physical annihilation of space.
>
> (MW 9: 92)

Dewey seeks individual and social growth through diversity. It further explains his democratic ideal, which derives directly from the two traits of inner and outer diversity, exchange, and participation that provide the above introduced democratic standards:

> The two elements in our criterion both point to democracy. The first signifies not only more numerous and more varied points of shared common interest, but greater reliance upon the recognition of mutual interests as a factor in social control. The second means not only freer interaction between social groups (once isolated so far as intention could keep up a separation) but change in social habit—its continuous readjustment through meeting the new situations produced by varied intercourse. And these two traits are precisely what characterize the democratically constituted society.
>
> (MW 9: 92)

Dewey reminds us that the "devotion of democracy to education is a familiar fact" (MW 9: 93). There is a good reason this is so: "Since a democratic society repudiates the principle of external authority, it must find a substitute in voluntary disposition and interest; these can be created only by education" (MW 9: 93). However, Dewey identifies an even deeper, hidden reason:

> A democracy is more than a form of government; it is primarily a mode of associated living, of conjoint communicated experience. The extension in space of the number of individuals who participate in an interest so that

each has to refer his own action to that of others, and to consider the action of others to give point and direction to his own, is equivalent to the breaking down of those barriers of class, race, and national territory which kept men from perceiving the full import of their activity. These more numerous and more varied points of contact denote a greater diversity of stimuli to which an individual has to respond; they consequently put a premium on variation in his action. They secure a liberation of powers which remain suppressed as long as the incitations to action are partial, as they must be in a group which in its exclusiveness shuts out many interests.

(MW 9: 93)

Here Dewey articulates his widely influential pluralistic communicative theory of democracy (cf. Barber, 1992). What matters for us as educators is that what Dewey says about societies as pluralistic communicative democracies applies to any society, including the classroom, the school, and, of course the local, regional, national, and global communities.

In the beginning of this chapter, we mentioned three epochs and traditions of political thought and action that Dewey uses in his text to critically clarify and justify his own ideal of democracy. These are not only of historical interest but constitute challenges for education until the present day. Dewey examines and rejects three ideals of education that represent influential, even dominant orientations. His criticisms provide further insight into his own commitment to pluralistic communicative democracy. The first is the educational philosophy of Plato:

No one could better express than did he the fact that a society is stably organized when each individual is doing that for which he has aptitude by nature in such a way as to be useful to others (or to contribute to the whole to which he belongs); and that it is the business of education to discover these aptitudes and progressively to train them for social use.

(MW 9: 94)

Dewey strongly endorses this stance. However, he points to a serious problem. Plato "never got any conception of the indefinite plurality of activities which may characterize an individual and a social group, and consequently limited his view to a limited number of *classes* of capacities and of social arrangements" (MW 9: 94). Plato thought there were only three basic human capacities, each of which should occupy only one of three rungs in his social hierarchy.

The first is well-trained skill as represented by "the laboring and trading class, which expresses and supplies human wants" (MW 9: 96). This is the level of the craftsperson. The next level is the "generous, outgoing, assertively courageous disposition" (MW 9: 96). Those with this capacity become "the citizen-subjects of the state; its defenders in war; its internal guardians in peace" (MW 9: 96).

Having sufficient rational capacity, an elite of few "philosophers or lovers of wisdom—or truth—may by study learn at least in outline the proper patterns of true existence" (MW 9: 95). Only these are fit to rule. Plato believed an "education could be given which would sift individuals, discovering what they were good for, and supplying a method of assigning each to the work in life for which his nature fits him" (MW 9: 95). Even today, many modern nations sift in terms of three categories; these are vocational, general, and elite (i.e., college-bound) track. Plato's ancient beliefs still hold in the twenty-first century in that "the testing and sifting function of education only shows to which one of three classes an individual belongs" (MW 9: 97). Such sifting has no interest in unique potential.

Plato's assumption is echoed today in many modern industrial and post-industrial societies in that they believe or make-believe there is a limited range of capacities and we may justify social chances and privileges based on innate differences. Such thinking supports as well as represents a sort of meritocracy that is a danger for democracy. It rests on narrow and relatively fixed assumptions about warranted privileges of vested interests on the one side, and a hardly concealed ideological version of *Survival of the Fittest* (cf. Chapter 11) on the other. Both aspects enforce the belief and expectation that the existing order of inequality goes unchallenged. Dewey identifies the undemocratic implications of Plato's classism:

> But it is true that lacking the perception of the uniqueness of every individual, his incommensurability with others, and consequently not recognizing that a society might change and yet be stable, his doctrine of limited powers and classes came in net effect to the idea of the subordination of individuality.
>
> (MW 9: 96)

A pluralistic democratic society has an endless array of actual and possible needs and opportunities that it must call upon the unique potentials and capacities of individuals. The development of societies depends on diverse contributions of individuals that develop and realize their unique potentials and grow in participation and exchange with the growth of society. Since growth is an open process on the level of individuals as well as society, it is often the case that necessary contributions for social reconstruction and for the solution of social challenges only become substantial and perceptible when the unique individual arrives that can perform the task. Therefore, diversity is the key to survival and growth in a changing world. Against this background, a Deweyan approach to democracy and education must be critical with respect to schools as sorting machines and the suppression of unique individuality in educational institutions. We will get back to these issues in the following chapters.

Dewey next examines the individualistic ideal of the eighteenth-century Enlightenment. We have already learned how he rejects and criticizes the ideal of a socially detached individual born with a mind, free will, and rationality. Dewey also rejects the romantic version of this ideal associated with Rousseau. Of course, Dewey endorses strong individuality and agrees with Rousseau in championing "the diversity of individual talent" and "the need of free development of individuality in all its variety" (MW 9: 97). However, his concern is that, for Rousseau, the individual, in his natural state, is essentially nonsocial: "Social arrangements were thought of as mere external expedients by which these nonsocial individuals might secure a greater amount of private happiness for themselves" (MW 9: 97). Education was to proceed according to "nature" with as little social influence as possible. Instead of trusting social orders that are admittedly often authoritarian and oppressive, romantic individualism would trust completely to the uncontrolled and often destructive contingencies of nature. In historical context, it is clear that Rousseau used his romanticized idea of nature as well as his concept of the "Social Contract" as an ideological weapon against the extremely fixed and hierarchical social order of French absolutism and its political and religious justifications. Therefore, Rousseau, at the same time, stands for the progress of republican and democratic principles and for a naturalistic understanding of individualism that underestimates the significance of social interaction. It would be historically inadequate and unjust, however, to isolate this understanding of individualism from the political and cultural contexts in which it was an important ideological tool of political modernization.

The third epoch and tradition of education Dewey addresses, is that of nineteenth -century idealism developed especially in Germany. This tradition emphasizes the social nature of the self, but harnesses it to nationalistic interests. While Dewey recognizes the cosmopolitan orientation in Kant's version of Enlightenment, he also observes the nationalistic twist that philosophy took in the early decades of the nineteenth century. He writes:

> Kant's philosophic successors, Fichte and Hegel, elaborated the idea that the chief function of the state is educational; that in particular the regeneration of Germany is to be accomplished by an education carried on in the interests of the state, and that the private individual is of necessity an egoistic, irrational being, enslaved to his appetites and to circumstances unless he submits voluntarily to the educative discipline of state institutions and laws. In this spirit, Germany was the first country to undertake a public, universal, and compulsory system of education extending from the primary school through the university, and to submit to jealous state regulation and supervision all private educational enterprises.
>
> (MW 9: 102)

The state sets not only the ends of public education, but its means. A modern notion of public schools "educating" students to be good and productive citizens follows this ideal. The result was the idealization of established social order, especially with regard to class society and an educational system that trained students to fit into compartmentalized functions including utilitarian ideas of social efficiency in a developing capitalist society. This situation led to the eclipse of the individual in the phrase "social individual."

Dewey poses a problem in terms of the internal and external criteria of his standard that is still with us: "Is it possible for an educational system to be conducted by a national state and yet the full social ends of the educative process not be restricted, constrained, and corrupted?" (MW 9: 104). He sees the problem as follows:

> Each nation lives in a state of suppressed hostility and incipient war with its neighbors. Each is supposed to be the supreme judge of its own interests, and it is assumed as matter of course that each has interests which are exclusively its own.
>
> (MW 9: 103)

He further refers the aspects of the problem to his two democratic criteria when he asks how the situation looks like from the inside and the outside:

> Internally, the question has to face the tendencies, due to present economic conditions, which split society into classes[,] some of which are made merely tools for the higher culture of others. Externally, the question is concerned with the reconciliation of national loyalty, of patriotism, with superior devotion to the things which unite men in common ends, irrespective of national political boundaries.
>
> (MW 9: 104)

Dewey leaves no doubt he does not limit his ideal of democracy to national borders nor defines it primarily on the basis of national communities (MW 9: 105).

Challenge for Today: Diversity and Participation

As we have seen above, Dewey's understanding of democracy is a deeply pluralistic and participatory concept that requires constant deliberation in the way of construction and criticism. The most general challenge in reconsidering *Democracy and Education* today therefore consists in a substantial reconstruction of the meanings of diversity and participation in and for our time. Here, we strive to give the reader such a general orientation, while the closing sections of all other chapters to follow will aim at providing implication that is more concrete while specifying more detailed consequences for educational theory and practice.

From a pragmatic perspective, political languages, practices, and institutions are always in the process of construction and reconstruction by each new generation. It is a transformative practice constituting democracy as an open-ended and revisable project of learning from experience. For instance, in our time we must ask ourselves what the risks and opportunities are of living with diversity in our local and global contexts. Obviously, there are many potential dark sides like getting lost in confusion and overwhelmed by an excess of opportunities and options that require much individual and social intelligence and wisdom of decision making. Against this background, social intelligence must take diversity seriously as a challenge to democratic living together. This involves issues posed by legal and illegal immigration, ethnic conflicts involving violence and even genocide, radical and fundamentalist religious movements, extreme and exclusive forms of community like nationalism or restrictive identity politics, etc.

Considering the opportunities and risks of democratic diversity, Dewey reminds us that the aim of democracy is growth in "ordered richness" (LW 14: 229). What is at stake here is the construction of ways of democratic deliberation based on a sustainable balance between necessary forms of direct as well as representative democracy. Judith Green (1999) has introduced the term "deep democracy" to indicate this necessary balance and especially emphasize the importance of democracy as a direct experience of partaking with others that has consequences for individual as well as social growth. Deep democracy is Green's expression for a participatory and deliberative ideal of democracy as a personal way of life.

At the bottom of this understanding of deep democracy lies the insight that direct face-to-face encounters are powerful experiences. This is not to deny that experiences of virtual communities using the new social media through the Internet can also be important as means for cultivating deep democracy. They provide new opportunities to participate and deliberate with others and show that today's advanced technologies have considerably broadened the realm of potential "face-to-face" encounters in comparison to Dewey's time.

Direct or deep democracy, however, is not opposed to necessary representative structures. With Dewey we may see representative democracy and all political institutions as an instrument that is at the same time necessary as well as always problematic and in need of critical revision with regard to its viability in practice and in relation to the needs of direct democracy. Any institution may be educative, as we noticed above, but it may also become a hindrance to growth and further education. Dewey is well aware that the tension between direct and representative democracy is constitutive of each modern society. It is precisely the challenge and opportunity of civil society and its means of public deliberation to mediate and reconstruct the terms of this very tension. We must expect that in a democracy, public interests and problems are continually emerging and developing. Therefore, political ideas and conceptions as well as political institutions are in need of current reconstruction (see Campbell 1992: 46 ff.). In *The Public and Its Problems*, Dewey observes: "By its very nature, a state is something to be scrutinized, investigated, searched for. Almost as soon as its form is stabilized, it needs to be re-made" (LW 2: 255).

Dewey has investigated the rich diversity of meanings lived in the concrete life-experiences of humans in many comprehensive studies. Basic to his philosophical pluralism is the idea of "experience" as starting point of all philosophical reflection. For him, belief and knowledge obtained in always culturally contextualized practices of human inquiry are of necessity surrounded by frames of ambiguous and ambivalent meanings. He insisted that experience has its dark, obscure, vague, or twilight aspects and that intelligent problem-solving, including scientific practices and philosophic reflections, can never do away with the precarious dimensions of experience. We believe this sense of ambivalence is a fundamentally important trait of any philosophical pluralism. Dewey urges us to encounter our world experimentally as an open universe that allows for many possible perspectives and interpretations. This philosophical attitude rejects narrow reductionisms as well as overgeneralizations or willful universalizations.

In Dewey's philosophy we find a thoroughgoing reflection on the diverse consequences of contextualism that in many respects equally applies to challenges in our time. This connects well with his theory of inquiry. On the grounds of his experimentalist philosophy, Dewey urges us to abandon the traditional philosophical habit of identifying reality with our systems of knowledge (see LW 1: 28). He rather suggests that our experience is characterized by an inevitable mixture of the precarious and the stable (see LW 1: 42 ff.). Contingency, ambiguity, and ambivalence are therefore genuine traits of living in an unfinished and pluralistic cultural universe.

Dewey introduces the term "warranted assertibilty" to give a name to a contextualized understanding of truth claims as experimental constructions with temporal, spatial, individual, social, and cultural background. His philosophical experimentalism underlies his notion of social intelligence and democratic method. He argues that the experimental method "is, in short, the method of democracy, of a positive toleration which amounts to sympathetic regard for the intelligence and personality of others, even if they hold views opposed to ours, and of scientific inquiry into facts and testing of ideas" (LW 7: 329). The social power of intelligence is decisive as an instrument for social welfare and prosperity.

Dewey observes that the "problem of bringing about an effective socialization of intelligence is probably the greatest problem of democracy today" (LW 7: 365–366). We suggest that this observation still applies in our contemporary context. Upon the whole, the task does not seem to be easier today despite the technological advancements that have contributed, for instance, to facilitate communication.

It accords with Dewey's notion of social intelligence that he was very critical of the idea that experts should control or even rule modern democracy. He argues that a "class of experts is inevitably so removed from common interests as to become a class with private interests and private knowledge, which in social matters in not knowledge at all" (LW 2: 364 f.). The democratic ideal that the people shall rule implies that the multitude of people must be involved, as comprehensively as possible, in all political actions, decisions, plans, and so on. If participation in government of affairs—from everyday life to global politics—is not provided to a sufficient extent, democracy is at risk. It all too easily degenerates into "an oligarchy managed in the interests of the few" (LW 2: 364 f.). Dewey believes that it is the responsibility of public intellectuals in fields like science, philosophy, art, literature, journalism, etc. to add productively to the realization of social intelligence. He distinguishes, among other things, four important functions experts may perform in this connection (see Garrison, Neubert & Reich, 2012, part 3): (1) to promote an experimental attitude toward social events throughout the democratic public; (2) to entertain systematic and continual inquiries into social and human affairs; (3) to further free access to information regarding issues that affect the public; and (4) to cultivate forms of free and full intercommunication as well as multilayered articulations of knowledge of public import, including, for example, artistic, journalistic, scientific as well as other discursive constructions (see LW 2: 339–350).

In many respects, Dewey's position is close to contemporary post-structuralist and constructivist approaches that speak of discourses and cultural viabilities. To indicate the relevance and actual applicability of his concepts of truth, belief, and knowledge, we may think of current challenges that are articulated, for example, in debates about globalization. To the degree that globalization has increased since Dewey's time, the challenges of diversity and participation have partially changed and even in some respects gained an increased importance. If we think of capitalism, for example, the old solid form of capitalism characterized by Fordist production has given way to much more liquid, flexible, and light versions of capitalist organization that have produced new dangers for democracy. Behind the curtains, capitalism has changed:

> The present-day "liquefied," "flowing," dispersed, scattered and deregulated version of modernity may not portend divorce and the final break of communication, but it does argue the advent of light, free-floating capitalism, marked by the disengagement and loosening of ties linking capital and labour.
>
> (Bauman, 2000: 149)

New forms of capital have emerged, and most of them have taken a lighter character than in former times: "Having shed the ballast of bulky machinery and massive factory crews, capital travels light with no more than cabin luggage—a briefcase, laptop computer and cellular telephone" (Bauman, 2000: 150). The consequence, among other things, is the emergence of new forms of social precariousness and insecurity that have become apparent in our time:

> No jobs are guaranteed, no positions are foolproof, no skills are of lasting utility, experience and know-how turn into liability as soon as they become assets, seductive careers all too often prove to be suicide tracks. In their

present rendering, human rights do not entail the acquisition of a right to a job, however well performed, or—more generally—the right to care and consideration for the sake of past merits. Livelihood, social position, acknowledgement of usefulness and the entitlement to self-dignity may all vanish together, overnight and without notice.

(Bauman, 1997: 22)

It is helpful at this point to remind the reader of the three perspectives of construction, reconstruction, and deconstruction introduced in Chapter 4. Among other things, interactive constructivism employs these perspectives in order to distinguish important aspects of democracy and education. First, "education as construction" supports the possibilities of learners attaining their own constructions of reality in active and self-determined learning experiences. Constructivists think humans are the makers of their own meanings and insofar the inventors of their own realities. But learning is not only a subjective process; it involves interaction. As a construction, it relies on co-constructions within a community of learners. Interaction, co-construction, communication, and coordination would of course be impossible if each individual had to invent her/his purely subjective reality completely on her/his own.

Second, education as reconstruction work means that learners come to discover the abundant richness and wide variety of reality constructions already accomplished by others in culture. These reality constructions are now available as symbolic resources of the lived cultures that the learners inhabit. In a democracy, construction and reconstruction should freely work together and mutually enrich each other. This is a basic tenet of democracy and education and a challenge for the reconstruction and continual critical development of educational institutions. Given the diversity and heterogeneity of discourses and symbolic representations in liquid modernity, education as reconstruction work is impossible without selection of contexts, interests, contents, and methods. Constructivists claim that already the choice of contexts, subject matter, and methods of learning is not only a task for administrators and curriculum experts. All those who are actively involved in learning should participate according to their capacities in making these choices. To achieve this goal, constructivist educators must take account of the different viabilities of their learners, including their specific interests, needs, requirements, capacities, situations, and environments.

Third, to take diversity seriously, we need an additional perspective besides constructions and reconstructions, namely education as deconstruction. This perspective reminds us that, in an open and pluralist universe, all cultural (re)constructions of reality are always contingent and incomplete. They always tend to neglect other possible perspectives and interpretations. Deconstruction is a starting point in education for new constructions and reconstructions. The famous French philosopher, Jacques Derrida, who launched the term *deconstruction*, argued that it is a necessary method for democracy. We suggest that Dewey, who died decades before the term became popular, would have agreed. In contrast to Derrida and many other social philosophies and political theories, however, we think it is a particular strength in Dewey to connect such crucial insights concerning democracy with insights about the necessity of education. To him, democracy and education mutually condition and constitute each other. It is a weakness of social and political thought to neglect this very interdependence. On the other hand, educational theories have often shown a tendency to neglect the relevance of power relations for educational practices, routines, institutions, theories, and philosophies. Among other things, the challenge is to take seriously the influence of power in direct face-to-face relations, formations of communities, as well as social, cultural, and political institutions. More recent approaches speak of hegemony as a construction of cultural power. Hegemony includes the struggle over powerful interpretations, for example regarding social, political, and economic relations and inequalities. The challenge is not to do away with power altogether. That would seem impossible from the very start. The challenge rather consists in struggling against one-sided asymmetries of power that delimit and obstruct the realization of lived diversity and participation in a democratic culture.

> For education this implies that against the background of their socialization learners must be given opportunities to participate in the negotiation of norms, values, rules, standards, limits of living together under conditions of diversity. They must have the chance to develop their own powers and discover their limits in interaction with others.
>
> (Reich in Green, Neubert & Reich, 2012: 208)

Dewey's Summary

> Since education is a social process, and there are many kinds of societies, a criterion for educational criticism and construction implies a *particular* social ideal. The two points selected by which to measure the worth of a form of social life are the extent in which the interests of a group are shared by all its members, and the fullness and freedom with which it interacts with other groups. An undesirable society, in other words, is one which internally and externally sets up barriers to free intercourse and communication of experience. A society which makes provision for participation in its good of all its members on equal terms and which secures flexible readjustment of its institutions through interaction of the different forms of associated life is in so far democratic. Such a society must have a type of education that gives individuals a personal interest in social relationships and control, and the habits of mind that secure social changes without introducing disorder.
>
> Three typical historic philosophies of education were considered from this point of view. The Platonic was found to have an ideal formally quite

similar to that stated, but which was compromised in its working out by making a class rather than an individual the social unit. The so-called individualism of the eighteenth-century Enlightenment was found to involve the notion of a society as broad as humanity, of whose progress the individual was to be the organ. But it lacked any agency for securing the development of its ideal as was evidenced in its falling back upon Nature. The institutional idealistic philosophies of the nineteenth century supplied this lack by making the national state the agency, but in so doing narrowed the conception of the social aim to those who were members of the same political unit, and reintroduced the idea of the subordination of the individual to the institution.

(MW 9: 105–106)

Our Summary

Dewey's insistence on the relevance of the conception of democracy for education still applies in our time. We have argued that we can only justify the democratic ideal against the background of cultural, social, political, and economic developments and changes. We must take Dewey's sense for the need of historical contextualization, which he shows especially in reflecting democracy through the medium of selected historical periods, seriously while extending them in the sense that we need to transfer and reconstruct his theories for our time. His reflections on democracy circulate around the two criteria that define the conditions of constituting democracy as a lived experience. We believe that these criteria are of fundamental importance in our time, as well. Dewey already saw that every criterion of democracy in order to be efficient in social life must be developed or constructed out of concrete experiences and practices and must use the resources of construction that are being provided by social intelligence. Obviously, this crucial insight demands application to our time and in the same moment requires reconstruction with regard to changed contexts. There are core problems and challenges for us to address in our contemporary situation with regard to the two criteria that require taking up repeatedly. Issues like diversity and pluralism, power and hegemony, experimentalism and knowledge, specialized and public interests, experts and the multitude, deep and representative democracy, change and ordered richness, individual and social growth, rule and participation, constitute recurring contexts that we must respond to constructively as challenges for furthering democracy. Education is indispensable for finding constructive solutions, but to further democracy, educational practices, routines, and institutions must be truly participatory and appreciative of all the above mentioned challenges.

6

AIMS AND COMPETENCIES IN EDUCATION

In this chapter, we look at Chapter 8, "Aims of Education" and Chapter 9, "Natural Development and Social Efficiency" in *Democracy and Education*. We will extend the account given by Dewey by introducing the now influential debate about competencies in education. Dewey starts Chapter 8 by reiterating that "the aim of education is to enable individuals to continue their education" (MW 9: 107). As we have seen, personal and social growth is the goal of education. Dewey wishes to connect aims in education to aims in democracy:

> Now this idea cannot be applied to *all* the members of a society except where intercourse of man with man is mutual, and except where there is adequate provision for the reconstruction of social habits and institutions by means of wide stimulation arising from equitably distributed interests. And this means a democratic society.
>
> (MW 9: 106)

An important aim of education in a democracy is helping all individuals actualize their unique potential so they can make their unique contribution to groups and the larger community. Dewey contrasts the conditions that prevail "when aims belong within the process in which they operate and when they are set up from without" (MW 9: 107). This is the core idea behind the now commonplace distinction between intrinsic and extrinsic motivation in learning. When the tendency prevails to impose aims one-sidedly from without, "some portions of the whole social group will find their aims determined by an external dictation; their aims will not arise from the free growth of their own experience" (MW 9: 107). This is typical of groups or societies built on hierarchical power relations and forms of organization. Externally dictating aims for individuals is the essence of dictatorship; it imposes a threat to democracy.

Before attempting to state the criteria of good aims, Dewey analyzes the characteristics of any aim, good or bad. He first discriminates between mere results and ends of experience. Any redistribution of energy has results. Dewey gives the example of wind blowing the sands of the desert resulting in a spatial redistribution of grains. This result of energy expended is not an aim because "there is nothing in the outcome which completes or fulfills what went before it" (MW 9: 107). In the case of mere results from the redistribution of material due to the expenditure of physical energy, there is "no basis upon which to select an earlier state of affairs as a beginning, a later as an end, and to consider what intervenes as a process of transformation and realization" (MW 9: 107). The determination of beginnings, processes, and products involves the exercise of intelligence, however limited.

We often confuse intelligent intervention with intentionality and purpose. The distinction is an important one with significant pedagogical consequences. Dewey urges us to consider the difference between the energetic event of blowing sand and the energetic event of bees gathering pollen, making wax, building cells in their nest in which the queen lays eggs that are sealed, and brooded over until they are hatched. What is essential about the second event is "the significance of the temporal place and order of each element" (MW 9: 108). Further, we should consider the way "each prior event leads into its successor while the successor takes up what is furnished and utilizes it for some other stage, until we arrive at the end, which, as it were, summarizes and finishes off the process" (MW 9: 108). When a process displays continuity in moving toward an integral fulfillment as its product, we may speak of ends and not just results of energy redistribution. In order to appreciate the relevance and role of aims in education, Dewey carefully distinguishes among results, ends, and aims.

"The results of the bees' actions may be called ends not because they are designed or consciously intended," insists Dewey, "but because they are true terminations or completions of what has preceded" (MW 9: 108). Seen from a constructivist perspective, we may add that this description itself is an observation based on cultural constructions and not just a statement given by nature. In this sense then, the very distinction between results, ends, and aims is constructed and not essentially given in the order of things. It implies and takes for granted a specific order of language and discourse. While following Dewey's account, we should keep in mind our earlier discussion of nature and culture as fields of discourse in Chapter 1.

For Dewey, the event of sand blowing is a result while nest-tending by bees is a result that we may call an end. But what is the difference between an end and an aim? For one thing, educational aims must display "intrinsic continuity" instead of "a mere serial aggregate of acts" where one thing follows another (MW 9: 108). Learning and growth are processes of experience and cannot just be imposed from outside. Dewey uses a pedagogical example to make his point:

To talk about an educational aim when approximately each act of a pupil is dictated by the teacher, when the only order in the sequence of his acts is that which comes from the assignment of lessons and the giving of directions by another, is to talk nonsense. It is equally fatal to an aim to permit capricious or discontinuous action in the name of spontaneous self-expression.

(MW 9: 108)

Here Dewey is scolding not only traditional forms of education, but also a widely held misinterpretation of "child-centered" progressive education, implicitly including many kinds of contemporary subjectivist constructivism. In the former case, the student has no aims other than to satisfy the teacher, parent, or other external authority. We may say the same for teachers forced to teach an externally imposed lock-step curriculum keyed to standardized tests. There is no intrinsic continuity to such a sequence.

Dewey is now ready to define what it means to have an aim that is not merely a result or even an end:

An aim implies an orderly and ordered activity, one in which the order consists in the progressive completing of a process. Given an activity having a time span and cumulative growth within the time succession, and aim means foresight in advance of the end or possible termination.

(MW 9: 108)

Ideally, in such a process there is intrinsic continuity where each stage is itself an integral fulfillment of what precedes and a constant anticipation of the final product. Dewey helped popularize the concept of educational development. However, he was always wary of the notion of fixed predetermined stages leading to predetermined ends. Such approaches ignore the unique capacities, aims, and purposes of the learner, or the teacher for that matter.

The ability to form aims—that is, imagine possibilities and anticipate consequences—"gives direction" to our activities and "influences the steps taken to reach the end" (MW 9: 109). Foresight of future events may reflect back on and control present action. Dewey lists three functions of foresight:

In the first place, it involves careful observation of the given conditions to see what are the means available for reaching the end, and to discover the hindrances in the way. In the second place, it suggests the proper order or sequence in the use of means. It facilitates an economical selection and arrangement. In the third place, it makes choice of alternatives possible. If we can predict the outcome of acting this way or that, we can then compare the value of the two courses of action; we can pass judgment upon their relative desirability.

(LW 9: 109)

Dewey concludes that "acting with an aim is all one with acting intelligently" or having a mind, "for mind is precisely intentional purposeful activity controlled by perception of facts and their relationships to one another" (MW 9: 110). Such intentional, purposeful, meaningful conduct is obviously crucial to education. In what follows, we will talk about aims in education, i.e., consciously intended ends of human action. In this context, we will use the terms "ends" and "aims" synonymously like Dewey does when talking about education.

Having exposited his definition of aims, good or bad, Dewey next turns to establishing three criteria of good aims. The first is that the "aim set up must be an outgrowth of existing conditions. It must be based upon a consideration of what is already going on; upon the resources and difficulties of the situation" (MW 9: 111). Often, educational theories ignore the students' and teachers' actual situations and impose on them external aims:

> Theories about the proper end of our activities—educational and moral theories—often violate this principle. They assume ends lying *outside* our activities; ends foreign to the concrete make-up of the situation; ends which issue from some outside source. Then the problem is to bring our activities to bear upon the realization of these externally supplied ends.
>
> (MW 9: 111)

Second, we should not proceed "as if aims could be completely formed prior to the attempt to actualize them" (MW 9: 111). The foresight imparted by having aims-in-view directs activity intelligently, but once we begin to act, contextual constraints become apparent, perhaps along with the absence of resources we thought we had or the recognition of resources of which we were unaware. Hence, "An aim must, then, be *flexible*; it must be capable of alteration to meet circumstances" (MW 9: 111). Dewey draws the following conclusion for educational practice:

> A good aim surveys the present state of experience of pupils, and forming a tentative plan of treatment, keeps the plan constantly in view and yet modifies it as conditions develop. The aim, in short, is experimental, and hence constantly growing as it is tested in action.
>
> (MW 9: 111)

By contrast, an "end established externally to the process of action is always rigid" (MW 9: 111). That is one of the main things wrong with rigid curricula and inflexible standards.

Third, "The aim must always represent a freeing of activities" (MW 9: 112). Clearly, the liberation of action stands in stark contrast with "the static character of an end which is imposed from without the activity" (MW 9: 112). Dewey is a logical instrumentalist; that is, he believes all reasoning is practical means-ends (or means-consequence) reasoning. In his 1938 *Logic*, he writes: "Rationality as an abstract conception is precisely the generalized idea of the means-consequence relation as such" (LW 12: 17). Most forms of instrumentalism are what Larry Hickman (1990: 12–14) calls "naïve" or "straight-line" instrumentalism. Such instrumentalism assumes we may detach means from the end, which is the *telos* of action. Hans Joas (1996) argues that Dewey has a non-teleological understanding of the intentionality of acting. Dewey remarks that:

> [T]he external idea of the aim leads to a separation of means from end, while an end which grows up within an activity as plan for its direction is always both ends and means, the distinction being only one of convenience.
>
> (MW 9: 113)

Said differently, like the blueprints for building a house, the "aim is as definitely a *means* of action as is any other portion of an activity" (MW 9: 113). An ideal end-in-view projected into the future reflects back to guide present action. Dewey advocates means-ends continuity:

> Every means is a temporary end until we have attained it. Every end becomes a means of carrying activity further as soon as it is achieved. We call it end when it marks off the future direction of the activity in which we are engaged; means when it marks off the present direction.
>
> (MW 9: 113)

There are no means without ends and no ends without means; they constitute each other. In any development of practical reasoning, an achieved end then becomes the means to further ends. Likewise, in seeking means to an end-in-view, we might decide at any point in the process that the means assembled up to that point are good enough or even better than what we had first set out to secure. Many unintentionally sacrifice superior ends to secure their original goal. Rigid thinking and straight-line instrumentalism go together.

Having analyzed the general idea of aims, Dewey turns to aims in education noting that there "is nothing peculiar about educational aims" that differentiates them from other ends (MW 9: 113). However, he does remark that "education as such has no aims. Only persons, parents, and teachers, etc., have aims, not an abstract idea like education. And consequently their purposes are infinitely varied" (MW 9: 114). This is why Dewey refuses to specify any one ideal as *the* aim of education. All we can say in the abstract is that the aim of education is more education and that any aim that interferes with individual growth is harmful to that person.

Dewey lists three characteristics of good educational aims. First, an "educational aim must be founded upon the intrinsic activities and needs (including original instincts and acquired habits) of the given individual to be educated" (MW 9:

114). In student-centered teaching, the aims of education emerge within the life experience of the student and draw on present individual capacities.

Next, an "aim must be capable of translation into a method of cooperating with the activities of those undergoing instruction. It must suggest the kind of environment needed to liberate and to organize *their* capacities" (MW 9: 115). Student-centered teachers adapt their pedagogical method to the individual student needs, desires, and capacities if they are to help them actualize their unique potential for growth. Teachers must avoid straight-line instrumentalism, seek aims intrinsic to the student's capacities, and pursue their own teaching intentions non-teleologically. However, not only is the development of the student's capacities at stake, but also that of the teacher. Teachers who accept the aims of their teaching from external sources give up their own creative autonomy and, with it, the realization of their own capacities.

Third, "Educators have to be on their guard against ends that are alleged to be general and ultimate" (MW 9: 116). We should be wary because "'general' means 'abstract' or detached from all specific context" (MW 9: 116). Education and social context was the challenge for today in Chapter 2, and, while we will not repeat that discussion here, we do urge the reader to go back and reconsider our remarks. Dewey calls attention to still something else. Remember that aims and purposes may be infinitely varied. There is an endless array of possible ends "differing with different children, changing as children grow and with the growth of experience on the part of the one who teaches" (MW 9: 114). *There are no general aims such that one size always fits all.* Which aim to choose requires considerable knowledge about the individual student and careful deliberation since "one statement of an end may suggest certain questions and observations, and another statement another set of questions, calling for other observations" (MW 9: 117). "What a plurality of hypotheses does for the scientific investigator," Dewey surmises, "a plurality of stated aims may do for the instructor" (MW 9: 117). Creative student-centered teaching requires selecting the right aim to pursue at the right time and is part of the art of teaching.

Dewey begins Chapter 9, "Natural Development and Social Efficiency," by reminding us of "the futility of trying to establish *the* aim of education—some one final aim which subordinates all others to itself" (MW 9: 118). Selection of aims depends on the needs of the students and circumstances. Unfortunately, it is often also dictated by the desires of those with power and privilege to shape the lives of others. That is the democratic challenge for our times, as it was in Dewey's day.

Acknowledging an infinite array of possible aims, Dewey decides to focus on three general aims that had influence in his day. All three of these continue to hold sway in ours as well. In the first, "Nature is supposed to furnish the law and the end of development; ours it is to follow and conform to her ways" (MW 9: 119). The excessive preoccupation with natural development called out—as a second aim—"the antithetical conception of social efficiency, which often opposes social to natural" (MW 9: 119). The third aim he discusses is culture. Because culture itself is an emergent actualization of nature's potential, Dewey sees no opposition between them. Once we properly understand nature along with a reconstructed meaning of social efficiency and culture, it is easy to reconcile all three.

The notion of natural development has become a dominant idea in educational thinking. All too often, natural development as an aim assumes latent potentials unfolding in a fixed sequence terminating in a predetermined, fixed, and final end. We have already criticized that idea. If every individual "naturally" has unique potential to make their unique contribution to society, then the ideas of "normal" or "standard" are of little use to educators who seek to help students actualize their potential. Further, the idea of normativity and standardization is often associated with the workings of power in defining what it means to be "normal."

One influential idea of natural development originated with Jean-Jacques Rousseau, to whom we also owe some of its most serious errors. Dewey turns to Rousseau's own text to discuss the strengths and weaknesses of natural development. With appropriate changes, Dewey's conclusions apply more or less to any other notion of nature as supplying the aim of education. Let us begin with the strength of Rousseau's ideas:

> The three factors of educative development are (a) the native structure of our bodily organs and their functional activities; (b) the uses to which the activities of these organs are put under the influence of other persons; (c) their direct interaction with the environment. This statement certainly covers the ground. His other two propositions are equally sound; namely, (a) that only when the three factors of education are consonant and cooperative does adequate development of the individual occur, and (b) that the native activities of the organs, being original, are basic in conceiving consonance.
>
> (MW 9: 119–120)

Rousseau's first mistake is to consider the three factors as independent when in fact they always work together. Instead, he assumes "'spontaneous' development" unless someone or something interferes with the natural unfolding of latent potential. Rousseau also "thinks that this development can go on irrespective of the use to which they are put" (MW 9: 120). As we have seen, potentiality is the capacity for change that depends on the kind of interactions in which something or someone (e.g., a student or teacher) participates. Further, it implies progressively intensifying diversification. Dewey approves of using "native activities in accord with those activities themselves—as distinct from forcing them and perverting them," but condemns "supposing they have a normal development apart from use, which development furnishes the standard and norm of all learning by use" (MW 9: 120). Dewey's counter-example is the acquisition of language, which depends upon "vocal apparatus, organs of hearing, etc.," which left alone could never evolve into language use. "The natural, or native, powers furnish the initiating and limiting forces in all education," Dewey concedes, but nonetheless "they do not furnish its ends or aims" (MW 9: 121). This observation will become especially important when we discuss "disability" in Chapter 9 and 11.

Dewey comments on four more of Rousseau's positive insights. First, "natural development as an aim fixes attention upon the bodily organs and the need of health and vigor" (MW 9: 122). Second, "the aim of natural development translates into the aim of respect for physical mobility" (MW 9: 122). This is one reason that it is more important to give students the right thing to do, the right learning activity, rather than simply something to learn. It is also why mere symbolic manipulation has serious limits. We should never ignore the role of the body in learning. Third, we must pay "regard for individual differences" (MW 9: 122).

Differentiated instruction has become part of the canon of good teaching; however, institutional forces often subordinate it to a one-size-fits-all curriculum and norm-referenced standardized tests. Regard for differences also has significant implications for the role of gender, race, ethnicity, disability, sexual orientation, and such in education. Finally, "the aim of following nature means to note the origin, the waxing, and waning, of preferences and interests. Capacities bud and bloom irregularly" (MW 9: 122). Dewey notes that we may most readily observe and respond to these natural tendencies when the children are free from excessive restraint and free to express themselves. This insight is critical to student-centered constructivist teaching. Every individual develops in a unique way depending on "natural" endowments and the kinds of physical, biological, and social interactions in which they participate. We can only educate indirectly by properly shaping these environments.

Rousseau challenges one of the most influential ideas in Western thought; that is, the idea that as the legacy of Adam's sin in the Garden of Eden, "Man" is fallen and intrinsically evil. Instead, Rousseau argues that "Man" is innately good, but society corrupts him. Dewey denies both positions asserting that "primitive impulses are of themselves neither good nor evil, but become one or the other according to the objects for which they are employed" (MW 9: 121). Human beings are what their environmental transactions make of their unique potential.

Dewey indicates: "A conception which made nature supply the end of a true education and society the end of an evil one, could hardly fail to call out a protest" (MW 9: 125). Here, education functions to secure what nature alone cannot, which is the "habituation of an individual to social control; subordination of natural powers to social rules" (MW 9: 121). We have seen why socialization and social control is necessary (just imagine driving a vehicle on roads where there are no rules). However, Dewey makes an important qualification:

> The error is in implying that we must adopt measures of subordination rather than of utilization to secure efficiency. The doctrine is rendered

adequate when we recognize that social efficiency is attained not by negative constraint but by positive use of native individual capacities in occupations having a social meaning.

(MW 9: 125)

Recall our discussion of moral equality in Chapter 4. Positive use of individual capacities requires developing each individual's unique potential to make their unique contribution. Moral equality also means educating in accordance with the democratic criteria discussed in the last chapter.

Larry Hickman (2006: 69) states that "it is not the *fact* of socialization that concerns the educator, but its *context*, its *means*, and its *consequences*." Good socialization enables individual intellectual, moral, and aesthetic growth while expanding the group's openness to otherness and differences that provide a more pluralistic community open to novel forms of socialization. As Hickman remarks, Dewey's democratic criteria allow us to judge any social institution by "the extent to which they produce a form of socialization that is *reductive* and the extent to which they produce a form of socialization that is *exclusive*" (69). Dewey wishes to avoid those forms of socialization and social efficiency that are reductive and exclusive in favor of forms that are expansive and inclusive.

Dewey discusses two aspects of social efficiency: industrial competency and citizenship. We begin with the former. He understands that people need to be able to make a living, so he does not deride economic participation; indeed, he praises it:

> Translated into specific aims, social efficiency indicates the importance of industrial competency. Persons cannot live without means of subsistence; hence, the ways in which we employ and consume these have a profound influence upon all the relationships of persons to one another. If an individual is not able to earn his own living and that of the children dependent upon him, he is a drag or parasite upon the activities of others. He misses for himself one of the most educative experiences of life. If he is not trained in the right use of the products of industry, there is grave danger that he may deprave himself and injure others in his possession of wealth. No scheme of education can afford to neglect such basic considerations.

(MW 9: 125–126)

Similar remarks apply to today's post-industrial global economy. What Dewey says here is easily misunderstood; he is not an apologist for the *status quo*; indeed, quite the opposite. Practically, there is the problem that arises when industries change and those who are narrowly specialized cannot "readjust themselves." Still there is something far more serious:

> But, most of all, the present industrial constitution of society is, like every society which has ever existed, full of inequities. It is the aim of progressive education to take part in correcting unfair privilege and unfair deprivation, not to perpetuate them. Wherever social control means subordination of individual activities to class authority, there is danger that industrial education will be dominated by acceptance of the *status quo*.
>
> (MW 9: 126)

The ideal for Dewey is the ability to participate in economic affairs actively and intelligently.

As Dewey was writing *Democracy and Education*, he was engaged in a much-publicized debate over the establishment of government legislation that would put an end to educating all students in the same classroom and establish a tracking system that sorts large numbers of students into vocational education classes. He was a strident opponent of such legislation. Dewey lost this debate when the Smith-Hughes National Vocational Education Act passed the year after the publication of *Democracy and Education*. In an essay published in *The New Republic*, Dewey replied to one of the leaders of the vocational education movement, David Snedden. At first, what he says seems surprising: "I would go farther than he [Snedden] is apparently willing to go in holding that education should be vocational" (MW 8: 411). He means it! As we have already seen in the previous chapters, for Dewey, "education *through* occupations consequently combines within itself more of the factors conducive to learning than any other method" (MW 9: 319). Notice Dewey does not support education in the public schools *for* an occupation. That can come later at the employer's expense. Engaging in the various skilled practices of a culture prompts the formation of cognitive and emotional dispositions without separating the mind from the body. The typical result of tracking is to invoke a dualism wherein those on the higher track are destined to work with their minds while those on the lower tracks prepare to work with their bodies; both are alienated from the wholeness of their being.

In his reply, Dewey is very explicit about what he would reject in vocational education as Snedden conceives it and as it was eventually legislated a century ago:

> [I]n the name of a genuinely vocational education I object to the identification of vocation with such trades as can be learned before the age of, say, eighteen or twenty; and to the identification of education with acquisition of specialized skill in the management of machines at the expense of an industrial intelligence based on science and a knowledge of social problems and conditions. I object to regarding as vocational education any training which does not have as its supreme regard the development of such intelligent initiative, ingenuity and executive capacity as shall make workers, as far as may be, the masters of their own industrial fate.
>
> (MW 8: 411)

Vocational education should make everyone an active intelligent, skillful, reflective, critical, and creative participant in the economic affairs of the national and global economy instead of passive, docile, and dependent slaves of a system they do not understand. Dewey summarizes:

> I am regretfully forced to the conclusion that the difference between us is not so much narrowly educational as it is profoundly political and social. The kind of vocational education in which I am interested is not one which will "adapt" workers to the existing industrial régime; I am not sufficiently in love with the régime for that. It seems to me that the business of all who would not be educational timeservers is to resist every move in this direction, and to strive for a kind of vocational education which will first alter the existing industrial system, and ultimately transform it.
>
> (MW 8: 112)

Dewey is indeed the philosopher of reconstruction. Nonetheless, he underestimated the role of power in the socio-political realm and human affairs more generally, which is something we will look at in our next chapter.

The other aspect of social efficiency discussed by Dewey is "civic efficiency, or good citizenship" (MW 9: 127). Dewey quickly notes we cannot separate industrial competency from capacity for good citizenship. Dewey wants efficient "industrial intelligence" to contribute to civic efficiency by fostering democratic participation. The traits of good citizenship are many:

> These traits run from whatever make an individual a more agreeable companion to citizenship in the political sense: it denotes ability to judge men and measures wisely and to take a determining part in making as well as obeying laws. It calls attention to the fact that power must be relative to doing something, and to the fact that the things which most need to be done are things which involve one's relationships with others.
>
> (MW 9: 127)

In spite of such a wide range of positive traits, he warns: "Here again we have to be on guard against understanding the aim too narrowly" (MW 9: 127). For instance, we must be wary of the reduction of civic efficiency to economic efficiency. Here is what worries Dewey in his response to Snedden:

> The curriculum on this narrow trade plan will neglect as useless for its ends the topics in history and civics which make future workers aware of their rightful claims as citizens in a democracy . . . So far as it takes in civic and social studies at all, it will emphasize those things which emphasize duties to the established order and a blind patriotism which accounts it a great privilege to defend things in which the workers themselves have little or no share.
>
> (MW 8: 148)

Not mincing his words, Dewey warns that narrow trade training contributes to a static social order resembling "feudal control of industry" (MW 8: 150). Dewey is using the idea of "feudalism" loosely, but what he means by it is social, political, and economic structural inequality. The old medieval feudalism was primarily agrarian and land based. It assumed a predetermined, fixed, and final hierarchical elite composed of the military, economic, and priestly social classes and the subordinate peasants and social classes of the commoners, which included serfs, peasants, and those skilled in the trades that no one from top to bottom could alter. Dewey has mostly this hierarchical rigidity in mind when he speaks of feudalism in modern capitalist contexts. That is why he champions the kind of education that provides critical and creative "industrial intelligence" capable of "a reorganization of industry as will change it from a feudalistic to a democratic order" (MW 8: 150).

The third aim Dewey discusses is culture, which in one sense is completely incompatible with natural development as an aim: "Culture means at least something cultivated, something ripened; it is opposed to the raw and crude. When the 'natural' is identified with this rawness, culture is opposed to what is called natural development" (MW 9: 128). However, we have already seen that Dewey rejects the nature-versus-culture dualism. There is also a sense in which it is incompatible with constrained social efficiency:

> Culture is also something personal; it is cultivation with respect to appreciation of ideas and art and broad human interests. When efficiency is identified with a narrow range of *acts*, instead of with the spirit and meaning of *activity*, culture is opposed to efficiency.
>
> (MW 9: 128)

Notice how Dewey here champions personal cultivation and not just culture in either the anthropological or elitist sense. This changes everything and makes it possible to understand the cultivation of unique individuality as the synthesis of both the natural development of everyone's distinctive characteristics as well as democratic social efficiency:

> Whether called culture or complete development of personality, the outcome is identical with the true meaning of social efficiency whenever attention is given to what is unique in an individual—and he would not be an individual if there were not something incommensurable about him.
>
> (MW 9: 128)

Dewey is thinking in terms of moral equality—the "democratic faith in human equality is belief that every human being, independent of the quantity or range of his personal endowment, has the right to equal opportunity with every other person for development of whatever gifts he has" (LW 14: 226–227).

Structural inequality is a serious threat to democracy that moral equality helps us to oppose. Structural inequality persists and is at least as severe in our time as in Dewey's day. The aim of education in a pluralistic, participatory, and communicative democratic society is individual and social growth. This implies that each unique individual should have sufficient opportunity to make their unique social contribution. This can only be realized if steps are taken towards more equal chances and equitable support for all not only in education but in all areas of social life. That remains as much of a challenge for democracy and education today as in Dewey's time.

Challenge for Today: The Aims of Education, Learning by Doing, and Learning by Testing

In the view of many, contemporary capitalism with its dependencies, power relations, and forms of exploitation look pretty much like a new version of feudalism or rule by the few. While Dewey does not use the term hegemony, he understands the danger that capitalist elitism poses on democracy. In public debate today, the talk is often that, instead of the divine right of kings anointed by God, we have the divine right of aristocratic capitalists anointed by the market. Today's money managers interpret the will of the market to wealthy capitalists like the priests of yore interpreted God's will to the princes.[1] This account, however, is too simple to describe the contemporary situation adequately. However accurate in Dewey's day, feudalistic analogies oversimplify conditions of late modernity.

In the present, not only the feudal order of old but also the economic, social, and cultural order and organization of early modernity have given way to processes of liquefaction (cf. Bauman, 2000) that render the comparison with feudalistic institutions of power and rule questionable. The liquefied market is not like the medieval marketplace from which early and modern capitalism arose, but is itself the very product of accelerated, flexible, dynamic, growing capitalism. Against this background, we may observe that the military today often protects the postcolonial global markets, but does so in decidedly different fashion than the medieval knight defended the old feudal manor or the nineteenth and twentieth centuries nation-state defended its national market and goods (cf. Sassen, 2008). Tendencies of capitalism influence and threaten democracy and education in our time as in Dewey's, but there are relatively new manifestations of such influence that require a new account. Without going too much into details, here, we focus on some especially important examples.

The widespread and commonsense use of the term "human capital" indicates how much capitalism has pervaded human experience in liquid modernity. Human capital theory assumes we may refine and render everything, including people, fit to circulate as a commodity. Public education then becomes an investment in refining raw human resources into standardized interchangeable and readily replaceable parts for circulation along with other non-human commodities that comprise the global economy. That is why one-size-fits-all educational standards and standardized tests become so important. They pretend to ensure quality control of the product. However, the power relations in liquid modernity benefit mostly wealthy capitalists, and education increasingly becomes a means for this benefit. It is obvious that the diversity of individual experiences and interests and needs—of fundamental significance for democratic coexistence—cannot be captured and done justice to by one-size-fits-all measures or reduction to "human capital" invested in the market. What is at stake today in debates around "human capital" including critical approaches to capitalization of society and education is the discussion about the role of competencies and capacities in education. Regarding capitalism, we may use both terms in an affirmative or a critical sense.

The concept of competencies can allow for a more generous openness to diversity and experiences than the term aim in its general usage. This comes close to Dewey's criticism of narrow reductionism and merely external ends in education. A tendency that we often observe in connection with programs that define aims in education is that they have a relatively narrow focus on contents and forget about action, communication, participation, and construction in learning. Dewey's plea for understanding aims as means that help us to make the process of education a rich, diverse, and resourceful experience is reflected in the present-day appeal to competencies (instead of aims) as an educational orientation that provides a more open and expansive approach. This appeal regards aims as constructions in experience and emphasizes the malleability and variability of aims in educational growth. In part, the use of the concept "competencies" implies a shift of perspectives away from predefined contents or skills towards capabilities of learners as resources in and for their own experiences. There is also an inter- and trans-disciplinary implication because we often identify competencies as so-called "key-competencies" transcending specific contexts, disciplines, contents, or skills. Rather, they are seen as means and instruments for disciplinary border crossing and transfer. At the same time, however, this conceptual shift also expresses a growing adaptation to market interests and especially the requirements of flexible, dynamic, and disposable attitudes and skills in learning and work. The crucial challenge for democracy and education in the tradition of Dewey is to use the strength of the concept "competencies" to empower the experiences of all learners and to resist the reductionist tendencies to mere market adoption by emphasizing and furthering participation and diversity of interests. The terms of this challenge very much resemble the stakes of the Snedden–Dewey controversy about vocational education mentioned above.

In this context, the primary claim is to the necessary funding of education and educational practices and institutions. In an increasingly globalized world, we can observe two fundamental trends that seem highly problematic because they put democracy and education at risk: First, we observe that societies in the global

South are continually and, in many cases, even increasingly deprived of the resources needed to furnish their educational systems with sustainable potentials for growth. Here we face a growing inequality between rich and poor societies worldwide. Second, we observe the growing tendency for capitalism to pervade all fields of experience in the developed and relatively rich countries to a degree where the gap between haves and have-nots, those who are well educated or fall back, those who win or lose, is increasing. In relation to the prosperity produced by capitalist societies, the underfunding of educational institutions and practices is a permanent scandal for democracy and education.

Against this background, the critical debate about the role and importance of capacities in education can be used as a conceptual instrument for responding to what Bauman has insightfully characterized as one of the main challenges of emancipation and autonomy in liquid modernity: namely overcoming the growing gap between individuality *de jure* and individuality *de facto* in social life. Bauman claims that in a democracy being an individual *de facto* is equivalent to being a citizen in the full political sense of that term. His account resonates with many aspects on which Dewey had already reflected in his 1930 "Individualism, Old and New" (LW 5: 41–123). Individuality *de jure*, for Bauman, represents the expectations, roles, requirements, and responsibilities imposed on men and women by an increasingly individualized society. To be an individual *de jure* implies that one has to care for and take responsibility for one's life and education without the possibility of blaming anybody but oneself for success or failure. Individuality *de facto*, on the other hand, represents the capacities and competencies for making one's own decisions and following one's own life plans in productive and participatory exchanges and cooperation with others. In Dewey's words: "Freedom or individuality, in short, is not an original possession or gift. It is something to be achieved, to be wrought out" (LW 2: 61). If we fail to provide individuals with opportunities and resources for personal growth and autonomy—which necessarily includes the most advanced opportunities and resource of education for all—the risk is that *de facto* they will fall into the gap instead of bridging it.

We may conclude that the term "competencies" in itself is vague and that we need to fill it substantively. The debates about competencies in education are therefore necessarily ambivalent and ambiguous in our time. They are part of hegemonic controversies and struggles. To construct the concept as a critical instrument for democracy and education, we need to focus on the importance of conditions for autonomy and individuality *de facto* that include all learners as democratic participants.

Let us now address some more concrete challenges in the contemporary global educational scene. Along with the Trends in International Mathematics and Science Study (National Center for Education Statistics) and Progress in International Reading Literacy Study, we have already mentioned OECD's PISA program. OECD is a member of the United Nations Global Compact. Among the agencies of the United Nations are the World Bank and United Nations Educational,

Scientific and Cultural Organization (UNESCO). Meyer, Tröhler, Laberee & Hutt (2014) observe: "As the PISA juggernaut gathers momentum, it paves the way for an ever broader menu of services, including costly consulting and restructuring services, delivered by private multinationals, which address the educational shortcomings that PISA presumably uncovered." Currently, one of the fastest growing global service industries is for-profit education at all levels as well as the associated textbook publishing industry, all of which are keyed to the needs of the global economy and human capital theory. For example, the Educational Testing Service (ETS) is a rapidly expanding global company based in the United States that vends its products internationally. In the United States, it provides the test about half of the students take for admission to the university, as well as the tests most students have to pass for admission to graduate school (GRE) and many professional schools such as law (LSAT). ETS also provides a test of reading, writing, and mathematics (PRAXIS I) as well as general and subject-specific teaching skills for entering teaching (PRAXIS II), both of which most pre-service teachers must pass to become public school teachers. ETS content is keyed to the global economy.

We will concentrate on the PISA exam. Given every three years, PISA is a two-hour summative test on reading, mathematics, and science representing about 28 million 15-year-olds globally. Many assume it is a highly reliable indirect measure of the productivity of a nation's economic system that allows state technocrats to accurately compare educational performances across nations (cf. OECD, 2010). These comparisons rank nations according to their scores on the tests that many interpret as indicators of the quality of the job each nation's educational system is doing to refine its human resources. Hence, nations compete for good PISA test scores as an extension of their global economic competition.

Internationally, many nations and localities have aligned their curriculum standards and teaching methods to PISA or other standardized tests that closely resemble it. One result of globalization is the transformation of schooling from a cultural to a technological system. This technological turn has rather ambivalent aspects with regard to democracy and education. Obviously, the reductionism contained in the will to measurement and testing leads to a narrow concept and practice of education and schooling insofar as the PISA results are taken to represent a universal and unequivocal standard of comparison for all systems worldwide. From a Deweyan perspective, this is nonsensical, because it involves a disastrous neglect of context and a loss of the qualitative dimension of experience and growth. However, if we take the PISA studies as a contextualized measurement with limited results, we may simultaneously find some productive and even critical use for them. For example, in the German context, the first publication of PISA in 2001 started a public discussion about the detrimental connections of low social status and income with chances for educational success. This discussion has continued until the present day, fueled by new publications of PISA results. One of the main effects has been a shift in public opinion toward a critical view on state politics regarding inequality in education. This shows the ambivalence of PISA as an instrument developed in the contexts of capitalization of learning, while at the same time producing critical evaluations of this very capitalization. What is more, we find that even the PISA catalogues contain assignments that in some respects involve rather pragmatic and communicative issues that do not rely on mere reproductive learning but rather inspire constructive applications. Therefore, it would be unfair to say that they totally lack qualitative dimensions.

Drawing conclusions on a more general level, we must say that PISA as an instrument for assessing and comparing learning achievements is necessarily captured in the tensions between capitalism, democracy, and education. As such, we must avoid using it uncritically as well as rejecting it blindly.

First, if we look at the discussions and debates that PISA has effected, especially in those countries that are relatively low in ranking, like Germany previously and the United States more recently, we find that one core issue is the increasing role of state funding. Schools worldwide need reform, and reform needs money. Therefore, the situation after PISA at least involves growing public awareness of the tension between the political will to austerity and the democratic need of proper, well-funded, and sustainable educational systems.

Second, from a Deweyan perspective, we must remember its limits and contexts as an instrument. But we must also consider that we need instruments that are viable in the present contexts of capitalization and that allow for comparison insofar as they do not distort what they measure. They should at least give reliable information about the correlations of the necessary resources and the expectable results in different societies. While PISA is useful in this respect, we require more contextualized and qualitatively based evaluations from local to global levels.

Third, critics of PISA should ask what the situation was like before the test: Having no considerable and broadly comparative information, there was a strong temptation for educators, politicians, and public opinion to sugar-coat the growing capitalization of learning and education with romanticized fantasies about qualitative and contextualized learning and schooling. We should not put the cart before the horse: It was not PISA that started the capitalization, although PISA certainly has been produced by and is representative of some parts of global capitalization in education.

Fourth, PISA tends to produce a general attitude in education worldwide that takes "human capital" and the will to measurement for granted as generalized orientations for the evaluation of educative practices. To the degree in which this attitude becomes hegemonic and constitutive of a mainstream that allows for hardly any alternatives, it is detrimental and even catastrophic for claims to democracy and education, especially with regard to the necessary participation and diversity, the uniqueness of individuals, and the qualitative dimensions of experience and growth.

Finally, PISA may help to make inequalities within a country and between countries visible, but it alone will not aid in ameliorating injustices and unfair distributions. This applies not only with regard to developed countries like the United States, Germany, or others, but even more to countries characterized by underdevelopment, poverty, and global powerlessness. Measuring and ranking neglect context, especially when the standards and instruments are implemented without taking the specific resources, challenges, cultural and linguistic contexts and so forth into account.

Against this background, we note there is a more general effect to be considered that goes with the increasing popularity of PISA and other forms of standardized testing. There is a change in attitude that we can observe on many levels in education, from the individual teacher and school to public debates and politics. Increasingly, schooling seems to involve for many the belief that teaching to the test is the best orientation. This attitude tends to block or even crush a teacher's creative autonomy and communicative ability to connect to individuals in a moral and aesthetic manner. In the United States, school administrators and teachers often even depend on good test scores for their very jobs. Around the world, many regional, state, and local tests are reductionist, quantitatively oriented for measurement, multiple choice, paper and pencil, norm referenced, and machine graded. Let us reflect some on what this means.

First, the emphasis is largely on lower-order thinking skills such as discrimination, identification, classification, comprehension, and knowledge as opposed to application, analysis, synthesis, and evaluation. Higher-order thinking skills are harder to define and assess. Tests often measure what is cheap to assess and does not cause controversy. True higher-order thinking skills are more vague and indeterminate, or what we sometimes call "subjective." Of course, what we call "objective" is also a human construct subject to error and falsification. What is at issue is called "construct validity." It concerns whether or not a test measures what it claims to measure and whether or not inferences from those measurements are sound and valid. If we rely on testing in any form, we must consider these limits.

Second, these tests are measures yielding whole numbers (e.g., 570, 580, 613). At first that appears so obvious as to seem irrelevant. However, numbers are commensurable. They can always be compared such that 613 is greater than 580 and 580 greater than 570. That is, they assign a position for every tested individual in a predetermined population with respect to the measured trait. For instance, a norm-referenced test given to 100 Nobel Prize winners in science would rank them from below average, to average, to above average—provided that we consider the Nobel Prize Committee as a valid "universal" judge anyway. Most tests are norm referenced and, hence, assume every individual is commensurable to every other. Furthermore, we might ask, why some traits or items are preferred to others. Who decides? From the perspective of democracy and education, these are public decisions that should rely on the most generous and comprehensive participation of all in society. They should reflect the diversity of interests in the multitude of people. This perspective gives us a good standard for estimating the role and status of measurement and ranking in education. The qualitative dimensions of experience and the uniqueness of individuals should always count more than numbers. Against the generalized will to measurement we must cultivate an educational will to diversity, participation, and growth. Here again, we encounter the tension between democracy and capitalism. Under the present capitalist global order, norms of capacity and conduct are contingent social constructions erected because of social power and market mechanisms that rely on comparison and standardization for exchange. Numbers and rankings are feasible instruments for the distribution of positions involving income, prestige, influence, and so on.

Third, confidence in numbers and measurement implies the commitment to a culturally entrenched positivistic, rationalistic, and scientistic prejudice. In her biography of Thorndike titled *The Sane Positivist*, Geraldine Joncich Clifford (1984: 282) begins one chapter with a passage from Thorndike's *Educational Psychology*: "We conquer the facts of nature when we observe and experiment upon them. When we measure them we have made them our servants." The famous Thorndike principle is a statement of his metaphysical commitment to measurement: "Whatever exists exists in some amount. To measure it is simply to know its varying amounts" (Clifford, 1994: 262). Thorndike is one among other modern scientists who immensely influenced the global fetish with norm-referenced educational testing. The Thorndike principle—as one representative formulation of this general attitude and approach—has dominated not only educational research, but also many other forms of social research for the last 100 years. This principle is the preeminent guide to governmental policy research (now compiled as statistical facts such as PISA results), while most social legislation, including educational legislation, provides for the quantitative measurement of output productivity. Bureaucrats and technocrats rely on such data to carry out cost–benefit analysis and spend taxpayer funds where they seek to yield the most benefit for the least expense. Today, as they have for decades, educational reformers talk Dewey, but do Thorndike. The result is a democratic crisis in American or other countries' public schools and universities.

Fourth, many examples of standardized testing confine themselves exclusively to symbolic manipulation. That is the only kind of action involved. Recall Dewey's worries that exclusively symbolic book learning will not allow us to adequately address all the complexity of "ordinary vital experience" such as the practical and the emotional. Symbols are always secondary and representative of primary experience. Their strength is in their abstract mobility. However, they always involve the danger that the "pupil learns symbols without the key to their meaning. He acquires a technical body of information without ability to trace its connections with the objects and operations with which he is familiar—often he acquires simply a peculiar vocabulary" (LW 9: 228). We must not confuse symbols for the reality they represent thereby falling into "intellectualism." Learning by testing harms learning by doing and, worse still, being able to do anything personally meaningful with what we learn.

Democracy and education is not just an ideal-typical claim of political romanticism but can be a pragmatic program that takes account of and comes to terms with actual conditions, possibilities, and challenges. We have argued in this and other chapters that this program, among other things, needs to offer resistance against reductionisms in education in many forms. One example is our taking for granted an understanding of intelligence as an individual possession to be measured by standardized intelligence tests (IQ). We have seen that in *The Mismeasure of Man*, Stephen Gould, bemoaned the fact that we have reduced intelligence as the "wondrously complex multifaceted set of human capabilities" to "its dubious status as a unitary thing" (Gould, 1996: 56). One way of understanding intelligence as a larger set of human capabilities is Howard Gardner's theory of multiple intelligences. Rather than seeing intelligence as a single general capacity, Gardner (2000) proposes an array of capacities that include: visual–spatial, musical–rhythmic, logical–mathematical, bodily–kinesthetic, interpersonal, verbal–linguistic, intrapersonal, and naturalistic. Gardner thinks we might also include existential and moral intelligence, although he is less sure of them. There is also the dimension of "emotional intelligence" identified by Daniel Goleman (1995). The Nobel Prize-winning economist James J. Heckman (see Heckman, Stixrud & Urzua, 2006) has made a strong and widely influential case for the importance of non-cognitive skills, which many call "soft skills." The United States Department of Labor lists six soft skills especially valuable in the workplace: communication, enthusiasm and attitude, teamwork, networking, problem solving and critical thinking (including making ethical decisions), and professionalism (understood as integrating the other skills). Many of these are traits of good citizenship. Of course, economic efficiency is among the by-products of helping every individual actualize their unique capacities. Finally, there is also "cultural competence," which is the ability not only to comprehend one's own cultural practices and attitudes, but also that of others along with the skill to work well with others from different cultures. Inter- and transcultural competencies not only tolerate diversity but also genuinely appreciate it. Because many of the capacities mentioned in this paragraph are non-cognitive, it is not possible to develop them merely by symbolic manipulation much less adequately measure and assess them that way.

We have seen that Deweyan pragmatism and interactive constructivism are companions in contemporary education. They both emphasize the construction of meaning and knowledge through shared social action within a community. Acquiring language is a noteworthy example, but it is only one among many social practices. Dewey especially emphasizes sharing social practices in a pluralistic and communicative democratic community. He also stresses the embodied character of practice and the acquisition of dispositions to act (i.e., habits) in ways other forms of constructivism do not. Pragmatism derives from the ancient Greek word *pragma*, meaning deed or a thing done. While emphasizing action, the goal is to make action, and especially shared action, cognitively intelligent as well as emotionally sensitive. Dewey's emphasis on developing individual capacities *through* occupations having social meaning, but not *for* predetermined occupations, is a strong expression of his democratic social constructivism.

Both Deweyan and interactive constructivism emphasize learning by doing. Dewey maintains:

> The most direct blow at the traditional separation of doing and knowing and at the traditional prestige of purely "intellectual" studies, however, has been given by the progress of experimental science. If this progress has demonstrated anything, it is that there is no such thing as genuine knowledge and fruitful understanding except as the offspring of *doing*. The analysis and rearrangement of facts which is indispensable to the growth of knowledge and power of explanation and right classification cannot be attained purely mentally—just inside the head.
>
> (MW 9: 284)

What is critical here is that experience stops being passive sensation and becomes active experimentation upon the world. Dewey emphasizes the necessary qualitative dimension of experience that education must retain. Active doing is essential to good learning; while necessary, symbolic representation is secondary. In this way, everyone may engage in a wide variety of social practices to find what they are good at and most interested in doing for their life's work. Dewey envisioned a society in which everyone was morally equal.

Dewey's Summary

> An aim denotes the result of any natural process brought to consciousness and made a factor in determining present observation and choice of ways of acting. It signifies that an activity has become intelligent. Specifically it means foresight of the alternative consequences attendant upon acting in a given situation in different ways, and the use of what is anticipated to direct observation and experiment. A true aim is thus opposed at every point to an aim that is imposed upon a process of action from without. The latter is fixed and rigid; it is not a stimulus to intelligence in the given situation, but is an externally dictated order to do such and such things. Instead of connecting directly with present activities, it is remote, divorced from the means by which it is to be reached. Instead of suggesting a freer and better balanced activity, it is a limit set to activity. In education, the currency of these externally imposed aims is responsible for the emphasis put upon the notion of preparation for a remote future and for rendering the work of both teacher and pupil mechanical and slavish.
>
> (MW 9: 117)

Our Summary

The aim of education is to enable individuals to continue their education. Hence, the ideal of democracy and education demands that aims should arise within the impulse to personal growth of experience. But there is a tensional relation between the experience of learners and the aims and expectations representing powerful interests in society as articulated by the curriculum. We here find a main source for distinguishing between intrinsic and extrinsic aspects of learning. Dewey rightly observes that education has to take this tensional relationship seriously. His famous claim that education has no end beyond itself suggests we must never impose aims from without; rather, they must be genuine components within the very process of learning and growth. Enabling every individual to actualize their unique potential that they may make their unique contribution to the community is a primary aim of education in a democracy. Societies characterized by compartmentalization, division of labor, diversity of interests, and unequal power relations tend to impose aims and contents on learners to make them fit for their purposes and channel their experiences and energies into utilitarian opportunities. This is true for capitalist societies in our time as it was in Dewey's. Therefore, it is equally important today as it was in his day to emphasize the necessary tension between capitalism, and especially human capital theory, and democratic education. With regard to aims, this includes the insight that good educational aims counteract external imposition. Education and democracy should provide opportunities for learners to participate in the development of aims that are intrinsic to their ongoing activities, needs, desires, and purposes. This is the way to facilitate social intelligence in learning and to provide opportunities so learners may construct and develop competencies to solve relevant problems in their experience. In this sense, we must insist with Dewey that it is not enough to formulate standardized aims for students and teachers. Teachers should tailor aims to fit each individual student, while students need sufficient opportunities to partake substantively in communities of learning they themselves construct with others. Competencies within democracy and education must be understood as an outgrowth of personal and social experience and not as something entirely defined from without. This is a main insight of Dewey's criticisms of the narrow vocational training programs in his time, and it must be a main insight for us in criticizing the reductionist tendencies in current measures like standardized testing, multiple choice, reproductive learning strategies, learning for the test, and the general will to measurement.

Note

1   See Cox (1999). An ordained Baptist minister, Cox is among the most influential religious scholars in North America.

7

INTEREST, DISCIPLINE, AND POWER

In Chapter 10 of his *Democracy and Education*, titled "Interest and Discipline," Dewey introduces the distinction between the roles or perspectives of a *spectator*, *participant*, and *agent* (MW 9: 131) in order to discuss the meaning and import of the terms "interest" and "discipline" in his pragmatist philosophy and their implications for education. The mentioned distinction of the three roles comes very close to current constructivist terminology in the humanities, social sciences, and educational theory. The Cologne program of interactive constructivism uses the concepts of "observer," "participant," and "agent" as a systematic theoretical distinction in its account of the social and cultural constructions of reality (see Reich, 2009).

In the course of this chapter, we will first give a condensed account of Dewey's approach to "interest" and "discipline" against the background of this crucial distinction. Second, we will further extend the theoretical reflection of the three roles by giving a more extensive consideration of the cultural dimensions and contexts involved. Third, we will expand the scope of reflection by introducing some thoughts of a more recent philosopher who has also given us important theoretical perspectives on the question of the emergence of "problems" in cultural and historical contexts: Michel Foucault. With Foucault, we will come to the third term in the title of our chapter—the issue of "power" and how it relates to Dewey's pragmatist and our constructivist understanding of "interest" and "discipline." We here encounter another challenge for today's democracy and education if we want to connect our approach with Dewey's and at the same time go beyond Dewey and his time.

We start with "interest" and "discipline." At the very outset of his chapter, Dewey offers the following remarks to pave the way towards his understanding of the term "interest":

> We have already noticed the difference in the attitude of a spectator and
> of an agent or participant. The former is indifferent to what is going on
> ... The latter is bound up with what is going on; its outcome makes a
> difference to him ... The attitude of a participant in the course of affairs
> is thus a double one: there is solicitude, anxiety concerning future
> consequences, and a tendency to act to assure better, and avert worse,
> consequences.
>
> (MW 9: 131)

It is this double attitude in the perspective of a participant that provides us
with a starting point. Dewey observes that there "are words which denote this
attitude: concern, interest" (MW 9: 131). In his pragmatic philosophy, participation means a way of interacting and transacting with a world filled with interests
and concerns, since the results of such interaction make an actual and real
difference to those involved. "Interest, concern, means that self and world are
engaged with each other in a developing situation" (MW 9: 132). The words
suggest

> that a person is bound up with the possibilities inhering in objects; that he
> is accordingly on the lookout for what they are likely to do to him; and
> that, on the basis of his expectation or foresight, he is eager to act so as to
> give things one turn rather than another.
>
> (MW 9: 131)

It accords with Dewey's overall interactional approach that "interest," for him
is simultaneously personal and objective. The more personal side involves
affections, purposes, and motives, while the more objective side involves aims,
ends, and results. Participation and interaction imply that both sides are inseparable
in experience. Rather, they condition each other and develop together:

> While such words as affection, concern, and motive indicate an attitude of
> personal preference, they are always attitudes toward *objects*—toward what
> is foreseen. We may call the phase of objective foresight intellectual, and
> the phase of personal concern emotional and volitional, but there is no
> separation in the facts of the situation.
>
> (MW 9: 132)

Dewey reminds us of the necessary connection between interest and imagination. Obviously, it is impossible to have interests without having imagination.
"The difference imaginatively foreseen makes a present difference, which finds
expression in solicitude and effort" (MW 9: 132). This brings us to the original
meaning of the word "interest." Etymologically, i.e., in its Latin origin, the word
suggests what *is between*: "To be means for the achieving of present tendencies,

to be 'between' the agent and his end, to be of interest, are different names for the same thing" (MW 9: 134). This necessary imaginative and in-between status of interests is of the utmost importance for education. In learning and educational growth, interest is what makes for development and growth.

The moving and transcending character of the *no-more-here-and-not-yet-there* that is essential for any constructive learning process testifies to the intrinsic role of developing interests as authentically connecting as well as connected factors in experience:

> When material has to be made interesting, it signifies that as presented, it lacks connection with purposes and present power: or that if the connection be there, it is not perceived. To make it interesting by leading one to realize the connection that exists is simply good sense; to make it interesting by extraneous and artificial inducements deserves all the bad names which have been applied to the doctrine of interest in education.
>
> (MW 9: 134)

Against this background, Dewey believes that a reconstructed theory of the role of interest in education has immensely important implications. He claims:

> [T]he value of recognizing the dynamic place of interest in an educative development is that it leads to considering individual children in their specific capabilities, needs, and preferences. One who recognizes the importance of interest will not assume that all minds work in the same way because they happen to have the same teacher and textbook. Attitudes and methods of approach and response vary with the specific appeal the same material makes, this appeal itself varying with difference of natural aptitude, of past experience, of plan of life, and so on.
>
> (MW 9: 137)

Differences of interest help us better understand issues of difference between cultures, ethnic groups, genders, race, and such, which thereby contributes to our ability to appreciate issues of diversity.

For Dewey, "interest" and "discipline" necessarily complement each other in any intentional activity. He observes that "[d]iscipline is positive." It means "power at command" (MW 9: 136). It combines will and execution. More specifically, discipline consists of the "development of power to recognize what one is about" combined with "persistence in accomplishment" (MW 9: 136). On the one hand, therefore, discipline contains an intellectual phase of deliberation: "That the primary difference between strong and feeble volition is intellectual, consisting in the degree of persistent firmness and fullness with which consequences are thought out, cannot be overemphasized" (MW 9: 135). On the other hand, discipline implies an affective phase of engagement that makes persistent action possible:

Where an activity takes time, where many means and obstacles lie between its initiation and completion, deliberation and persistence are required. It is obvious that a very large part of the everyday meaning of will is precisely the deliberate or conscious disposition to persist and endure in a planned course of action in spite of difficulties and contrary solicitations.

(MW 9: 134)

Or in short: "To know what one is to do and to move to do it promptly and by use of the requisite means is to be disciplined, whether we are thinking of an army or a mind" (MW 9: 136).

In the following passage, Dewey gives a nice account of the context of intelligent action in which interest and discipline come to play as relevant factors. We quote this passage at length because it easily sums up the connections of interest and discipline with participation and interaction mentioned before:

[M]ind is not a name for something complete by itself; it is a name for a course of action in so far as that is intelligently directed; in so far, that is to say, as aims, ends, enter into it, with selection of means to further the attainment of aims. Intelligence is not a peculiar possession which a person owns; but a person is intelligent in so far as the activities in which he plays a part have the qualities mentioned. Nor are the activities in which a person engages, whether intelligently or not, exclusive properties of himself; they are something in which he *engages and partakes*. Other things, the independent changes of other things and persons, cooperate and hinder. The individual's act may be initial in a course of events, but the outcome depends upon the interaction of his response with energies supplied by other agencies. Conceive mind as anything but one factor partaking along with others in the production of consequences, and it becomes meaningless.

(MW 9: 139)

The implications for education are important. Generally speaking, Dewey believes that a pragmatic and interactional understanding of the roles of "interest" and "discipline" in learning and education can help us to avoid fruitless dualisms of mind and world or mind and subject matter in educational theory. He criticizes traditional education where mind too frequently "is set over the world of things and facts to be known; it is regarded as something existing in isolation" (MW 9: 137). This has serious consequences for our understanding of knowledge and subject matter because the dualism—as contained, e.g., in traditional rationalist and empiricist theories of learning—almost totally conceals the necessary roles of interest, partaking, and interaction in learning and knowing.

Dewey identifies one primary error behind the empirical and rationalistic educational traditions:

In short, the root of the error long prevalent in the conception of training
of mind consists in leaving out of account movements of things to future
results in which an individual shares, and in the direction of which
observation, imagination, and memory are enlisted. It consists in regarding
mind as complete in itself, ready to be directly applied to a present material.

(MW 9: 139–140)

And he goes on to observe:

In historic practice the error has cut two ways. On one hand, it has screened
and protected traditional studies and methods of teaching from intelligent
criticism and needed revisions . . . In the other direction, the tendency was
towards a negative conception of discipline, instead of an identification of
it with growth in constructive power of achievement.

(MW 9: 140)

However, the release and cultivation of powers of construction and criticism
in education is especially important in and for democracy.

Dewey has a clear awareness that a reconstructed vision of the roles of
"interest" and "discipline" in educational theory and practice has important social
implications. Above all, it provides necessary conditions for the development and
growth of individuals who have the ability to contribute with their own activities
to the growth and well-being of social life for all:

Persons whose interests have been enlarged and intelligence trained by
dealing with things and facts in active occupations having a purpose
(whether in play or work) will be those most likely to escape the alternatives
of an academic and aloof knowledge and a hard, narrow, and merely
"practical" practice. To organize education so that natural active tendencies shall be fully enlisted in doing something, while seeing to it that the
doing requires observation, the acquisition of information, and the use of
constructive imagination, is what most needs to be done to improve social
conditions.

(MW 9: 144)

We now turn to a somewhat more comprehensive reflection on the emergence
of problems in culture. This section of the present chapter has a double purpose:
First, our aim is to further embed and contextualize the issues of "interest" and
"discipline" in a broader perspective on culture and cultural history and ask for
the general conditions of the cultural emergence of the kind of situations that
frame these issues and their import for education. For this intention, we use a
reflection on philosophical method from the later Dewey focused on the question
of what it is to be a problem in the philosophical, scientific, and broader cultural

sense. Our second aim is to prepare, in this way, the connection that we want to draw between Dewey's perspectives and some important aspects in the work of Foucault in the challenge for today section. The latter, like Dewey, was deeply concerned throughout his entire philosophical career with the question of the cultural and historical emergence of problems. He has developed—with his genealogical method—a unique and helpful approach we can use fruitfully to further reflect and extend Dewey's own use of genetic method, especially with regard to the mutual involvements of interest, discipline, and power in the specific constellations that underlie the historic constitution of "problems."

In a methodological excursus contained in the unfinished book project *Unmodern Philosophy and Modern Philosophy* (Dewey, 2012) from the 1940s, recently edited and published by Phillip Deen, Dewey gives an informative account of the social and cultural emergence or construction of problems.

> I shall say something about the nature of problems in general. For a clear view of the conditions under which problems come into existence and take the special forms which mark off one problem from another will greatly facilitate consideration of the problems of philosophy . . . For the main point regarding the existence of such conditions is that problems have definite connections and can be understood only in terms of what they are connected with—the fact of connection extending to their occurrence, existence and to the specific terms in which they are formulated, a matter that regulates the way in which they are gone at and hence regulates the terms in which "solutions" will be sought for and formulated. The import of this "main point" will probably be most readily gathered by saying what it negates, namely, the notion that there is such a thing as problems "in general," or without relation to conditions outside themselves.
>
> (Dewey, 2012: 136)

Dewey observes that in a narrow sense and "within the scope of restricted fields" it may be said that a problem is "given" as a "practical matter" (Dewey, 2012: 136): e.g., in everyday problem-solving or scientific research where a given context, say, of an established state of practice, science, art, or technology is simply taken for granted. However, when we convert the notion that problems "exist directly *per se* and are given" into a statement of general theory of knowing, it inevitably leads to a fallacy (Dewey, 2012: 136). For the notion involves forgetfulness about the necessary contexts of experience in which a problem arises. It thus "leads to the assumption, tacit or avowed, that the existence of a problem is simply an affair between something termed 'mind,' knowing subject, consciousness . . . on one side and something called 'object' on the other side" (Dewey, 2012: 137).

Dewey further elaborates on the implications of this insight for a pragmatist theory of observing. He notes that in concrete cases of observation—like perceiving "a wire strung along on poles by the highway" as part of a telephone or telegraph network—"we recognize the dependence of the event of observing and of *what* is observed upon the antecedent existence of a constellation of habits, including attitudes of belief operating as facilities, resources" (Dewey, 2012: 138). He points out that it is important to understand that the observation of an event "which gives it rank as *fact* (which is a precedent condition of noting . . . a *problem*)" depends on conditions that are determined by social practices "including language, or the meanings current as means and material of communication" (Dewey, 2012: 138). Dewey's social constructivism is apparent, here—*facts* as well as *problems* are socially constructed (see also Neubert & Reich, 2006; Garrison, 2009; Hickman, Neubert & Reich, 2009). Dewey (2012) pretty well summarizes his social constructivist theory of observing in the sentence that follows: "The true statement that we know (observe) *with* what we have known (that is, learned) needs to be supplemented by recognition that what is learned is a function of the social group and groups of which one is a member" (Dewey, 2012: 138).

This statement reminds us of the above mentioned distinction between the necessarily interconnected roles of observers, participants, and agents. Dewey gives an example that is as insightful as it is revealing.

> We are familiar, in some cases only too much so, with the existence of sects, parties, denominations, factions, schools, cliques, sets, economic classes, 'organizations.' We are also aware that each one of these consists of human beings who in that particular capacity are followers, adherents, votaries, devotees, partisans.
>
> (Dewey, 2012: 138 f.)

Obviously, these terms refer to the participant role that informs and influences observation and action. Dewey further specifies this participant role by observing that upon reflection it becomes obvious that these groups are informed and constituted by commonly held "formulated doctrines, creeds, tenets, platforms, etc." (Dewey, 2012: 139). And what is more, he explains that he has used these examples because they specifically help understand the necessary relation between participant and observer perspectives, for "it is so obvious in their case that the belief that determines what is admitted and excluded as facts and the manner in which observation is carried on (including deflections and distortions . . .) is a matter of group, constitution and behavior" (Dewey, 2012: 139). If we look at these groups and their beliefs and observations from outside (as distant observers, to use the term of the Cologne interactive constructivism program), we will probably find that, at least in some of these cases, the influence between participation and observation "suggests undesirable, objectionable qualities," especially in the case of those groups "with which we do not agree" (Dewey, 2012: 139). However, for our present purposes, the most important point of Dewey's argumentation lies not in this critical view on specific cases of rather narrow partisanship, but in the general conclusion that he draws from these considerations with regard to a necessary cultural self-criticism. He continues:

I have used these cases because their somewhat extreme character illustrates the sort of thing *which happens in all cases*, including those which are regarded as highly desirable. For the contrast between the undesirable and the desirable is not that of determination of belief-constellations (and consequent facts and problems) in one case by socio-cultural conditions and in the other case by mind or intellect free from any such social influence but is that between *habits and the attitudes which are characteristic of the methods used by different groups*.

(Dewey, 2012: 139, our italics)

The turn from criticism to necessary self-criticism (comp. also his essay "Construction and Criticism," LW: 5: 127–143) is of utmost importance. It rests upon his keen cultural sense for the importance of context (see also his essay "Context and Thought," LW 6: 3–21). Dewey's insistence on the necessary contextuality of facts and problems reminds us that, in any case, as humans, we are participants, agents, and observers in culture, and that our participation influences our observations and actions as well as the other way around. Therefore, Dewey goes on to claim that we are always "partisans" of sorts. "In the etymological sense of the word, all of us are partisans in that we are parts along with others, of groups which are with respect to their 'parts' wholes of a sort" (Dewey, 2012: 139).

He even speaks of a cultural relativity "of beliefs, facts and problems" which must not be confused with the idea that beliefs are arbitrary and all of equal value (Dewey, 2012: 139). Relativity does not exclude comparison and evaluation of beliefs and practices. Rather, as Dewey observes, the "fact of relativity is an indirect way of calling attention to the differences which exist in the attitudes and practices of different cultural groups as to the methods and criteria by which their beliefs are respectively reached and modified" (Dewey, 2012: 139). A scientific community as well as a religious sect implies a cultural context of observing, participating, and acting under specific cultural conditions. There is no difference with regard to this general condition of cultural relativity. Yet, there is all the difference in the world between both groups with regard to the methods used, the criteria employed, the attitudes formed, and the practices performed in the constitution and formation of beliefs.

Challenge for Today: Self, Agency, and Power Relations

The examples of sects, parties, partisanships, and the like show that, for Dewey, the constitution of a problem in the comprehensive social and cultural sense has a political dimension to it—at least potentially. Social problems can be connected and pervaded with issues of power—e.g., in the sense of relations of domination. That Dewey has a clear awareness of this potential connection becomes even more evident from a passage that follows shortly after the section discussed in the foregoing part. There he introduces the term "*pseudo*-problems" to characterize social problems framed or at least kept alive in the interests of maintaining power and the privileges of domination (Dewey, 2012: 140). Such "pseudo-problems," he argues, conduce to the perpetuation of established prestige, doctrines, and beliefs. From the democratic point of view, he observes that they are "genuine *social* problems, since their perpetuation is hostile to the formation of a society [whose] operations are marked by greater intelligence" (Dewey, 2012: 140). Dewey here uses a concept of power that is rather typical of his time—power as something that obstructs, oppresses, denies, mystifies and so on. Let us elaborate a bit further on the relations and connections between interest, discipline, and power by referring to the ideas and works of Foucault, who has dedicated his research to the socio-cultural analysis of power relations in many ways and different contexts.

Foucault provides extended perspectives on the relations between self, agency, and power that can be very fruitful for a reconstructed pragmatic and constructivist understanding. As we have discussed repeatedly in the foregoing chapters, Dewey has an excellent understanding of what today is often meant by the terms self and agency. In this chapter, the account of his use of "interest" and "discipline" has added to understanding his pragmatic perspectives on these issues. In all of these discussions, there has been a connection with questions of power in human relations, at least by implication. But now we must turn to a more explicit rendering of a theory of power adequate for our own time. In the recent human sciences, debates on power relations almost always build on Foucault's work in one or another way.

Like Dewey, Foucault was an author who was equally interested in the historical emergence and cultural construction of problems. There are many affinities between their perspectives. For example, both authors regard the Social as the most comprehensive and inclusive philosophical idea, they both have a thoroughly interactionist view on social realities in all of their complex inter-relations, both are philosophers of contextuality, and they share a pragmatic and constructivist understanding of the world of action as meaning-making practices in culture (cf. Rabinow, 2011). They both see "problems" in the larger social and cultural senses, not as something "given," but as constructed under specifiable social conditions and in the context of complex constellations of experiences, practices, institutions, habits, beliefs (Dewey) or discourses, epistemologies, "dispositifs," technologies of the self (Foucault). Although they use different terminologies, their ideas and theoretical philosophical perspectives have many aspects in common. For example, one can even define what Foucault means by the rather abstract concept of "dispositive" using Deweyan terminology.

We may say that what Foucault calls a "dispositif" consists of a historically specific complex of mutually related practices, institutions, and discourses that imply what Dewey—as already quoted above—called a "constellation of habits, including attitudes of belief operating as facilities, resources" (Dewey, 2012: 138).

Within a dispositif in this sense, subjects observe, participate, and act in communication and interaction with each other, and they thereby construct forms of selfhood and agency in relations with each other. Foucault explicitly and penetratingly shows us that power pervades all such relations, although power never fully determines selfhood and agency. As such, a dispositif may and often does contain ambivalences and even contradictions, but the ambivalent or contradictory positions and articulations necessarily connect with each other within a common frame of reference. For example, you look at a dispositif in the Foucauldian sense when you consider how in a given time and society, say ours, operations of measurement in education form a constellation of practices, ways of talking and using specific ideas or concepts, methods of research, terms of theoretical reflection, reconstruction of institutions, framing of horizons, mainstreaming of opinions with consequences for the life of many. From Foucault's pragmatic perspective, we can recognize such dispositifs from the effects they produce. Let us take an example.

The dispositif of measurement is highly productive. It produces not only such worldwide recognized programs like PISA, but, at the same time, the very effects and changes, e.g., in the attitudes and expectations of teachers and students, the general public, scientific communities, governments, and educational bureaucracies. Even on a global scale, measurement in education appears as a dispositif with mighty power effects if we think of poor societies and cultures that need development in all areas of social life, including cultural and political contexts in great diversity, but are driven by the dominant will to measurement to reduce their educational perspectives to the production of "human capitals." Generally speaking, we can say that a dispositif is part of the cultural emergence of problems. It responds to actual perceived problems in society and at the same time constitutes the conditions and terms for "solutions." Thereby, it reproduces and reconstructs the contexts of problems and the conditions of the emergence of new problems.

We have seen in the foregoing chapters that it is possible to creatively analyze, reflect upon, and criticize many aspects of such developments from a Deweyan perspective and contemporary constructivist considerations that connect with Dewey. With Foucault, we get an additional perspective that focuses on power. His works help us understand how—in a larger social and cultural sense—the historical constitution of problems implies, presupposes, and reproduces relations of power that must be understood as complex, systemic, and productive interactions in which all those who observe, partake, and act are involved.

One of Foucault's most well-known studies is his *Discipline and Punish* (Foucault, 1979). With his theory of disciplinary power, Foucault offers us a quite different understanding of the meaning of "discipline" in larger social and cultural contexts than does Dewey. Foucault and Dewey agree that discipline is something "positive." But, for Foucault, this means that it is a productive form of modern power relations. Discipline as a historical dispositif is a social force and resource that implies the subjection of individuals in practices, routines, institutions, and discourses pervaded by power. Such power, for Foucault, is productive because it constitutes forms of individuality, subject positions, knowledge, and a will to knowledge with specific discursive frames—i.e., the order of discourse. Generally speaking, it constitutes ways as well as limits of observation, participation, and action in culture. Foucault connects the history of modern knowledge in the humanities and human sciences with the history of modern power and especially of disciplinary power, e.g., in prisons, at the workplace, in hospitals, in the army, in schools, etc. He sees individuality itself as an effect of discipline and power.

The *panopticon* is a paradigmatic instance. Originally conceived as a type of architecture, the core idea of the *panopticon* is to implement as well as to increase the power of observation and surveillance. The central principle is to enforce a division of the possibilities to see (observe) others and to be seen (observed) by others. Those subjected to surveillance—and in a panoptic society this potentially applies to all of its members—do not encounter power as an external and physical constraint or attack. Rather, because of the division between observing and being observed, it is impossible for them to escape surveillance. In original prison architecture, for instance, there was a central tower of surveillance around which the cells were positioned in an outer circle. Thus, it was always possible to observe the prisoners, but the prisoners could not see the guards as observers. The necessary consequence was the internalization of the power relation by the prisoners in the form of self-surveillance and self-discipline. This constitutes a transformation of social constraints into self-restraints. The idea of *panopticism* started with the wish for total surveillance in institutions like prisons, factories, the military, schools, etc. Foucault observes, however, that starting within the late eighteenth century, it has increasingly been generalized as an organizational principle of society, and in our own time, we can observe many facets of *panopticism* in society, like surveillance by video cameras in public spaces, access to data by electronic media, and the increasing diffusion between the spheres of the private and the public. The more thoroughly an institution or whole societies are organized on panoptic principles the more power relations must be internalized by those who are subjected to surveillance as generalized attitudes, expectations, orientations, etc. As we have seen in Chapter 3, the self interacts with others. The tension between self and generalized other that we discussed there gets new implications and meanings in the present context. With Foucault, we see that power relations, like the principles of *panopticism*, pervade the generalized other and are always involved in the formation of the self.

We can take a second example from the first volume of *The History of Sexuality* (Foucault, 1978). He speaks of a modern *dispositif* of sexuality that accounts for the ways in which sexuality becomes a theme of deliberate concern in societies. His study focuses largely on European eighteenth- and nineteenth-century societies that develop a dramatized concern and interest in the following four aspects: (1) the hysterical woman, (2) the masturbating child, (3) the "perverse" or homosexual adult, and (4) state population planning. The extent to which these themes have become obsessive subjects of discourse in modernity and still influence views on sexuality in liquid modernity shows that a powerful dispositif in the Foucauldian sense is at work and produces many pragmatically important results. In all of these fields, Foucault observes that the relations between power and sexuality pervade the interactions of all members. In that sense, power is omnipresent and distributed among all in the multitude. However, this does not deny that there are at the same time asymmetries between different members. For example, with regard to the modern dispositif of sexuality, we observe that, in many respects, men are more powerful than women, adults are more powerful than children, the state is more powerful than the family or couple, and the norms of heterosexuality dominate society and exclude other forms of sexuality. In all of these cases, however, Foucault insists that modern power relations are never unilateral and total. They allow for partial reversals and forms of resistance that subvert the apparently fixed hierarchies.

In his reflections on the *Technologies of the Self*, Foucault (1988) further explores the opportunities and risks of subjects acting under conditions of power. He provides a comprehensive account of the cultural role of technologies in modern societies that is highly interesting considered from a Deweyan pragmatic point of view. It underlines the Deweyan insight that the cultural relations of means and ends in human practice are historical constructions that emerge out of changing contexts. For Foucault, we can distinguish at least four dimensions of technology:

1. Technologies of production, which create and sustain the practices of constructing things, means, instruments, tools, ideas, etc., that are necessary for sustaining and developing life in culture and producing economic wealth in society. They produce the material basis for all other technologies and constitute conditions and constellations that frame human action but do not determine its ways and results completely.

2. Technologies of sign systems, which create and sustain the meanings of cultural practices and organize or order them in structures like symbols, texts, and discourses to be constructed, reconstructed, and deconstructed by individuals or social groups who partake in signifying practices. They produce the semiotic basis for all other technologies and constitute conditions and constellations of meaning-making and representation. Even if a system of representation may be dominant at a given time, its influence is always limited and open to reconstruction because the sign process itself is necessarily ambiguous and never complete.

3. Technologies of power or domination, which create and sustain the practices of submitting subjects to positions in the social order combined with, for example, hierarchies, rankings, status, coordination of functions in divisions of labor, judicial relations, political organization, and taking appropriate roles in institutions like the family, the school, the military, the court, the prison,

the hospital, the workplace, the state. They produce apparently objective conditions and constellations for the positioning of individuals in relation to each other and the existing forms of power represented and enacted by all individuals who partake in the prevailing dispositifs.

4. Technologies of the self, which create and sustain practices of individuals and groups to develop their creative and constructive capabilities of living under conditions and constellations constituted by the effects of the other technologies in culture. If they succeed, relatively, Foucault speaks of "arts of living." Technologies of the self are the diverse "operations on their own bodies and souls, thoughts, conduct, and way of being" that individuals employ deliberately by themselves and in relationships with others. They are means for individual and social growth as well as self-transformation to reach a "state of happiness, purity, wisdom, perfection, or immortality" (Foucault, 1988: 18).

Foucault suggests that we must see these four dimensions of technology in their interdependence and mutual relations. From our point of view and with regard to what has been argued throughout this chapter concerning the educational significance of "interest," "discipline," and "power," it seems necessary to connect these considerations with the pragmatic and constructivist distinction of observers, participants, and agents in culture. We can learn from Foucault that when we are most intimately involved in contexts of participation, the tendency is the strongest to forget about the implicit connections between our own observations and actions with power. This brings us back into interactive constructivism's distinction between the roles of observer, participant, and agent that we use here for a concluding reflection.

> As observers, we see, hear, sense, perceive, and interpret our world. We construct our versions of reality on the basis of our beliefs and expectations, our interests, habits and reflections. As participants, we partake in the larger contexts of the multiple and often heterogeneous communities of interpreters that provide basic orientation in our cultural universe. We participate in social groups, communities, networks and institutions of all kinds. Our partaking is an indispensable cultural resource, but it also implies commitments, responsibilities, loyalties, and the exclusion of certain alternatives. As agents, we act and experience. We communicate and co-operate and struggle with others. We devise plans and projects to carry out our intentions. We articulate ourselves and respond to the articulation of others.
>
> (Neubert, 2008: 108)

The emergence of problems in culture always connects with contexts of observation, participation, and action. Let us connect this pragmatic and constructivist insight with the four dimensions of technologies discussed by Foucault. We then get a considerably broadened approach to the complex and highly relevant question of the emergence of problems in culture as the necessary contexts and resources of learning and educational growth. In this connection, again, we encounter many forms of reductionism in education as a main challenge for democracy and education in our time. We close by considering some important examples with regard to the four dimensions:

1. On the level of technologies of production, we often find that educators too easily accept market conditions as given or even an indubitable and just order of exchange. In doing so, their role as participants in the given technologies of production one-sidedly dominates and limits their imagination as observers and their creativity as agents. To struggle against narrow reductionism, democracy and education implies that the actual never exhausts the potential. We have to overcome taken for granted adaptations to capitalism and its logics of competition and unequal distribution that often restrict a clear and comprehensive understanding of the interrelations between the economic system and education. The principles of democracy and education are denied if educators and learners lose their imaginative powers as observers to appreciate experiences in all their diversity and uniqueness beyond the imperatives of the market. They are equally denied if they lose their capability as agents to cultivate creative and critical practices of shared educational growth. Although we cannot ignore the power of market mechanisms in the lives of all in liquid modernity, we must nonetheless conceive education as a power to construct a balance between the standardized expectations of the markets and the qualitatively unique potentials of every individual's growing experience. Thus considered, we can say that education is necessarily a part of the technologies of production and actually contributes to their work. We suggest that educators take a broad view on the interconnection of their theories and practices with the world of production.

2. On the level of technologies of sign systems, we frequently encounter narrow and reductionist systems of representation that are connected with apparently strict and fixed concepts like selection, evaluation, ranking, measurement, labeling, etc., that are based on seemingly static categories and procedures. Throughout this book, we discuss a number of examples of such representational systems. Think of categories like "human capital," procedures like the standardized measurement, or the capitalization of learning (see Chapter 10). For democracy and education, the challenge lies in the task to balance out the needs for symbolic representation as necessary conditions and resources for making a living in complex capitalist societies and the equal opportunities for the articulation of diverse experiences of unique learners that are never exhausted by the categories of representation (like types of learners, forms of skill, bodies of knowledge, methods of measurements, credit

points, levels of achievement, etc.). Democracy and education have the best chance to grow when the educational system, institutions, and practices take this necessary balance into account and provide conditions for the inclusion of all learners and their diverse resources and experiences and support them in all their unique needs. Thus considered, education is never confined to a given system of representation—or a given group of such systems—but must be seen as a necessary and active part in the creation and use of technologies of signs. This creation and use presupposes that we overcome limited perspectives that we often take for granted in our roles as participants within the given context of representation. Teachers and learners who partake in procedures of standardized measurement must cultivate not only an ironical attitude towards the limits and apparent claims of this reductionist practice (as observers), but also struggle for conditions and opportunities for educational growth beyond the mere will to measurement (as agents).

3. On the level of technologies of power or domination, the Foucauldian observation that power pervades the individual applies especially to the roles of teachers, educators, and learners in liquid modernity. Although we can never completely evade power relations, it is possible to act against asymmetries and hegemonic forms of one-sided domination. The democratic project consists of the deliberate attempt to employ the technologies of power on the part of the multitude in society as well as in education. The necessary tension requiring balancing in education on this level is between leadership and participation. As participants, learners and educators often take the models of leadership and participation for granted that they themselves have experienced in their previous learning. The challenge with regard to the technologies of power consists on the one hand in developing and cultivating a constructive and critical awareness of the justification and the effects of specific power relations including all lines of difference (as observers). On the other hand, it consists in the attempt to include all in processes of deliberation and decision making (as agents). It further consists in finding appropriate measures to avoid fixed hierarchies and asymmetries beyond the possibility of critique. To achieve this aim, we need schools with a deliberate program to further participation on all levels and in all areas of school life. In this sense, we suggest that direct democracy cannot succeed without inclusion in school.

4. On the level of technologies of the self, each individual must actually construct the best possible degree of balance with regard to the tensions discussed in 1—3. It is part in the arts of living as well as the arts of education that this challenge necessarily implies the cultivation of relationships, because each individual can only achieve a balance and, thereby, grow in experience in transaction with others. Whereas in earlier phases of modernity, like the times of Fordism, the individual could easily appear as a part of a clockwork with relatively limited and determined chances of participation and action,

it is a characteristic of liquid modernity that the individual *de jure* increasingly has to take responsibility him- or herself for the necessary balancing out of tensions, contradictions, challenges, opportunities, resources, costs, risks, and the like. Education in a democratic sense has to prepare sufficient opportunities for individuals to realize their autonomy *de facto* in the complex contexts of modern power constellations.

Dewey's Summary

Interest and discipline are correlative aspects of activity having an aim. Interest means that one is identified with the objects which define the activity and which furnish the means and obstacles to its realization. Any activity with an aim implies a distinction between an earlier incomplete phase and later completing phase; it implies also intermediate steps. To have an interest is to take things as entering into such a continuously developing situation, instead of taking them in isolation. The time difference between the given incomplete state of affairs and the desired fulfillment exacts effort in transformation; it demands continuity of attention and endurance. This attitude is what is practically meant by will. Discipline or development of power of continuous attention is its fruit. The significance of this doctrine for the theory of education is twofold. On the one hand it protects us from the notion that mind and mental states are something complete in themselves, which then happen to be applied to some ready-made objects and topics so that knowledge results. It shows that mind and intelligent or purposeful engagement in a course of action into which things enter are identical. Hence to develop and train mind is to provide an environment which induces such activity. On the other side, it protects us from the notion that subject matter on its side is something isolated and independent. It shows that subject matter of learning is identical with all the objects, ideas, and principles which enter as resources or obstacles into the continuous intentional pursuit of a course of action. The developing course of action, whose end and conditions are perceived, is the unity which holds together what are often divided into an independent mind on one side and an independent world of objects and facts on the other.

(MW 9: 145–146)

Our Summary

Dewey frames his concepts of interests and discipline in accord with his understanding of the necessary intrinsic dimension of learning by experience. Here again, we encounter a tensional relationship that has to do with the role of motivation, will, methods, and effectiveness in learning as a personal and social experience of problem-solving. We have argued that—especially if we look on his broader philosophical work—Dewey has a unique sense of the necessary cultural and historical contexts in which problems of all kinds arise. In this sense, we suggest sharpening and enriching his educational view on interests and discipline by connecting it with his philosophical reflections on the emergence of problems in culture. We have seen that the distinction between the perspectives of observers, participants, and agents in experience is helpful to deepen our understanding of the cultural relativity of interests and disciplines. Further, we suggest that the reference to the work of the more recent philosopher Michel Foucault, and his penetrating analysis of the involvement of interests and disciplines with power relations in culture, can be helpful to reconstruct and further develop the Deweyan project. Whereas Dewey largely relied on an idea of power that was typical of his time and came close to understanding power as oppression, domination, rule, and the like, Foucault gives us much more concise and detailed accounts of the productive, omnipresent, dynamic, and network-like qualities of power relations in modern societies and especially in liquid modernity. Foucault's perspectives improve our understanding of how power relations constitute not only pseudo-problems but also all problems in culture while comprising an important part of hegemonic articulations and interpretations. From this point of view, democracy and education represent a tensional field in which we may experience selective interest as well as spatial and temporal backgrounds and contexts in constructive as well as re- and deconstructive ways. With Foucault, we see how much and how inextricably power pervades these ways, contexts, and backgrounds. Democracy and education is itself a hegemonic project and must reflect on all power relations contained in the field.

8

CONTENTS, METHODS, AND RELATIONSHIPS IN EDUCATION

We now turn to a discussion of Dewey's perspectives on contents and methods in education. Again, we supplement his insights with more recent considerations, especially with regard to the role of contents and relationships in communication and education generally, and among other things with regard to "new learning." Here we examine Chapters 11 ("Experience and Thinking"), 12 ("Thinking in Education"), 13 ("The Nature of Method"), and 14 ("The Nature of Subject Matter") of *Democracy and Education*. As their titles suggest, each chapter depends upon and further refines the ideas of the foregoing chapter in the sequence.

Dewey begins Chapter 11 by distinguishing two phases *within* every experience. There is the active phase when "experience is *trying*" and the passive when "it is undergoing" (MW 9: 146). We act and we suffer the consequences of our actions good or bad, which is the basis of learning:

> To "learn from experience" is to make a backward and forward connection between what we do to things and what we enjoy or suffer from things in consequence. Under such conditions, doing becomes a trying; an experiment with the world to find out what it is like; the undergoing becomes instruction—discovery of the connection of things.
>
> (MW 9: 147; see also 151)

Thinking and learning is about making connections. Dewey immediately draws two important conclusions for education from this observation:

> (1) Experience is primarily an active-passive affair; it is not primarily cognitive. But (2) the *measure of the value* of an experience lies in the perception of relationships or continuities to which it leads up. It includes

cognition in the degree in which it is cumulative or amounts to something, or has meaning.

(MW 9: 147)

Recall that Dewey decries "intellectualism"; nonetheless to have a mind is to have meaning and meanings are cognitive.

We learn (acquire meaning) as participants in affairs and not as "theoretical spectators" that "appropriate knowledge by direct energy of intellect" (MW 9: 147). Unfortunately, "the mind and body dualism" has led us to believe that the body acts while the mind passively acquires meaning (MW 9: 147). The body-mind is one. Dewey believes most of the problems of discipline result from educators "suppressing the bodily activities" they believe "take the mind away from its material" (MW 9: 148). Learning involves embodied activity. Our senses contribute to knowledge not by passively conveying information to the brain as in the Turing machine model, but "because they are *used* in doing something with a purpose" (MW 9: 149). Finally, "on the intellectual side, the separation of 'mind' from direct occupation with things throws emphasis on *things* at the expense of *relations* or connections" (MW 9: 150). However, perceptual judgment that some "thing" is thus and so with specific properties determining its essence involves thought: "Judgment is employed in the perception; otherwise the perception is mere sensory excitation or else a recognition of the result of a prior judgment, as in the case of familiar objects" (MW 9: 150). Constructing connections is the function of thought.

"Thought or reflection," according to Dewey, is "the discernment of the relation between what we try to do and what happens in consequence" (MW 9: 151). It is "the intentional endeavor to discover *specific* connections between something which we do and the consequences which result, so that the two become continuous" (MW 9: 152). There is a pattern to systematic reflective thought as opposed to guessing, although trial and error is never entirely eliminable. Dewey provides a summary of the five general phases of a distinctively reflective process of thought (see MW 9: 157). He presents these five phases somewhat differently in different places. For instance, the five phases of the 1910 version of *How We Think* are somewhat different from those of the 1933 version. Further, while the five phases of the 1910 version line up well with the five phases in *Democracy and Education* (1916), he transposes phases two and three. Chapter 6, "The Pattern of Inquiry" in Dewey's 1938 *Logic: The Theory of Inquiry* also offers useful insights. What follows is one useful synthesis of these disparate expositions adapted to the phases offered in *Democracy and Education*.[1]

Before beginning, we must first note that in actual practice the phases of reflective thought are such that we may enter and exit at any point; there is no fixed sequence. Therefore, we should not be surprised at Dewey's different arrangements of their order. Sometimes, we may omit steps and frequently we can telescope phases into one movement of thought while other times we can expand them. Further, the phases are recursive. Finally, each phase blends into the other. Sharply separating the process of inquiry into separate five phases is solely for the analytic purposes of distinguishing the most prominent aspects of the process. As Dewey himself says, "no set rules can be laid down on such matters"; moreover, there "is nothing especially sacred about the number five" (LW 8: 207).

In the 1933 version of *How We Think*, Dewey identifies two limits of reflective thinking. First, there is "a perplexed, troubled, or confused situation at the beginning and a cleared-up, unified, resolved situation at the close" (LW 8: 200). The first is "*pre*-reflective," the latter is "*post*-reflective" (LW 8: 200). Reflective thinking occurs between these limits. Here is Dewey's definition of inquiry: "*Inquiry is the controlled or directed transformation of an indeterminate situation into one that is so determinate in its constituent distinctions and relations as to convert the elements of the original situation into a unified whole*" (LW 12: 108, original italics).

In *Democracy and Education*, Dewey depicts the first phase as "(i) perplexity, confusion, doubt, due to the fact that one is implicated in an incomplete situation whose full character is not yet determined" (MW 9: 157). The "situation as such is not and cannot be stated or made explicit"; it "cannot present itself as an element in a proposition" (LW 5: 247). We begin with a "tensional" problematic situation, but not a statable problem. (MW 10: 326). To be able to state a problem is to be half done. Dewey does not believe we can be in existential doubt at will. A genuine doubt is initially precognitive, embodied, intuitive, and passionate, never abstract. We *feel* it before we think it and have an urge to actively *do* something about it. As participants in such situations of "imbalance in organic-environmental interactions," we feel disoriented, anxious, confused, and unsure how to act (LW 12: 110). We passionately "desire this or that outcome". However, "born in partiality, in order to accomplish its tasks it [thinking] must achieve a certain detached impartiality" (MW 9: 154). Indeed,

> The almost insurmountable difficulty of achieving this detachment is evidence that thinking originates in situations where the course of thinking is an actual part of the course of events and is designed to influence the result. Only gradually and with a widening of the area of vision through a growth of social sympathies does thinking develop to include what lies beyond our *direct* interests: a fact of great significance for education.
>
> (LW 9: 154–155)

For Dewey, reflective objectivity does not mean the rejection of emotions, which for him constitute the very context of inquiry and propel the inquiry to its conclusion. It does mean controlling them properly.

The second phase of reflection is "(ii) conjectural anticipation—a tentative interpretation of the given elements, attributing to them a tendency to effect certain consequences" (LW 9: 157). This stage involves the imaginative construction of a tentative hypothesis that provides "the guiding idea" for subsequent inquiry (LW 8: 202). Dewey observes:

> [A]ll thinking involves a risk. Certainty cannot be guaranteed in advance. The invasion of the unknown is of the nature of an adventure; we cannot be sure in advance. The conclusions of thinking, till confirmed by the event, are, accordingly, more or less tentative or hypothetical.
>
> (MW 9: 155)

Such an "idea is first of all an anticipation of something that may happen; it marks a *possibility*"; hence its imaginative characteristic (LW 12: 113). Imagination perceives the possible in the actual. Initially, we only have a tentative *working* hypothesis: "Tentative means trying out, feeling one's way along provisionally" (MW 9: 156). We use working hypotheses to direct subsequent inquiry.

Once we have a working hypothesis, we may employ it to collect additional facts (data) and link the hypothesis to other concepts already in our command, which we may then use to collect more data that may lead to further conceptual connections. This is what Dewey means when he identifies the third phase as "(iii) a careful survey (examination, inspection, exploration, analysis) of all attainable consideration which will define and clarify the problem in hand" (MW 9: 157). That part of the process involves reasoning in the narrow sense of mental cogitation. Along the way, "conjectures that seem plausible at first sight are often found unfit or even absurd when their full consequences are traced out" (LW 8: 204). In his *Logic*, Dewey calls attention to "The Operational Character of Facts-Meanings" (LW 12: 116). Concrete facts and abstract meanings are correlated "functional divisions in the work of inquiry" that must "cooperate with each other" (LW 12: 116). We must reject the theory versus fact dualism. Ideas are operational in that "they instigate and direct further operations of observation" while facts "are selected and described . . . for a purpose" (LW 12: 116). Selected facts "are evidential and are tests of an idea insofar as they are capable of being organized with one another. The organization can be achieved only as they correspond with one another" (LW 12). When facts and meanings conflict we may use one to correct the other.

What we experience is meaningless unless we have concepts to interpret events. All inquiry is theory-laden (concepts, ideas, hypotheses, etc.).[2] Collecting all the relevant facts requires some idea of which facts are, indeed, relevant to take and use as data. However, if the ideas used to collect facts do not work out, the data might be *mis*taken. If we are mistaken about our data, inquiry falters and hypotheses as well as data must undergo revision. Ultimately, it is the task of the inquirer to reconcile theory with data. In the process of using the working hypothesis to collect and refine additional data and connect to other concepts, the working hypothesis may become refined. This is how we interpret the fourth phase in *Democracy and Education*: "(iv) a consequent elaboration of the tentative

="2"

hypothesis to make it more precise and more consistent, because squaring with a wider range of facts" (MW 9: 157). The elaborated *working* hypothesis may now become an *explanatory* hypothesis that, if it works, will serve to resolve the problematic situation.

The final phase involves "(v) taking one stand upon the projected hypothesis as a plan of action which is applied to the existing state of affairs: doing something overtly to bring about the anticipated result, and thereby testing the hypothesis" (MW 9: 157). Dewey concludes by observing, "it is the extent and accuracy of steps three and four which mark off a distinctive reflective experience from one on the trial and error plane" (MW 9: 157). Controlled experiments are best and these often involve apparatus especially designed for the purpose. In any case, "some active steps are taken which actually change *some* physical conditions. And apart from such steps and the consequent modification of the situation, there is no completion of the act of thinking" (MW 9: 157). Of course, sometimes the results of testing fail to confirm the hypothesis. "Nothing shows the trained thinker better," Dewey maintains, "than the use he makes of his errors and mistakes" (LW 8: 206). Education and school practice can still learn much from this insight.

In his summary of Chapter 12, Dewey observes that "thinking is the method of an educative experience"; hence, the "essentials of method are therefore identical with the essentials of reflection" (MW 9: 170). He then lists five phases of thinking as "the method of an educative experience" (MW 9: 170). These line up rather well with the five phases of reflection summarized in Chapter 11 (MW 9: 157). Let us caution the reader that what Dewey said about there being nothing sacred about the number five regarding reflective experience extends to the experience of constructing good instruction.

We begin with a genuine situation of experience. Such a situation comprises the "sort of situation that presents itself outside of school; the sort of occupations that interest and engage activity in ordinary life" (MW 9: 161). Successful methods of instruction "give the pupils something to do, not something to learn; and the doing is of such a nature as to demand thinking, or the intentional noting of connections; learning naturally results" (MW 9: 161). The situation should be neither something "routine or capricious" (MW 9: 161).

Next, a genuine problem must arise for the students within the situation. Dewey offers two criteria for distinguishing genuine from mock problems. First,

> Is there anything but a problem? Does the question naturally suggest itself within some situation of personal experience? Or is it an aloof thing, a problem only for the purposes of conveying instruction in some school topic? Is it the sort of trying that would arouse observation and engage experimentation outside of school?
>
> (MW 9: 161)

Second, "is it the pupils [sic] own problem, or is it the teacher's or textbook's problem, made a problem for the pupil only because he cannot get the required mark or be promoted or win the teachers approval, unless he deals with it?" (LW 9: 161–162). With problems imposed from without, "the pupil's problem is simply to meet the external requirement" (LW 9: 162). At worst, "the problem of the pupil is not how to meet the requirements of school life, but how to *seem* to meet them" (LW 9: 163). Genuine problems interest the student and provide internal discipline; they are intrinsically motivating. Thus, such pedagogical situations should be sufficiently familiar to the student as to enable intelligent responses, but neither routine or entirely disconnected from their background knowledge.

Third, there must be data (facts) that students are capable of recognizing and operating upon: "The material of thinking is not thoughts, but actions, facts, events, and the relations of things" (MW 9: 163). It matters little where they acquire the material; it might come from memory, observation, reading, communication, and so on. Students must have had previous experiences of actions, events, problems, ideas, and theories that allow them to cope with the confounding situation; otherwise, they will simply become overwhelmed and unable to think at all. Far too often in an age of standardized tests and narrowly prescribed curricula, knowledge is not a resource of further inquiry "of finding out, or learning, more things" (MW 9: 165). Instead, we treat is as if it was an end in itself. When this happens, "then the goal becomes to heap it up and display it when called for. This static, cold-storage ideal of knowledge is inimical to educative development. It not only lets occasions for thinking go unused, but it swamps thinking" (MW 9: 165). Instead, we should give students something to do and not something to learn, and then work with them to develop their inquiry. Accordingly,

> The perplexing situation must be sufficiently like situations which have already been dealt with so that pupils will have some control of the means of handling it. A large part of the art of instruction lies in making the difficulty of new problems large enough to challenge thought, and small enough so that, in addition to the confusion naturally attending the novel elements, there shall be luminous familiar spots from which helpful suggestions may spring.
>
> (MW 9: 163–164)

Herein lies the creative art of student-centered teaching. There is no art in simply allowing students do whatever they wish without internal discipline born of deep interest far beyond mere amusement. At the very least, student-centered teaching involves knowing our students' cognitive state. Good teaching involves knowing something of our students' social and emotional lives as well. It also requires the teacher to express a degree of vulnerability that the students may also know them.

The fourth phase involves the construction of hypotheses: "The correlate in thinking of facts, data, knowledge already acquired, is suggestions, inferences, conjectured meanings, suppositions, tentative explanations:—*ideas*, in short" (MW 9: 165). Ideas emerge to guide future inquiry, but they must arise from prior data and remain subject to revision as subsequent data are collected and earlier collections undergo correction. This is the operational character of facts-meanings. Dewey urges us to recognize that "*all* thinking is original in a projection of considerations which have not been previously apprehended" (MW 9: 165). "Thinking is preeminently an art," Dewey asserts, "knowledge and propositions which are the products of thinking are works of art, as much so as statuary and symphonies" (LW 1: 283). Dewey judges that the "joy which children themselves experience is the joy of intellectual constructiveness—of creativeness, if the word may be used without misunderstanding" (MW 9: 165). Creativity is common to all transformative activity for Dewey; it is not the prerogative of a few special people called artists. Everyone is an artist who thinks and acts constructively to transform the world. In his essay, "Construction and Criticism," Dewey comments: "I have used the word construction rather than creation because it seems less pretentious. But what I mean by it is the creative mind, the mind that is genuinely productive in its operations" (LW 5: 127). Constructivism is creative; reflective constructivism is critical. Student-centered teaching requires critical-creative thinking on the part of the teacher as well as student. We should think of good teaching as a co-constructive activity where teachers and students create meanings together.

The final phase is "some kind of testing by overt action to give *experimental corroboration*, or *verification*, of the conjectural idea" (LW 8: 205). Our hypotheses are just tentative conjectures; "only testing confers full meaning and a sense of their reality" (MW 9: 168). As abstract ideas, our hypotheses need have no specific concrete connection to the actual world. Just think about escapist fantasy or much of traditional cold-storage school knowledge. Dewey writes that "[t]here can be no doubt that a peculiar artificiality attaches to much of what is learned in schools" (MW 9: 168). Most students most of the time work with inert ideas; such ideas are not fully real to students in the way ideas are outside of school. Dewey observes, "where schools are equipped with laboratories, shops, and gardens, where dramatizations, plays, and games are freely used, opportunities exist for reproducing situations of life, and for acquiring and applying information and ideas in the carrying forward of progressive experiences" (MW 9: 169). Of course, we may misuse such facilities to acquire "just bodily skill," that while useful, limits intellectual development. In the formal setting of schooling, wise teachers give students something to do that engages them in critical-creative reflection of the kind that already occurs informally in settings outside of school. In this way, subject matter becomes fully real to students in ways that invoke internal motivation and discipline.

Chapter 13 of Dewey's book refines and provides further insights into the references to "method" in Chapters 11–12. It also explains the relation of method to subject matter, which prepares the way for the discussion of subject matter in

Chapter 14. The most striking claim of the chapter occurs in the very first paragraph and arises out of Dewey's famous anti-dualism: "The idea that mind and the world of things and persons are two separate and independent realms—a theory which philosophically is known as dualism—carries with it the conclusion that method and subject matter of instruction are separate affairs" (MW 9: 171).

We have already identified and discussed a host of dualisms including nature versus culture, thought versus feeling, self versus society, and organism versus environment. In one way or another, the mind-versus-world dualism involves all these. Dewey gives the helpful example of eating food. When we are eating, we are engaged in a single act of eating food. We do not divide the activity into eating something else called food. We may however sometimes find it useful to distinguish two sub-functions within the single functional act of eating, just as we may distinguish oxygen and lungs in the act of breathing. This reflective distinction "gives rise to a distinction of *what* we experience (the experience*d*) and the experienc*ing*—the *how*. When we give names to this distinction we have subject matter and method as our terms" (MW 9: 173). Method and subject matter do not exist separately. However, for "the purpose of *controlling* the course or direction which the moving unity of experience takes we draw a mental distinction between the how and the what" (MW 9: 174). We must not convert useful distinctions into misleading dualisms.

Dualisms arise as the result of the following series of steps. First, we detach the products from the process of thought. Next, we forget the process. Finally, we reify the product as an object that existed prior to the process. Often, we follow the last step by placing the objects produced by the process into a dominion separate from the experiential realm from whence they emerged. Dewey condemns what he calls "*the* philosophic fallacy," by which he means the "conversion of eventual functions into antecedent existence" whether performed on "behalf of mathematical subsistences, esthetic essences, the purely physical order of nature, or God" (LW 1: 389). According to Dewey, we can never separate the process of thinking from the subject matter that is its product. It makes no difference whether we are talking about the original discovery that yielded the subject matter or the pedagogical methods by which we communicate it to others. After all, the joy of intellectual constructiveness is the same for those that originally constructed the knowledge as for those that later learn about it.

In educational practice, it is common for the state to mandate standardized subject matter within a fixed curriculum and system of testing. It is also often common for some authorities to require educators to adapt certain prescribed methods instead of learning how to creatively respond to students by developing their own methods tailored to the specific teaching context of the day and place. Bureaucracy institutionalizes the pedagogical method-versus-subject matter dualism. It does not understand the nature of thinking: "But since thinking is a directed movement of subject matter to a completing issue, and since mind is the deliberate and intentional phase of the process, the notion of any such split is radically false" (MW 9: 172). The foregoing states what thinking is not; the following makes the positive point: "Method means that arrangement *of* subject matter which makes it most effective in use. Never is method something outside of the material" (MW 9: 172). Therefore, we may structure subject matter one way for one purpose and another for other purposes. For instance, the structure of subject matter for further discovery is likely to vary greatly from the structure of subject matter for teaching beginners. Indeed, this is the insight that validates the very idea of differentiated instruction, which adapts to the student's different developmental levels, different learning styles, and different ways of expressing the same subject matter.

Dewey identifies four "evils" that arise from isolating method from subject matter. First, "there is the neglect . . . of concrete situations of experience" (MW 9: 175). For Dewey, pedagogical method derives from what actually happens in the process of teaching and learning. Sadly, in Dewey's day as well as ours, "there is rarely sufficient opportunity for children and youth to have the direct normal experiences from which educators might derive an idea of method or order of best development" (MW 9: 175). With the loss of ordinary experience for teachers to observe and develop, methods "have then to be authoritatively recommended to teachers, instead of being an expression of their own intelligent observation" (MW 9: 175). Many teachers enter teaching seeking creative self-expression, which the system then sacrifices to a mindless "mechanical uniformity," a phrase that well describes public education globally (MW 9: 175). Today, global capitalism winds the mechanical clockwork of technocratic conformity. Many that teach feel a sense of vocation, of being called or summoned by a power higher than themselves (vocation from the Latin *vocare*). The best and brightest leave when they fail to find creative self-expression.

"In the second place," Dewey continues, "the notion of methods isolated from subject matter is responsible for the false conceptions of discipline and interest already noted" (MW 9: 175). Here, the dualism leads us to "utilize excitement" to engage the student, or perhaps to "make the consequences of not attending painful," or perchance "direct appeal may be made to the person to put forth effort without any reason" (MW 9: 175). Third, "the act of learning is made a direct and conscious end in itself" when normally it is "a product and reward of occupation with subject matter" (MW 9: 176). We learn effortlessly when we are intrinsically interested in subject matter for its own sake. Finally, "method tends to be reduced to a cut and dried routine, to following mechanically prescribed steps" (MW 9: 176). When this happens, "it is assumed that there is one fixed method to follow" (MW 9: 176). The vast majority of practicing teachers know this obsession well. "Nothing has brought pedagogical theory into greater disrepute," Dewey goes on to say, "than the belief that it is identified with handing out to teachers recipes and models to be followed in teaching" (MW 9: 176–177).

Dewey affirms that "the method of teaching is the method of an art, of action intelligently directed by ends" (MW 9: 176–177). The art of teaching is not entirely spontaneous, although there are plenty of opportunities for improvisation equal to the most innovative forms of jazz. Dewey wants us to recognize the middle ground between the inspiration of the moment and ready-made rules. Those most creative at improvisation are those that know their discipline well and allow it to properly discipline them. In a footnote, Dewey refers to the comments in his Chapter 17 "Science in the Course of Study." Since it also illustrates the difference between subject matter structured for the purpose of discovery versus teaching, it is quite valuable; so, let us look at it.

Dewey distinguishes between the logical and the psychological. Regarding the logical, he writes: "Science, in short, signifies a realization of the *logical* implications of any knowledge. Logical order is not a form imposed upon what is known; it is the proper form of knowledge as perfected" (MW 9: 227). "To the non-expert," Dewey maintains, "this perfected form is a stumbling block. Just because the material is stated with reference to the furtherance of knowledge as an end in itself, its connections with the material of everyday life are hidden" (MW 9: 227). At first, we just drink water. Only later do we learn to manipulate the abstract chemical formula H_2O. For the learner, the logical structure is the goal not the point of departure. Dewey urges us to think developmentally: "The chronological method which begins with the experience of the learner and develops from that the proper modes of scientific treatment is often called the 'psychological' method in distinction from the logical method of the expert or specialist" (MW 9: 228). In this approach, the student may not so quickly memorize facts and ideas, but whatever "the pupil learns he at least understands" (MW 9: 228). This way, we avoid the cold-storage ideal of knowledge that leads to inert ideas.

In Chapter 14, "The Nature of Subject Matter," Dewey expands on two themes previously discussed: (1) the role of the educator and (2) "the necessity of a social environment" (MW 9: 188). He looks at each from the standpoint of both the instructor and student. Society charges the educator with passing on those cultural meanings the culture deems "desirable to transmit" (MW 9: 190). Educators must acknowledge that although very familiar to them, much of the material taught is of necessity remote from the learner. Dewey's remarks here set the stage for the psychologizing of the subject matter we discussed earlier. He also points out that the educator must have complete and flexible command of the subject matter and her or his "attention should be upon the attitude and response of the pupil" (MW 9: 191). More exactly, "the teacher should be occupied not with subject matter in itself but in its interaction with the pupil's present needs and capacities. Hence simple scholarship is not enough" (MW 9: 191). Knowledge of subject matter is necessary for teaching, but alone it will not make anyone a teacher. In this connection, Dewey reminds us in a footnote that since "the learned man should also still be a learner" the distinctions between teacher and student "are relative, not absolute" (MW 9: fn. 191). No one is a good teacher that does not enjoy learning, and as Dewey notes even the roles of teacher and learner may ultimately be exchangeable.

Dewey next turns to the learner; here he distinguishes three broad stages in the growth of subject matter. First, "knowledge exists as the content of intelligent ability—power to do" (MW 9: 192). Second, "material gradually is surcharged and deepened through communicated knowledge or information" (MW 9: 192). Third, "it is enlarged and worked over into rationally or logically organized material—that of the one who, relatively speaking, is expert in the subject" (MW 9: 192). Let us consider these in order.

The knowledge we first acquire "and that remains most deeply engrained, is knowledge of *how to do*; how to walk, talk, read, write, skate, ride a bicycle" (MW 9: 192). Notice such doing may involve other persons as well as things. Such "primary or initial subject matter always exists as matter of an active doing, involving the use of the body and the handling of material" (MW 9: 192). We should start with learning by doing. Skilled "know how" precedes propositional "knowing that." The latter builds upon the former. This is why good teachers give their students "something to do, not something to learn" (op. cit.). When we fail to do this, we end up with subject matter detached from "the needs and purposes of the learner" that "becomes just a something to be memorized and reproduced upon demand" (MW 9: 192). This is the common fate of most schooling; it is not education in a Deweyan sense.

At the next level, learning from doing things with others leads to linguistic communication that, as we saw in earlier chapters, involves possession of and response to meanings. Although immensely powerful, propositional "knowing that" may mislead us: "the propositions, in which knowledge, the issue of active concern with problems, is deposited, are taken to be themselves knowledge" (MW 9: 195). Such propositions are the refined product of inquiry. We must not confuse them with the entire process, which includes skilled "knowing how." Lamentably, almost all formal school knowledge comes in the form of abstract "knowing that," which easily translates into inert ideas suitable for cold storage. It is often largely meaningless: If "what is communicated cannot be organized into the existing experience of the learner, it becomes *mere* words: that is, pure sense-stimuli, lacking in meaning. Then it operates to call out mechanical reactions" (MW 9: 196). Such learning cannot alter the content of our character and thereby affect conduct. There is no reason it should. It is not our knowledge, but someone else's. Because they cannot imagine doing anything with it, such knowledge does concern the students only because they cannot win the teacher's approval without it.

We now come to science or rationalized knowledge. Such knowledge is "the perfected outcome of learning . . . that which we think *with* rather than that which we think about" (MW 9: 196). We have already discussed this kind of knowledge organized by experts for "the enterprise of knowledge as a specialized under-taking" (MW 9: 198). We should not consider knowledge logically organized for inquiry as necessarily depicting a superior reality to other modes of description and narration. We organize knowledge differently for different purposes:

> Strictly speaking, it [H_2O] does not indicate the objective relations of water any more than does a statement that water is transparent, fluid, without

taste or odor, satisfying to thirst, etc. It is just as true that water has these relations as that it is constituted by two molecules of hydrogen in combination with one of oxygen. But for the *particular purpose* of conducting discovery with a view to ascertainment of fact, the latter relations are fundamental.

(MW 9: 198–199)

The last section reminds us that subject matter is always social. In our first chapter, we saw that education is the site of cultural reproduction. What knowledge is of most worth to future generations is not only the supreme question of curriculum; it is among the most important problems of all education. Dewey offers some valuable criteria for answering this question. First, we "must select with the intention of improving the life we live in common so that the future shall be better than the past." Therefore, we should select first from "the experiences in which the widest groups share." Those of "specialized groups and technical pursuits are secondary" (MW 9: 199). Specialized and technical groups are necessary, especially in a modern pluralistic democracy. However, we must not allow special interests to seize our educational system and deflect it from pursuing the common good by privileging the exclusive interests of the rich, business and industry, the military, academics, and others. Indeed, as Dewey indicates:

> Democratic society is peculiarly dependent for its maintenance upon the use in forming a course of study of criteria which are broadly human. Democracy cannot flourish where the chief influences in selecting subject matter of instruction are utilitarian ends narrowly conceived for the masses, and, for the higher education of the few, the traditions of a specialized cultivated class.

(MW 9: 199)

The next three chapters of our book will therefore investigate the role of education in democratic society by taking into account more recent cultural, economic, and political constellations and conditions.

The last section of Dewey's Chapter 14 begins by informing us that the next chapters of *Democracy and Education* "will take up various school activities and studies and discuss them as successive stages in that evolution of knowledge which we have just been discussing" (MW 9: 198–199). These chapters include "The Significance of Geography and History" (Chapter 16), "Science in the Course of Study", (Chapter 19), "Physical and Social Studies: Naturalism and Humanism" (Chapter 21), and "Vocational Aspects of Education" (Chapter 23). These and other chapters are quite interesting, but fit within the framework of interest, discipline, method, and subject matter we have been discussing here and in Chapter 7. Although immensely valuable to those with different technical interests, and of general interest to all, we have decided to skip over these chapters to pursue contemporary issues in democratic global education.

Challenge for Today: Instruction and Construction

The topics of this chapter, contents, methods, and relationships, all fall into Dewey's comprehensive concept of inquiry as a cultural and constructive process of problem solving taken in a generous social and cultural sense. They constitute aspects of this process because inquiry always implies the experience of subject matter (contents), the ways of experiencing these contents (methods), as well as communication and cooperation (relationships) in order to develop social intelligence. Even today the Deweyan model of inquiry offers a fine and fruitful orientation for developing learning and understanding the necessary contexts and conditions of learning. The highly elaborated five-step model of inquiry we have discussed in the first section of this chapter opens abundant possibilities of application. In the course of arguments in our book so far, we have repeatedly used perspectives from the Cologne program of interactive constructivism, such as the distinction of observer, participant, and agent role or the perspectives of construction, reconstruction, and deconstruction. Here, we intend to introduce another relevant metatheoretical consideration, namely the constructivist theory of discourse.

We can understand Dewey's model of inquiry as a practice deeply involved in social and cultural contexts. It requires reflection regarding the connections between culture and discourse. Foucault and others have introduced discourse as a preeminent topic in philosophical debate after Dewey's time. Today, we must recognize that the meanings involved in any social and cultural practice are products of discourse. What is meant by discourse here? We suggest an understanding of discourse that contains at least four dimensions.

First, discourse is frequently about the production of knowledge. That is to say, discourses provide fields of what we can say and justify about a respective topic. They connect statements to each other involving agreement or disagreement. Significantly, the relation of discourse to knowledge is never static, fully stabilized, and all comprehensive. Discourse theory points to the omissions and blind spots that go with the very constitution of knowledge because the construction of knowledge always relies on selective interests.

Second, human beings constitute and produce not only knowledge in discourses but engage in lived relationships. This dimension is also a part of discourse because it frames and pervades the modes of communication. It is an important question, especially for discourse in education, whether these relational frames communicate a general atmosphere of respect, care, responsibility for each other along with self-esteem and esteem for others and such. It makes a huge difference for learning whether or not competition or cooperation, homogeneous norms or diversity, repletion or creativity, domination or participation, and so on pervade the relations of educational discourse.

Third, this brings us to a consideration of the connections between discourse and power. According to our view, there are no innocent discourses regarding power (compare Hall, 1996: 203 ff.); power relations pervade all human relationships and therefore all discourses. What is especially important is to follow the implication that this observation has for a general theory of knowledge. As constructed in discourse and based on lived human relationships, we may never separate knowledge from effects of power with which it is inextricably interwoven.

Fourth, our selective interests in discourses necessarily restrict and condition our knowledge and understanding of them. Therefore, we must consider the limits of our abilities to understand, reflect, control, construct, etc. In this perspective, discourses are seen as events in experience that contain precarious as well as stable aspects, which we can never completely foresee, plan, execute, and so on.

For example, let us come back to the critical discussion about standardized testing in connection, e.g., with PISA, given in Chapter 6. Here we consider PISA or other forms of standardized testing as instances of inquiry and discourse. Already with Dewey, we can aptly reflect on the limits of general measurement approaches. Think of the five steps in his model of learning:

(i)   The necessary first step is "perplexity" and an emotional response to the situation by the learner. Standardized learning often violates this fist condition because the very idea of standardization implies neglect of individual and diverse interests and responses. Therefore, such measures must take refuge in extrinsic motivation from the very outset of their strategies.

(ii) The second step consists of the formulation of tentative hypotheses constructed by learners in cooperation with each other, learning materials, and teachers, which they use to construct the problematic situation. This necessarily involves an intellectual response by the learners themselves. Standardized testing provides only very limited space for experimenting with ideas, tentative and imaginative projections, or collaborative ways of developing creative and intelligent perspectives.

(iii) The third step consists of the necessity of a careful survey (examination, inspection, exploration, and analysis) with regard to the problem. Learners must have occasions for actively exploring problems and their contexts and constructively gathering facts they consider relevant to find solutions. In standardized measurements, by contrast, the program always predefines the problem with very few degrees of freedom for and variation by individual ways of learning. It is often largely decontextualized and does not actually invite or inspire curiosity, creativity, and joy of exploration. The premium on reproduction in generalized measurement makes creative and experimental approaches highly improbable.

(iv) The transition from the tentative working hypothesis to an explanatory hypothesis based on the constructive work of the learners done in the previous step is an active intellectual refinement of conceptions, observations, imaginations, etc. that again builds on skills of communication and cooperation, creativity, and experimentation. Standardized testing usually leaves only limited opportunities for constructions and deviations concerning the ways of moving from tentative hypotheses to explanatory ideas. In many cases, the program only allows one way of proceeding. In other more intelligent cases, like PISA in this respect, the program at least concedes and values a limited amount of alternatives.

(v) The course of the five steps comes to a provisional, but never final, close as learners attempt to solve the problem by acting out and testing their hypotheses. In generalized measurement, this is usually the moment when teachers take the papers out of the learners' hands and hand them over to somebody who assigns grades or rankings.

In our constructivist perspective on inquiry as discourse, we agree with all these observations while at the same time extending the critical interpretation to a meta-theoretical level of observation:

(1) Taking into consideration the four dimensions of discourse we have been speaking of, we may say with regard to the production of knowledge in discourse, programs of standardized testing support and utilize a very restrictive view of knowledge because they have to operationalize items that work in their predefined programs. They must define indicators and operators that apparently represent a comprehensive body of knowledge. The tendency is often to regard this body as necessary and complete. They tend to neglect the fact that it is itself a construction based on selective interests with many omissions and only seemingly reasonable claims to closure. The effect, though, on the general level of widespread beliefs about schooling is to produce a mainstream of privileged disciplinary knowledge and ways to teach, learn, and test.

(2) Concerning the dimension of relationships in discourses, we often observe that standardized measurement explicitly claims to avoid this dimension altogether because it supposedly has nothing to do with test results. Some even claim that giving relationships a substantial role would spoil the objectivity of the test. From a critical distance, however, we easily observe that relationships driven out the front door return through the back because human interaction cannot do away with this dimension. One way in which the dimension of human relationships returns is the often almost obsessive worship of tests and the agents of testing as authorities, not only for the classroom, students and teachers, or school boards, but also on the level of the general public and the global ranking among countries. Especially harmful is the effect of one-sided generalized measurement approaches on student–teacher relationships and interactions. One cannot overemphasize the reductionism contained in the rather cold, distanced, "objective,"

and merely instrumental qualities supported by excessive measurement. One-sided orientations toward fixed and predefined standards seriously hamper the arts of living teachers and students need to construct good, caring, and responsible relationships.

(3)   There is a strict order of power relations in discourse contained in the standardized measurement programs. These involve generalized norms defined and executed according to a top-down approach that narrows the diversity of experiences. There is a rather fixed hierarchy of levels descending from policies formed by educational technocrats and experts down to administrators, local school authorities, school boards, teachers, and students. We cannot ignore the attractiveness such an ordered hierarchy has, especially for many living in liquid modernity. Reductive programs like PISA appear to the general public as stable and secure anchors in the flux and flow of otherwise confusing and excessively complex realities. Likewise, we cannot ignore that this very characteristic imbues such programs and the agents who promote them with an immense amount of prestige and power. Yet, the hidden curriculum of PISA or other tests influences the role and responsibility of teachers and learners, thereby forming attitudes, expectations, social perceptions, and ways of communication in the classroom.

(4)   The will to control discourse is apparent—and even notorious for some—in standardized measurement. Equally apparent and notorious is the tendency of such programs to produce unintended consequences that belie the confessed intentions to further educational growth and success for all. The paradoxes of expert control appear in the belief that we can solve the problem of learning failure by more testing. It is obvious to many that teaching for the test does not contribute to growth in learning in any comprehensive and sustainable sense, but the response is still more testing. In a pluralistic and democratic society, the paradoxes of expert control are an especially important public issue that deserves public deliberation and solution through democratic rather than technocratic decisions. For one thing, there is the paradox that such programs—although they may attempt to control their own discourses and practices—usually forget to consider that they cannot control the constitutive contexts and broader conditions to which their programs respond. The capitalization of learning produces these effects. On the other hand, there is the paradox that lies in the fact that although the programs intend to further learning and growth, their effects in the long term are detrimental to constructive and creative learning cultures because of their discursive power to constrain critical, creative, and caring relationships. Characteristically, the scope of observation and public representation neglects these potential and actual effects.

Recent empirical studies on learning and teaching, like e.g., Hattie (2009, 2012), show that to be effective, classroom practices must involve all of the five steps described by Dewey, although they seldom refer directly to his educational theory. However, to contextualize learning in the broader frames of culture, society, politics, etc., we need educational philosophies like the one provided by Dewey or the above-mentioned discourse theory.

For the remainder of this chapter, we take a closer look at the conceptual, theoretical, as well as practical challenges posed by the critical distinction between instruction and construction in learning. Again, we connect with more recent theoretical and empirical findings on learning that show that the mixture of instruction and construction is a critical challenge in learning today. From our perspective, Dewey is on the way—or we might even say, he is one of the most important pathbreakers—from instruction to construction. Simplifying, we may say that instruction and construction constitute oppositional poles in a continual field of learning and teaching theories and practices. Speaking grossly, we may say instruction stands for teacher- and curriculum-centered positions, passive and reproductive acquisition, learning for the test, disciplinary subordination, homogenous norms, one-size-fits-all-expectations, top-down communication, competition, and ranking. Construction, on the other side, is associated with learner-centered positions, active and creative experiments and projects, learning by and for experience, participation, diversity of resources, ways, and results, bottom-up communication, cooperation, and personal and social growth (cf. Kalantzis & Cope, 2008). Thus stated, however, the picture is a bit too simple. What seems necessary from the perspective of contemporary learning theories is a well-balanced combination of instruction and construction. Such an approach must provide for sufficient access to important cultural and social resources—like knowledge, skills, competencies, methods etc.—while simultaneously creating sufficient opportunities for the constructive side of learning that includes possibilities of reconstructing relevant resources, deconstructing contents, approaches, methods, etc. as well as constructing new ways and perspectives in learning. In so doing, we must not forget the relevance of lived relationships as necessary social contexts of learning constituted by ways of cooperation and interaction (see Chapter 3 of our book).

Given the conditions of liquid modernity, it is not surprising that today the constructivist turn in learning theories and practices has become so apparent and omnipresent. The liquefaction of social and cultural life makes well-balanced responses in learning between the poles of instruction and construction unavoidable because only then can learning respond properly to the needs of rapidly changing, increasingly diverse, heterogeneous, mobile, and dynamic constellations. Social constructivists assume learning arises from social relationships and involves social institutions and the power they wield. We acquire our meanings and attitudes by participating in the meaning-making social, political, and economic practices and institutions of culture. That is why education is a basic social function. As already noted, it is the site of cultural reproduction. Social constructivism emphasizes the contingency and falsifiability of social constructions and the meanings that make up mind and self. In accord with the idea of intelligence discussed in our Chapter 1, our minds and selves are contingent social constructions constantly subject to re- and deconstruction as we encounter different contexts and different people. Social constructivism is the idea behind Deweyan democracy and education. Besides being a site of cultural reproduction, democratic society is a site of social reconstruction including the norms of social class, wealth distribution, gender, race, sexuality, and much more.

The challenge for today, much as in Dewey's time, centers on the difference between traditional instruction and progressive constructivist methods. We should understand this difference as a tension involving larger social, cultural, political, and economic interests that often affect the cultures of teaching and learning. Understanding this challenge requires synthesizing much of our previous argumentation. Recall our discussion of education as a social function in Chapter 2 and how education seeks to make the young "robust trustees of its own resources and ideals" (MW 9: 14). There we distinguished between socialization as narrow, unreflective, and relatively passive accommodation of individuals to the existing social order and critical-creative socialization enabling the development of "individual minds" and creative self-expression. There are different reasons why mere instruction and passive accommodation have become the mainstream approach in education:

First, instruction has considerable advantages seen from the perspective of discipline and power. The teacher as instructor seems to be in control of learning because s/he plans, conducts and evaluates the processes of input and output in learning. Ironically, teachers themselves become controllable by the very same pattern of discourse because not only the students, but also teachers and schools as institutions are put to test by standardized methods.

Second, most modernized societies have come to think of teaching and learning after the model of instruction as a typically modern imagination of sequential and ordered progress. Like the political leader and the military commander, many have seen the schoolteacher as a hero of modernization. The dark sides of modernity, however, have also become apparent, e.g., in power abuse and school tyranny. The traditional teacher model of instruction puts democracy at schools at risk because it excessively delimits opportunities of participation and chances for construction and criticism on the side of all learners including the teachers themselves.

Third, the capitalization of learning criticized above (and again in Chapter 10 of our book) puts a premium on "one-size-fits-all" strategies and delimits the chances for construction and criticism in education. In this context, the main point is that instruction is always cheaper than construction. In the politics of education, "one-size-fits-all" strategies are often preferred and propagated as being more effective for reducing costs and maximizing output. Training "individual[s] with minds" to be used as "human capital" is obviously very different from educating "individual minds" for the kind of creative self-expression and critical acumen needed for active democratic participation. Already a century ago, Dewey realized that private business would attempt to use the government to train its workers while the primary function of tax-supported public schools is to prepare democratic citizens.

> And some employers of labor would doubtless rejoice to have schools supported by public taxation supply them with additional food for their mills. All others should be united against every proposition, in whatever form advanced, to separate training of employees from training for citizenship, training of intelligence and character from training for narrow industrial efficiency.
>
> (MW 7: 102)

It seems unfortunate that the question of the role of government in building public schools even today often receives reductive answers in public debates. Narrow economic interests like those Dewey criticized in his time also appear in contemporary contexts like programs that focus on "human capital" and market adaptation for private employment. The public is in danger of forgetting that instead of only training standardized interchangeable parts for the global production function we should be educating for the individual, social, creative, critical, and moral growth of democratic citizens. "Human capital" and "one-size-fits-all" thinking fail to recognize that construction is more productive, in the long run, than teaching and learning for the test. This applies especially if we consider the necessities of sustainable learning, democratic participation, and educative growth. We will further extend this argument in Chapter 11.

Fourth, as already recommended, we must consider the transitions of modernity into liquid modernity. Liquefaction has important implications for democracy and education. We believe Dewey already critically anticipated this transition, because speaking in relation to his time he already foresees future developments and develops many concepts that today still respond to the liquefied conditions.

Traditional forms of education, like the teacher model of instruction that Dewey criticized, often tacitly support special interests groups. This is why Dewey says,

> Since the curriculum is always getting loaded down with purely inherited traditional matter and with subjects which represent mainly the energy of some influential person or group of persons in behalf of something dear to them, it requires constant inspection, criticism, and revision to make sure it is accomplishing its purpose.
>
> (MW 9: 250)

As a counter-strategy, democracy and education puts its hopes not on reproducing to the *status quo* but on providing and increasing opportunities for genuine participation and constructive as well as critical development of societal resources. Democracy is obviously a counter-factual ideal we cannot measure or test empirically, because we may only justify it as an *ethos* based on deep-seated attitudes of how we wish to live together morally.

In Chapter 6, we argued that in liquid modernity the democratic ideal of education of necessity involves opportunities for emancipation which means bridging the gap between individuality *de jure* and *de facto*. The aim of emancipation is to enable learners to become "masters of their own economic and social careers" (MW 9: 104). In a critical sense, this is what individuality *de facto* as an ideal-typical claim stands for. If we look at the actualities of capitalism in liquid modernity, however, we detect a quite different sense of the *de facto*: namely, the conditions, constraints, dependencies, and traps in which individuals struggle together with and against others in order to make a living on the best conditions and resources available to them at the time. Capitalists societies produce more wasted lives than market-oriented political ideologues are willing to admit. Following Bauman, individuality *de jure* means that individuals cannot hide themselves behind society as something static, solid, stable, and secure. "Come out, come out, wherever you are" is the slogan of liquid modernity. The human rights and capabilities approach includes critical perspectives for endowing the exposed individuals with more than just the naked skin of "human capitals." These become powerful perspectives that help us to understand more critically what individuality *de jure* means for democracy and education: claims to qualitative experience and learning, growth in diversity and participation, communication across differences, opportunities for all for the development of whatever gifts and resources they have. If we want to make progress towards bridging the gap between individuality *de jure* and *de facto* in educational practices and institutions, this reconstructed understanding of the *de jure* would be the necessary first step. Democracy and education begins with this reconstruction, which we must fight for time and again.

Dewey's Summary[3]

> Processes of instruction are unified in the degree in which they centre in the production of good habits of thinking. While we may speak, without error, of the method of thought, the important thing is that thinking is the method of an educative experience. The essentials of method are therefore identical with the essentials of reflection. They are first that the pupil have a genuine situation of experience—that there be a continuous activity in which he is interested for its own sake; secondly, that a genuine problem develop within this situation as a stimulus to thought; third, that he possess the information and make the observations needed to deal with it; fourth, that suggested solutions occur to him which he shall be responsible for

developing in an orderly way; fifth, that he have opportunity and occasion to test his ideas by application, to make their meaning clear and to discover for himself their validity.

(MW 9: 170)

Our Summary

To understand Dewey's theories of educational subject matter and methods it is essential to take his philosophical core concept of experience seriously. As has been shown, his distinction between experiencing and the experienced gives the clue for considering and interpreting the necessary mutual involvement of methods (as ways of experiencing) and subject matter or contents (as components of the experienced). His five-step model of reflective experience constructively connects both sides in an intelligent and experimental way. This is an ideal-typical postulation about learning from experience that can give educators a general orientation as to how to organize constructive learning and what conditions we must provide to give learners sufficient occasions for genuine and productive thinking. We may distinguish phases of intelligent thought and controlled inquiry for the practical purposes of identifying some of the phases of good thinking. Such identification involves interaction, emotional responses, personal and social experiences, communication, imagination, intuition, and embodied passions. All these components of social intelligence are necessary to release the possible in the actual. They also provide guidance as to what makes for good student-centered education. Instruction fails if it does not sufficiently contain constructive, creative, and artistic experiences for all who participate in the learning process. Sadly, externally imposed governmental bureaucratic standardization, often effected by special interests of business and industry, supports a method-versus-subject matter dualism in many contemporary practices and debates. With Dewey, we reject such dualism because it tends to destroy learners' and teachers' creative autonomy while rendering schooling mechanical and separate from the interests of ordinary lived experience. To avoid mere adaptation to existing social, political, and economic mainstream in capitalist society, democracy and education must support powers of resistance against conformism, compartmentalization, and passive adaptation. In the sense of Dewey's "Construction and Criticism," which uses the term construction as name for the unique and creative potentials of individuals and learners in cooperation and interaction with their world and each other, we may say that democracy and education puts a premium on construction over instruction.

Notes

1   For another, see Garrison, Neubert & Reich (2012, Part 2).
2   It is also value laden. See Putnam (2002). Putnam explicitly attributes his position to Dewey (9).

3   We chose to reproduce Dewey's summary of Chapter 12 as most representative of the four chapters of *Democracy and Education* we are combining in our present chapter on "Contents, Methods, and Relationships in Education," because it is most immediately relevant to educators who believe that teaching students to think for themselves is immensely important, especially in a democracy.

9

CLASS, RACE, GENDER, AND DISABILITY

The issues currently addressed by the terms "class," "race," and "gender" pose challenges for the critical and reconstructive continuation of the Deweyan program because they expose axes of discrimination in society that need to be addressed by *Democracy and Education*. In accord with more recent anti-discrimination programs (cf. OECD, 2009), we add as a further axis the issue of "disability." In what follows, we will first give a brief account and interpretation of Dewey's position with regard to each of these dimensions, drawing largely on a diverse selection of his writings, mostly from the later works. In this chapter, we discuss four instances of exclusion from full, free, and effective participation in democratic discourses and practices in social, economic, cultural, and political fields. With these instances, we focus on historically entrenched contexts of exclusion that accompany the emergence of modern societies. The first, social class, is one of which Dewey was well aware. The second, race, is one that Dewey addresses, but in ways that are partial, incomplete, and sometimes entirely inadequate. The same applies to the third, gender. The fourth is disability, of which he says nothing.

In the *Challenge for Today* section, we will expose some very general political, social, cultural, and educational implications of the matter. We will critique and reconstruct Dewey as necessary to respond to these four instances of exclusion and marginalization in our time. We believe that what we say about these four instances readily generalizes to how we may reconstruct Dewey for a perspective of democracy and education on issues like lesbian, gay, bisexual, transgender (LGBT), ethnic and cultural differences, and other marginalized populations, e.g., indigenous peoples. With regard to the latter, what little Dewey says about their conditions of life sometimes even seems to violate his own understanding of democratic participation.

The following two chapters will continue and expand the discussion. In Chapter 10, we will focus on the question of capitals and capitalization in liquid modernity as a necessary context for democracy and education. In Chapter 11, we will turn to the question of social inclusion and democratic participation for every individual in society. We will interpret the current turn to inclusion in education as a response to the needs of diversity and participation in contemporary democracy and education. All three chapters, therefore, should be read in their interconnections. Together they constitute an inseparable comprehensive account of aspects that are analytically distinguished only for reasons of a more detailed and elaborated understanding.

Social Class

Dewey lived in a class society whose classism was strongly contested and controversial. As a public intellectual of great national as well as international reputation, he was convinced that capitalist class barriers as well as revolutionary class struggle were essential challenges for democracy in modern Western society. Especially in the time after the First World War, he forcefully developed and publicly articulated his vision of a third way between or beyond untamed capitalism on one side and fictitious communism on the other. In writings such as *The Public and Its Problems* (1927; LW 2: 237–372), *Liberalism and Social Action* (1935; LW 11: 1–65), *Individualism, Old and New* (1930; LW 5: 41–123), *Art as Experience* (1934; LW 10), and *Freedom and Culture* (1939; LW 13 63–188), he addresses the social, cultural, economic, and political crises of his time and developed important philosophical foundations for a political program that was partly affine to European social democratic movements of the time and may be roughly characterized as a form of "democratic socialism." Besides these and other comprehensive and systematic contributions to social philosophy, he articulates his political positions in a large number of comments and criticisms on current affairs that were published in journals like *The New Republic*, newspapers like *The New York Times*, through radio programs, public talks, or by way of *News Reels* in the cinema.

In a world of global economic crises, growing tendencies of political totalitarianism, and increasing threats of international warfare, Dewey was convinced that it is not sufficient to simply recall the democratic principles and traditions of the past and to evoke their lasting efficacy. He criticizes the "conception of democracy as something static, as something that is like an inheritance that can be bequeathed" (LW 13: 298). For him, the challenge rather consists in giving new democratic responses to changed social, cultural, economic, and political constellations lest the democratic principles and traditions degenerate to mere lip services in a society that has already taken an undemocratic turn of development. As Dewey observes in his 1938 essay "Democracy and Education in the World of Today," whose title of course alludes to his famous 1916 book:

> The crisis that we are undergoing will turn out, I think, to be worthwhile if we learn through it that every generation has to accomplish democracy over again for itself; that its very nature, its essence, is something that cannot be handed on from one person or one generation to another, but has to be worked out in terms of needs, problems and conditions of the social life of which . . . we are a part, a social life that is changing with extreme rapidity from year to year.
>
> (LW 13: 299)

Of fundamental relevance, in this connection, is the capacity of criticism. Dewey believes that construction and criticism are twins or "companions" (see LW 5: 138). They belong to each other like two sides of a coin and complement each other like the "rhythm of output and intake, of expiration and inspiration, in our mental breath and spirit" (LW 5: 139). Together they constitute necessary attitudes of democratic culture and living together. "Creative activity is our great need," Dewey writes, "but criticism, self-criticism, is the road to its release" (LW 5: 143). He believes that the performance of social and cultural criticism in a most generous and comprehensive way belongs to the essential and indispensable tasks of philosophy. In accord with this belief, Dewey's idea and vision of democracy is indissolubly connected with his social and cultural criticism of capitalism. Having already elaborated his criticisms in the 1920s, he provided an even more decided twist in the 1930s after the experiences of the Great Depression and the rise of fascism. Dewey argues that during the advancements of industrialization, capitalist relations of private property and ownership have, on the one hand, furthered the liberation from the old feudal order. On the other hand, however, they have installed new hindrances to the effective realization of democratic communication, participation, and decision making. In the processes of overcoming the older social divisions that had been characteristic of the old feudal age, they have even furthered and multiplied the splitting up of society into separated, isolated, and non-communicating spheres of interest and exchange that, as we saw in Chapter 6, resemble "feudal control of industry" (MW 10: 150). The criticism of such fixed social hierarchies and divisions is a continual thread through Dewey's social-philosophical writings. For example, he complains in *Art as Experience*:

> Life is compartmentalized and the institutionalized compartments are classified as high and as low; their values as profane and spiritual, as material and ideal. Interests are related to one another externally and mechanically, through a system of checks and balances . . . Compartmentalization of occupations and interests brings about separation of that mode of activity commonly called "practice" from insight, of imagination from executive doing, of significant purpose from work, of emotion from thought and doing . . . Those who write the anatomy of experience then suppose that these divisions inhere in the very constitution of human nature.
>
> (LW 10: 26 f.)

Dewey points to the "present economic and legal institutional conditions" of living, which entail that, for large parts "of our experience," it is "only too true that these separations hold" (LW 10: 27). What he has in mind, here, is of course the institution of private property, in the first place, insofar as it concerns the ownership of the social means and forces of production. At the current stage in the development of capitalism, this ownership has anyway passed, upon the whole, from the hands of private businessmen and entrepreneurs into those of great corporations, banks, companies, and stock markets: "Capital is no longer the outcome of deliberate personal sacrifice, but is an institution of corporations and finance with massive political and social ramifications" (LW 1: 185). Under these conditions, capital and ownership to an even larger degree than before evade democratic control and influence because of the massive, complex, and often inscrutable interrelations of economic and political power.

From these developments, Dewey draws the conclusion that the classical liberal belief in the sacrosanct role of private property—as an indefeasible right of individuals thought of as socially isolated agents who act on behalf of their economic self-interests—and the attendant political conception of "laissez faire" can no longer constitute appropriate responses to the social and economic conditions and realities towards the middle of the twentieth century. He opts for a form of "democratic socialism" when he claims, e.g., in his 1935 book *Liberalism and Social Action*, that a contemporary liberalism that does not want to become politically and socially irrelevant needs to be radical in the sense that it cannot content itself with occasional reforms and social measures with respect to obvious social grievances, but has to envisage the necessity of fundamental institutional changes (comp. LW 11: 1–65). In his 1937 essay "Democracy is Radical," he observes:

> *The end of democracy is a radical end. For it is an end that has not been adequately realized in any country at any time.* It is radical because it requires great change in existing social institutions, economic, legal and cultural. A democratic liberalism that does not recognize these things in thought and action is not awake to its own meaning and to what that meaning demands.
>
> (LW 11: 298 f., original italics)

Dewey leaves no doubt that, for him, these necessary institutional changes imply, first of all, the socialization and public control of the essential economic and productive resources of society, the more equal and fair distribution of wealth, and the realization of effective opportunities for the democratic participation of all in social planning, regulation, and control. Among other things he writes in *Liberalism and Social Action*: "[T]he cause of liberalism will be lost for a considerable period if it is not prepared to go further and socialize the forces of production, now at hand, so that the liberty of individuals will be supported by the very structure of economic organization" (LW 11: 61 f.).

The partial affinity to Marxist positions that these quotes suggest evinces not only traces of a common Hegelian heritage, but also similarities regarding the turn to a philosophy of action that is characteristic for Marxism as well as Deweyan pragmatism (cf. Gavin, 1988). Nevertheless, there are also fundamental differences between both traditions. Dewey himself tended, for the most part, to emphasize these differences over the commonalities. He had visited the young Soviet Union in 1928 and at that time his statements and reports about the country and its new school system had been quite euphoric (see LW 3: 203–250). In his later writings, he was more concerned to distance himself from the prevailing Stalinist versions of Marxism that increasingly dominated the debates since the early 1930s. In theoretical respect, Dewey's criticism addressed, among other things, the concept of "science" in Marxism and the truth claims it raises. For example, Dewey writes in his 1938/39 book, *Freedom and Culture*: ". . . Marxism is 'dated' in the matter of its claims to be peculiarly scientific. For just as *necessity* and search for a *single* all-comprehensive law was typical of the intellectual atmosphere of the forties of the last [nineteenth] century, so *probability* and *pluralism* are the characteristics of the present state of science" (LW 13: 123). As Richard Rorty (1999: 23–26) aptly observed, the difference between Dewey and Marx consists, among other things, in their respective horizons with regard to social-philosophical hopes and expectations. Marx believed that he could grasp the contours of world history as a whole and recognize the present as a period of transition between the feudal age of the past and the necessary state of communism in the future. Dewey contented himself with the more modest claim that the present is a period of change and development toward something that could be inconceivably much better because of the effective use of social intelligence, participatory deliberation, and democratic reconstruction. But for him, there was no way of telling with necessity what the outcome would be. We have to take ambivalence and contingency seriously without losing our melioristic hope in the chances of a better future.

A second difference is a "practical" one. It concerns the choice of means. "*The fundamental principle of democracy is that the ends of freedom and individuality for all can be attained only by means that accord with those ends*" (LW 11: 298, original italics). For Dewey, the way to approach democracy and public socialism was not by enforcing class struggle and establishing the dictatorship of the proletariat. He was generally very skeptical about claims to elite rule, be it an elite of scientific experts, bureaucrats, or political leaders (see LW 2: 235–372). With a view to the developments in Russia and other countries, he observed: "In the light of what happens in non-democratic countries, it is pertinent to ask whether the rule of a class signifies the dictatorship of the majority, or dictatorship over the chosen class by a minority party" (LW 11: 60 f.). He also distrusted the idea that revolutionary violence could advance the development of democracy and insisted that—generally speaking—it is incompatible with the democratic principles: "It requires an unusually credulous faith in the Hegelian dialectic of opposites to think that all of a sudden the use of force by a class will be transmuted into a democratic classless society" (LW 11: 60). Dewey's democratic alternative—or third way—to the drift of capitalist laissez faire politics on the one hand and the dependence upon violence through the dictatorship of the proletariat on the other hand was "socially organized intelligence" (LW 11: 61). He hoped that the socialization of intelligence on behalf of more democratic ways of living was almost completely achievable without violence. In the controversies with proponents of Marxism, Dewey insisted on the premium put on democratic means and only occasionally admitted that this might include an intelligent and deliberate use of force:

> The one exception—and that apparent rather than real—to dependence upon organized intelligence as the method for directing social change is found when society through an authorized majority has entered upon the path of social experimentation leading to great social change, and a minority refuses by force to permit the method of intelligent action to go into effect. Then force may be intelligently employed to subdue and disarm the recalcitrant minority.
>
> (LW 11: 61)

Race

In his book *In a Shade of Blue*, Eddie S. Glaude Jr., Tod professor of Religion and African American Studies at Princeton remarks:

> I argue that pragmatism, when attentive to the darker dimensions of human living (what we often speak of as the blues), can address many of the conceptual problems that plague contemporary African American political life. How we think about black identity, how we imagine black history, and how we conceive of black agency can be rendered in ways that escape bad racial reasoning.
>
> (Glaude, 2007: IX–X)

Glaude calls on the African American writers James Baldwin, and especially Toni Morrison, to show how we may easily reconstruct Dewey's philosophy to sing the blues. He then uses the results to reconsider and reconstruct the very notion of African American identity. The book arose from a town meeting involving the leading African American Deweyan pragmatist and public intellectual Cornell West, and well-known African American media personality Tavis Smiley, both of whom endorse the book. Among other things, they respond to a young man's statement that "knowledge without action is useless." The remainder of the meeting reflects on John Dewey's definition of knowledge as the consequence of actions taken. Many African American intellectuals have followed West in finding Dewey's writings congenial to their social and political projects even as they reconstruct and recontextualize him for their purposes today (see Lawson and Koch, 2004).

Dewey lived in a society with historically deep-seated forms of racial discrimination—direct and indirect, personal and institutional—largely supported by racist ideologies. Racism was a component of social life that was as pervasive as it was often disavowed and neglected. If one looks through Dewey's writings, one will find him as a philosopher who was quite aware of the appearances of racism in the society of his time.[1] One will find passages where he criticizes racism in strong and unambiguous words as inconsistent with his democratic vision. We will cite some of these passages in the following paragraphs. However, such a survey also reveals that, in spite of Dewey's forceful and emphatic rejection of racist attitudes, behaviors, and structures, the problem of racism, upon the whole, plays a less significant role in his political writings than one would possibly expect from a perspective of today. His direct and explicit comments on "race" and racism are relatively limited in number, and one will hardly find a systematic, comprehensive, or thoroughgoing account of racism in Dewey. He does not address the issue at all in his 1926/27 book *The Public and Its Problems* that was one of his most important and influential political writings. While he is aware of the racist heritages from the age of slavery in the US and the current forms of discrimination against Afro-Americans, Jews, Catholics, and other ethnic and religious minorities, he hardly ever says a word about the history and life-conditions of Native Americans.

Dewey's direct engagement in anti-racist activities or campaigns was some-what limited (see Westbrook, 1991). Among the involvements that deserve to be mentioned here are his 1909 address to the "National Negro Conference" where he argues, among other things, that debates about substantial race differences and the conception of an "inferior race" are nonsensical and without scientific support (cf. MW 4: 156 f.). In the talk on "Racial Prejudice and Friction," given to a Chinese audience during his Asia trip in 1919–1921, he presents a multifactorial account of racial prejudice as a "practical reality" with psychological, social, cultural, economic, and political causes (cf. MW 13: 242–254). In 1932, he gives a talk to the NAACP (cf. LW 6: 224–230), "an organisation he helped to found" (Eldridge, 2004: 12). A further example would be Dewey's public intervention in "The Case of Odell Waller," an African American sharecropper from Virginia who had been sentenced to death by an exclusively white jury for allegedly shooting his white landlord (cf. LW 15: 356–358). Among other things, this case is interesting because it shows that Dewey regarded racism not only as a matter of personal prejudice and intolerance, but also as a problem with deep-seated social, structural, and institutional aspects (see also Neubert, 2012c).

In a recent essay with the title "Dewey on Race and Social Change," Michael Eldridge writes that "[r]acial prejudice was a concern of Dewey's . . . He was disturbed by the lynchings that were all too common in his time, but he participated in no crusade against them." (Eldridge, 2004: 19) Eldridge observes that "[g]iven the pervasive, deep problem of racism in American history, Dewey could have and perhaps should have said and written more. It was but one of many issues that he addressed" (Eldridge, 2004: 15). And he comes to the conclusion: "One committed to a multicultural society will find some help in Dewey's direct statements on race; he or she will, however, find greater assistance in Dewey's more general social and political thinking and overall philosophical approach" (Eldridge, 2004: 11). We share this general impression.

Let us now have a closer look at some of Dewey's direct statements and general positions in connection with "race" and racism. As to cultural differences between ethnic groups and their explanation on the basis of alleged biological or racial differences, he observes in his 1939 book *Freedom and Culture*: "Anthropologists are practically all agreed that the differences we find in different 'races' are not due to anything in inherent physiological structure but to the effects exercised upon members of various groups by the cultural conditions under which they are reared" (LW 13: 76). Note that he puts the word "race" in quotation marks— a strategy that he occasionally makes use of in order to show his skepticism and critical distance toward the prevailing usage of the term in debates that were apparent in his time. Dewey does not deny the influence of native individual differences, but he argues that collective and cultural differences cannot be explained on the grounds of biological heredity but only in terms of social and cultural influences:

> [B]iological heredity and native individual differences . . . operate within a given social form, they are shaped and take effect *within* that particular form. They are not indigenous traits that mark off one people, one group, one class, from another, but mark differences in every group. Whatever the "white man's burden," it was not imposed by heredity.
>
> (LW 13: 77)

And on another occasion he points out that "race" is an abstract idea. Although this idea has been influential in society and history, it must be regarded as a mythical construction from the standpoint of social and cultural science (see MW 13: 438).

Dewey's critical attitude toward the prevailing "race" discourses of his time is closely connected with his democratic vision. He believed that democracy as a way of life stands and falls with the general and undivided "belief in the potentialities of human nature" (LW 13: 153) or the "belief in the potentialities of every human being" (LW 14: 276). He insists that this humanistic and democratic attitude is put at risk by the social dismissal and intolerance that frequently emerge from labeling certain persons or groups in terms of "race," class, origin, religion etc. His rejection is unequivocal when he writes, e.g., in *Freedom and Culture*:

There is no physical acid which has the corrosive power possessed by intolerance directed against persons because they belong to a group that bears a certain name. Its corrosive potency gains with what it feeds on. An anti-humanist attitude is the essence of every form of intolerance. Movements that begin by stirring up hostility against a group of people end by denying to them all human qualities.

(LW 13: 153)

These lines were of course written with an eye to the fascist dictatorships in Europe of that time. But in the same breath, Dewey expresses his concern that American democracy is not only threatened from outside, but that the challenge and danger of intolerance first of all has to be faced and struggled against at home. He points to "racial prejudice" against African Americans—using the language of his time, Dewey speaks of "Negroes" or "colored people"—, Catholics, and Jews that has a history in American life. He claims that its present appearance represents not only a weakness of democracy, but even "a handle for the accusation that we do not act differently from Nazi Germany" (LW 13: 153). And in the 1941 short essay "The Basic Values and Loyalties of Democracy," Dewey observes that the American heritage of slavery and the use of religion to foster anti-Semitism have produced habits of racial intolerance and prejudice that continue to put the foundations of democracy at risk (cf. LW 14: 277). Lastly, Dewey develops a similar line of self-critical argumentation in the 1938 essay "Democracy and Education in the World of Today." In addition, he directly exposes the issue of "racial intolerance" as an educational challenge when he writes:

We are unfortunately familiar with the tragic racial intolerance of Germany and now of Italy. Are we entirely free from that racial intolerance, so that we can pride ourselves upon having achieved a complete democracy? Our treatment of the Negroes, anti-Semitism, the growing (at least I fear it is growing) serious opposition to the alien immigrant within our gates, is, I think, a sufficient answer to that question. Here, in relation to education, we have a problem; what are our schools doing to cultivate not merely passive toleration that will put up with people of different racial birth or different colored skin, but what are our schools doing positively and aggressively and constructively to cultivate understanding and goodwill which are essential to democratic society?

(LW 13: 301)

Democracy and education must respond to that problem. The challenge remains in our time, as we will point out later in this chapter.

Gender

Dewey lived in a patriarchal society with vibrant feminist movements. As in the case of "racism," it is clear from his works as well as correspondences that he was aware of feminist causes of his time, although he did not write extensively about them and only occasionally addressed issues of gender in substantial or somewhat systematic ways. In word and action, he supported important feminist issues like women's right to vote (see Westbrook, 1991: 167). One famous anecdote regarding the suffragette movement of the early twentieth century tells the story of the already well-known public intellectual Dewey carrying a poster that read, "Men can vote—Why can't I?" while he was walking with a march of protesters through the streets of New York City. His long-time acquaintance and cooperation with influential feminist intellectuals and reformers like Jane Addams at Hull House in Chicago helped him to deepen his sensitivity for issues of gender—probably more so than the average white, male philosopher of his time would have shown. Although he did not systematically and persistently question or criticize the underlying male-dominated structure of the society in which he lived or the academic and public culture in which he worked, his philosophy and political outlook were often sympathetic and supportive of women's issues. As Charlene Haddock Seigfried, one of the most influential pragmatist feminists of our time, has observed:

> Dewey's political activism included support for the many women's issues for which feminists were campaigning at the time, including women's suffrage, women's right to higher education and coeducation, unimpeded access to and legalization of birth control, and just wages and worker control of the conditions of work for women as well as men. Explicit references in his philosophical writings to issues as they differentially affect women or to feminist theory are sporadic but insightful and consistently supportive.
>
> (Seigfried, 2002: 48)

Seigfried goes on to argue that such feminist perspectives in Dewey are consistent with his pragmatism. Dewey himself had a clear understanding that a philosophy of experience—in the generous social sense that we have already discussed throughout the different chapters of this book—must of necessity be a pluralistic philosophy that appreciates the diversity of standpoints involved in the social process and that recognizes differences as a chance and resource for growth. With regard to gender difference, he explicitly observed:

> Women have as yet made little contribution to philosophy. But when women who are not mere students of other persons' philosophy set out to write it, we cannot conceive that it will be the same in viewpoint or tenor as that composed from the standpoint of the different masculine experience of things.
>
> (MW 11: 45)

Such feminist insights have been used as starting-points for constructing more explicit forms of Deweyan pragmatist feminism until today, as becomes evident in the work of Seigfried (2002) and many others.

> Pragmatist theory itself provides strong resources for feminist thinking, since many of its positions address current feminist interests and debates. Among these are a pluralism and perspectivism that go beyond theory to advocate the actual inclusiveness of appropriately diverse viewpoints, including those of class, color, ethnicity, and gender, as a precondition for resolving problematic situations . . . The pragmatic understanding of the developmental processes that characterize persons who dynamically interact with their physical and social environments dissolves a knot of problems evident in controversies over feminist standpoint theories as well as over the oscillation between affirming the individual subject as a unique Promethean entity or as a passive social construct.
>
> (Seigfried, 2002: 48)

On the other hand, though, Seigfried also observes and examines some important shortcomings in Dewey's treatment of social relations—and especially power relations—regarding differences like class, race, and gender. Three points deserve notice, here. First, Dewey often shows a tendency to (mis-)interpret conflicts of power as lack of common understanding about interests. "By locating conflicts in different approaches to life and not in struggles for power, he frequently underestimates what is required to overcome them. He seems to think that once someone has participated in a rational process of inquiry, she or he would not persist in holding onto prejudices or unilateral power." Therefore, "his analyses often do not go far enough" (Seigfried, 2002: 55 f.). Second, like many Marxists and other critics of his time, Dewey focuses his cultural criticism on economic inequalities and oppression. Compared with this overall concern with capitalism, though, he often rather tends to underestimate processes of discrimination and marginalization, e.g., due to racism (see also Sullivan, 2003) and gender prejudice. Seigfried believes that Dewey's rather optimistic views about social cooperation and goodwill lead him "to underestimate the extent and depth of misogyny, racism, homophobia, and classism in personal habits and social institutions" (Seigfried, 2002: 55). Seen from today's perspective, social developments and political movements like feminism, civil rights, and other minority movements sharpened our awareness in the course of the twentieth century of the complexities of power relations in late-capitalist societies or liquid modernity. For example, the complex intersections of classism, racism, and sexism (e.g., misogyny and homophobia)—as relatively independent lines of power that cannot be simply reduced to one another—have become the theme of many critical analyses of contemporary multicultural societies (see, e.g., Bradley, 1992). Third, as Seigfried observes, Dewey often "fails to follow through with an account of the role that power plays in human affairs". Especially, he does not sufficiently explore "in detail how it alters the lives of those affected by it" (Seigfried, 2002: 55), i.e., the consequences of power asymmetries in the experiences of those who are discriminated against or marginalized. A contemporary and reconstructed Deweyan approach to democracy and education that responds to the challenges of our time must go further, in this respect, and constructively address, as well as critically reflect, the multiple articulations and representations of diverse experiences in increasingly globalized multicultural societies. It must particularly address and respond to the marginalized or misrepresented voices of those who stand outside the mainstream of society—those whose lives are in danger of being wasted (see Bauman, 2004) and whose experiences are often particularly precarious, ambivalent, ambiguous, and often contradictory because of their in-between positions regarding culture and power (see Bhabha, 1996). Seigfried argues that Deweyan pragmatism has always been a hospitable philosophical perspective for the articulation of such diverse experiences—including the voices of the marginalized—even if Dewey himself has not always been prepared to "follow through."

> Women of many different ethnic groups and classes, and other groups whose lives were severely circumscribed by convention and who bore the brunt of sexist, ethnic, and racial prejudices, found a powerful resource in a philosophical position that questioned rather than justified convention and whose goal was transformation of given conditions to better meet the just needs of individuals and communities.
>
> (Seigfried, 2002: 51)

It remains to be said that, from today's perspective, what has been observed above about the necessary recognition and appreciation of female experiences and perspectives in pragmatic philosophy applies as well to the inclusion of LGBT or other gendered experiences and perspectives lest we abandon the necessary claim to philosophical pluralism as the basis for democracy and education.

Disability

As might be guessed with a sense for the historical emergence and articulation of problems, Dewey, in his time, never directly addressed issues of disability in connection with education in ways that would be comparable to what has become commonplace today in debates around special needs or inclusive education worldwide. Even less than with the case of "race," he did not address "disability" systematically as a potential axis of exclusion and discrimination in society and as a challenge for education. However, his general social philosophy and his approach to education as necessarily connected with democracy can provide many indirect clues and theoretical resources for current debates and developments. We start by looking at some of these clues and resources and discussing some of their important implications for educational philosophy. Generally speaking, we agree with John McDermott (1992) that the full inclusion of the handicapped would have pleased Dewey.

We will gather these clues and resources from topics discussed in earlier chapters. Of these, perhaps the most essential is Dewey's overcoming of the nature-versus-culture dualism and avoidance of reductionism. However, no less important is the notion of moral equality that connects to Dewey's ideas about growth, unique potential, and the development of capacities. This notion of equality brings us in direct contact with Dewey's unique notion of liberal, pluralistic, and communicative democracy, which allows him to respond much better to issues of diversity than traditional liberal notions of democracy. We have noted some elements of Dewey's critique of classical liberalism, and we will identify some more below. This critique equally applies to what we now call neoliberalism.

Danforth contends that debates regarding disability "hinge on a deep philosophical conflict between two different theories" (Danforth, 2008: 45). The first and traditionally dominant perspective is "an individual or medical concept" (Danforth, 2008: 45). Lekan calls it a "medical model of disabilities—treating these as biological defects that need to be corrected or mitigated" (Lekan, 2009: 215). The second is a "social constructionist orientation" (Danforth, 2008: 46).

The medical model assumes disability is an individual natural (i.e., biological) deficit we must treat through clinical diagnosis validated by psychometric measures (e.g., IQ tests) and cure or ameliorate in special classes apart from the mainstream. This approach reduces disability to natural phenomena; indeed, to a test score assumed to have construct validity according to a natural and fixed hierarchy that we may determine quantitatively. It ignores qualitative individuality. The second stance, one much closer to our own, asserts that disability is a social phenomenon. Here disabilities are conceived as "social phenomena that take shape and gain meaning within social processes and political structures" (Danforth, 2008: 46). Social constructivists conceive of disability as the result of linguistic, social, and political interpretation. Social constructionists shift the discourse away from pathology and treatment to democratic inclusion where we may not only tolerate a plurality of individual differences, but also appreciate and value them. As Lekan remarks, in Dewey's notion of growth, the disabled, indeed all students, achieve a moral position that allows them to "conceive of themselves as members of a community that values their contributions" (Lekan, 2009: 225).

Danforth identifies three Deweyan theses that allow us to balance the claims of both the medical model and social constructivists. We have already discussed all of these earlier in our book. First, Dewey rejects the "bifurcation of the natural and social" (Danforth, 2008: 51). This refutes the reductivist claims of the medical model. Danforth's reflections on Dewey resemble our own. He too calls attention to Dewey's emphasis on emergence. Culture and language themselves are natural, but with their emergence everything is transformed. Danforth reminds us of Dewey's conviction that "in the social the physical is taken up into a wider and more complex and delicate system of interactions so that it takes on new properties by release of potentialities previously confined because of the absence of full interaction" (LW 3: 47–48). Recall that Dewey rejects the idea of latent potentials in favor of the concept that we may only actualize potentials through interaction, which requires diversity and difference. This connects to the second Deweyan thesis Danforth discusses, which is the continuity of growth.

In Chapter 4, we saw that, although growth is the aim of education for Dewey, it is non-teleological; we have no fixed essence that we must develop. Lekan comments:

> Dewey's sense is not about developing those qualities that constitute some fixed species essence. For Dewey, growth is more radically individual. Whether a person is growing—and thus attaining an acceptable level of well-being—is determined by an idea of optimal functioning according to his or her own unique capacities.
>
> (Lekan, 2009: 220)

Lekan contrasts this "radical individualism" with traditional "liberal individu-alist" theories, which assume a human essence that predetermines the *telos* of development (Lekan, 2009: 220 ff.). Dewey's rejection of the very notion of a fixed human nature has a further consequence. As Danforth recognizes, "Dewey rendered the nature/nurture dichotomy useless" (Danforth, 2008: 53). In Chapter 1, we discussed the notion of cultivating one's garden. Because human nature is a part of the endlessly evolving interaction of events comprising nature, human nature is something we may nurture culturally.

The third thesis identified by Danforth is moral equality in democracy, which we also discussed in Chapter 4. Each individual is unique and incommensurable with every other. We have seen that understanding equality as sameness easily leads to social injustice. Sadly, it also leads us to underdevelopment of human capabilities and capacities. "Moral equality," Danforth indicates, "means that individuals are uniquely diversified in capacities, interests, and tastes such that comparisons between individuals on external standards of evaluation are not feasible" (Danforth, 2008: 55). It is a terrible mistake to think of human potential and capacity as fixed. The mistake, according to Lekan, would be "to ignore needed change in social conditions conducive to equal opportunity on the dubious grounds that some people are biologically barred from genuine growth" (Lekan, 2009: 221). Ironically, if we were to develop unique human potential to make its unique contribution, we could develop human capacities in ways that are not only morally and aesthetically worthwhile, but even materially rewarding as well. Our narrow notions of "human capital" are as socially imprudent as they are morally questionable from a democratic point of view. Their main justification is preserving the power of a privileged few in liquid modernity. It is here that we may identify some more of the problems with traditional liberal and current neoliberal theory.

We have already seen that Dewey decries many of the tenets of classical democratic liberalism—which extend to contemporary neoliberalism—including egoistic, unhistorical, context-blind, and atomistic individualism. He also rejects innate free will along with innate rationality and the liberal individualist theories that conceive equal rights as treating everyone the same. However, treating everyone the same when everyone is actually different is sure to secure inequality, since everyone has different needs and abilities. As Lekan indicates, Dewey's notion of growth is informed by an idea of optimal functioning according to the individual's own unique capacities (see Lekan, 2009: 220). As we saw in Chapters 3 and 6, the emphasis on moral equality of individual capacities makes Dewey's individualism more radical than that of traditional liberalism:

> Each person is a unique conflux of capabilities. Dewey would urge that this conflux is dependent on a variety of factors including the biological, psychological, and social dimensions of a person's life. Whatever else it is, individual growth consists in the successful exercise of capacities in the context of social functions. Given the rich, variegated permutation of factors that determine individual growth, evaluations about how well a person is growing must be made relative to that same individual's unique capacities.
>
> (Lekan, 2009: 221)

This observation holds for different cultures, genders, sexual orientations, or social classes or milieus as well as physical disabilities. Once we realize that the task of education is to actualize every individual's unique potential to make their unique social contribution, it is easy to see that while some populations require special consideration because of historical oppression, their demands are merely a special, and especially important, instance of democratic inclusion for all, which we will discuss in Chapter 11.

We may sum up some of the core implications of this chapter for a philosophy of democracy and education by drawing on three specifically pregnant passages from Dewey's writings in which he reflects on the meaning of equality as a democratic principle that stands against all forms of homogenization, reduction to fixed standards, one-size-fits-all procedures, as well as other forms of discrimination and exclusion of individuals and groups from full and generous participation in social life and growth. In his 1919 essay "Philosophy and Democracy," Dewey observes that the principle of equality means "a world in which an existence must be reckoned with on its own account, not as something capable of equation with and transformation into something else." It means a world "of the incommensurable in which each speaks for itself and demands consideration on its own behalf" (MW 11: 53). He further explores the democratic implications of equality when he observes, in his 1939 essay "Creative Democracy—the Task Before Us," that the "democratic faith in equality is belief that every human being, independent of the quantity or range of his [or her] personal endowment, has the right to equal opportunity with every other person for development of whatever gifts he [or she] has" (LW 14: 226 f.). And he draws the fundamental educational conclusion from this democratic vision of equality in his 1938 essay "Democracy and Education in the World of Today," when he points to the necessity of including the diverse experiences of all learners in participatory ways in order to make the classroom truly democratic:

> Even in the classroom we are beginning to learn that learning which develops intelligence and character does not come about when only the textbook and the teacher have a say; that every individual becomes educated only as he [or she] has an opportunity to contribute something from his [or her] own experience, no matter how meager or slender that background of experience may be at a given time; and finally that enlightenment comes from the give and take, from the exchange of experiences and ideas.
>
> (LW 13: 296)

Challenge for Today: Diversity as Opportunity and Risk

In liquid modernity, many proponents in fields like research on social inequality, cultural and postcolonial studies, gender and queer studies, disabilities studies, or other fields have developed powerful accounts and theoretical reflections on the experiences of those who live in ambivalent positions of inclusion and exclusion. They articulate minority positions in today's societies. These articulations must be seen against the background of historical developments including, for instance, the diverse social and political movements around issues of human rights, civil rights, feminism, claims for equality and equity, and claims for inclusion and participation. They also evoke an increased sensitivity for cultural diversity articulated especially through the often ambivalent and contradictory experiences of immigrants and other cultural minorities or marginalized groups. We believe that in the contexts of globalization these developments have become apparent in nearly all contemporary societies. They pose new challenges for Deweyan democracy and education.

According to Deweyan pragmatism, the openness to dissent as well as the willingness to cooperate across differences and to see the expression of difference as a potential enrichment of one's own life-experience is a necessary part of "the democratic way of life" (LW 14: 288). From the perspective of this fundamental democratic claim, the articulation and interpretation of experiences of marginalized groups can be seen as a challenge to continually further develop our sensitivity and openness to the precariousness that goes with diversity. The rich pragmatic understanding of experience as starting point and key concept of philosophical reflection is a particular advantage of pragmatism over many other contemporary approaches to welcome and take in the diverse articulations of living in cultures in all their ambiguity, ambivalence and contradiction (see Neubert 2012b, 148).

Dewey urges us to attend to the contingency of such social constructions as "class," "race," "gender," or "disability," while noting their inevitable ambivalences and their actual effects in social practices. In this context, we must connect the movement towards inclusion in education with the more general movement toward inclusion and participation in society. We must never separate education and democracy. Generally speaking, inclusion means the active and constructive struggle against discrimination in all forms and all contexts. This implies, for example, programs against exclusion not only in schools but also in many other social institutions like government, administration, companies, public life, etc. On the level of United Nations politics, we should mention the 2006 "Convention on the Rights of Persons with Disabilities," because it clearly states all subscribing countries must take measures for the inclusive and sustainable participation of people with disabilities or disadvantages in all areas of social life.

In education, international programs for equity commonly focus on five principles of participation and anti-discrimination. In these programs there is always a response to class, race, gender, and disability. Inclusive education in this sense is a necessary component of democracy (Toronto District School Board, 2011):

(1) *Ethno-cultural Equity and Antiracism*: A core demand of inclusive education is the recognition and appreciation of cultural and linguistic diversity as a resource of democratic living together and mutual growth. Diversity includes heterogeneity in the sense of the experience of difference as a necessary component of democratic experience. It also includes pluralism as an attitude of openness for varieties of experiences and perspectives. This always entails the necessary tolerance of ambivalences, ambiguities, uncertainties, and openness in social experience as a fundamental democratic attitude. Moreover, this attitude involves the will to live with differences and controversies while having productive contentions between opposing perspectives, interests, interpretations, etc., without using violence and negating the legitimate articulation of opposing opinions. As stated by the Equity Foundation Statement of the Toronto District School Board about the measures to be taken: "These shall reflect the diverse viewpoints, needs, and aspirations of community members, particularly those of aboriginal, racial, ethno-cultural, and faith groups whose voices traditionally and systemically have been marginalized and excluded" (4). We find a touchstone for the achievement of ethno-cultural equity in the degree to which we regard a person's ethnic background as irrelevant in comparison to the relevance of individual experience, achievement, and growth in and for education. Racism—even when we substitute the biological term "race" with a discriminatory use of cultural stereotypes—is, of course, a chief menace to cultural equity.

(2) *Gender Equity and Anti-sexism*: The modern heritage of constructing fixed order and homogenous groups constituted by binary oppositions has been particularly strong in the constructed difference of male and female as a social and apparently "natural" distinction. The distinction, however, is never simply given by nature. It is a powerful social distinction that produces and reproduces social power relations. The deconstruction of this discursive formation has even shown for some that not only the term "gender" but also the term "sex" is part of discourse and culturally constructed. Sexism is the name for all the diverse forms of discrimination that go with the distinction and definition of male and female. Like racism, we must consider it a main challenge and thread for inclusive education. For example, the Toronto statement mandates:

> [P]olicies, guidelines, and practices shall ensure that the needs and safety of all students, employees, trustees, parents, volunteers, visitors, permit-holders, contractors, and partners are addressed. These shall reflect the diverse viewpoints, needs, and aspirations of community members, particularly women whose voices traditionally and systemically have been marginalized and excluded. This includes aboriginal, racial, ethno-cultural, faith, lesbian, bisexual, transgender, disabled, working class, low-income, poor, and other historically-disadvantaged groups of women.
>
> (8)

Among other things, it is necessary to connect the recognition and appreciation of gender diversity with sensitiveness for the import of cultural and linguistic diversity along with awareness of discriminatory practices on the levels of culture and language. We must also complement it with active programs against sexual and gender harassment.

(3) *Diversity in Sexual Orientations and Anti-homophobia*: Inclusion must provide opportunities for the recognition and appreciation of diverse ways of living, including diverse sexual orientations and forms of sexual identity. Like racism and sexism, homophobia constitutes a major threat to democratic inclusion and participation of all. For example, the Toronto School Board claims for its measures:

> These shall reflect the diverse viewpoints, needs, and aspirations of members of these communities, particularly those of groups whose voices traditionally and systemically have been marginalized and excluded on the basis of their sexual orientation. This includes lesbians, gay men, bisexuals, two-spirited, transsexual, and transgender people and their families.
>
> (13)

Among other things, active programs against bullying and for social learning and competent conflict management must complement the attitude of anti-homophobia.

(4) *Socio-Economic Equity and Anti-classism*: The correlation between low socio-economic status and educational disadvantage calls for specific and deliberate measures for including marginalized and excluded students. The first among these measures is an attitude of solidarity among all in school and society. This attitude must be complemented by active programs to further equal opportunities and equity in education that include all socially and economically marginalized groups in society. Society must take measures to secure sufficient funding, and it is a fundamental claim of democracy and education that societies and governments increase the resources and financial support of a sustainable education for all. Among other things, inclusive schools should provide sufficient opportunities for learning in heterogeneous groups based on participation in shared resources, projects, communities, learning, and decision-making processes. It also involves active strategies for connecting the school with its urban or regional environments in all their diverse social and cultural aspects. The continuity in the experience of learners between learning and communicating outside and inside school, as well as across the artificial borders between the two, is of specific importance for the growth of learners from marginalized groups and relatively poor neighborhoods. Continual communication and cooperation between the school, the home, and the community-at-large is a precondition for contextualized schooling. Again, this includes a necessary sensitivity for the importance of language and linguistic differences and the development of multi-literacies (cf. Cope & Kalantzis, 2013). One key element in the furthering of inclusive education is the appreciation as well as cultivation of language skills.

(5) *Equity for Persons with Disability*: Traditionally in modern societies, disability in many different forms has been considered a personal characteristic—given by "nature" or accident—that constitutes specific educational needs and makes specific measures necessary, often accompanied by processes of exclusion and marginalization. Many such cases of exclusion and marginalization are even legitimated on behalf of their supposed benefit to the disabled. Inclusive education starts with a necessary paradigm shift away from this discursive formation. We must recognize, in the first place, that disability is a social construction with powerful social and individual consequences and not something given by nature or only inherent in a person. To some degree, we may say that the actual handicap or disability also lies in the practices of social communication, interaction, participation—all of these constituted and framed by institutional settings. To speak more concretely, the perspective of inclusion suggests that the handicap appears not only in the immobility of a person sitting in a wheelchair but also in the lack of an elevator in a

building. This critical turn has found expression in and is supported by statements and standards of the World Health Organization like the following:

> Disability is thus not just a health problem. It is a complex phenom-enon, reflecting the interaction between features of a person's body and features of the society in which he or she lives. Overcoming the difficulties faced by people with disabilities requires interventions to remove environmental and social barriers.
>
> (WHO, 2014)

Among other things, the attitude to include persons with disabilities must be complemented by active measures that cover areas from the school architecture to a general and generous community spirit and to concrete anti-bullying pro-grams. It is necessary for all learners as well as teachers, parents, and other people involved in inclusion, that they have sufficient opportunities to develop and further their social and individual competencies including knowledge as well as lived relationships. For all five of these—and other possible—principles it remains to emphasize that for democracy and education and for the realization of all specific measures one thing is of extreme importance, namely, that there is a general culture of communication and transparency that allows for participation as an "ongoing, constructive, and open dialogue in partnership" (Toronto District School Board, 2011: 14).

We need concepts and instruments to realize and continually evaluate these standards in inclusive practices (cf. Chapter 11). From a pragmatic perspective like Dewey's and from our interactive constructivist perspective today, education must consider such concepts, instruments, and standards as constructions requiring testing by application and continual reconstruction to improve inclusive practices and democratic participation.

Our Summary

"Democracy and Education" is essentially a program against discrimination in all possible forms. Dewey was critical of all forms of social injustice in his time and he often addressed issues of inequalities that threaten democratic living together. We have shown in our chapter that Dewey was very eloquent on class, while he did not say or write so much on race, gender, and disability. His concerns with the tension between capitalism and democracy still resonate with current challenges in our time. His insistence on the idea of equal opportunities in society and education and his powerful definition of education as personal and social growth that must include all in a democracy stand against exclusions, divisions, compartmentalizations that obstruct communication and exchange between individuals, groups, and societies. It is a strong argument for living in and with diversity. As we have seen, Dewey occasionally addressed problems of race and gender discrimination. But seen from today's perspective, his commentaries and criticisms on these issues are relatively scarce. Regarding disability, we found that he did not even anticipate issues and themes that today we find discussed under the names of special needs and inclusive education. With regard to all of these questions, however, his philosophy of democracy and education bears many fruitful insights by implication. For today, the task remains to take all forms of actual and potential discrimination seriously. Democracy and education necessarily include responses to current politics of identity and difference. Diversity and inclusion have become programs and orientations shared by many on a global scale to realize basic human and democratic rights. To the present day they pose challenges to educational reform in all countries.

Note

1   For a more comprehensive discussion, see Neubert (2012c). The following account partly draws on the arguments given there.

10
CAPITALS AS CONTEXTS FOR EDUCATION

Dewey was a lifelong advocate of "industrial democracy," i.e., he supported industrial competency, participation, and reconstruction along with citizenship.[1] He insisted on workers possessing critical and creative industrial intelligence that they might be masters of their own working life and fate. In this chapter, we consider capitals as contexts for education in twenty-first-century societies and the global economy. We intend to juxtapose and critically compare two perspectives on the contexts of capital in experience. We start by briefly reconstructing a Deweyan view on the tensions of production and consumption implied by the capitalist order of his time. For a second perspective this chapter draws on the argumentation in Reich (2013), who connects with the well-known approach of Pierre Bourdieu while also extending his concepts and categories. By drawing conclusions from the juxtaposition of these two perspectives, we approach the challenge for today which seems to us to consist in critically addressing the pervasive connections and tensions between capitalism, democracy, and education.

Dewey developed an evaluative approach based on his general understanding of experience, education, society, and culture to show how economic conditions affect the actualization of human potential and the development of capacities. His thinking was guided by democratic ideals of participation, social intelligence, and social self-actualization of individuals in diversity. He believed democratic self-government means individuals as partakers in groups, communities, and societies must be masters of their own lives and destinies in all social domains including, among others, the workplace and the school. We will examine necessary competencies of self-actualization in terms of capitals as contexts of education and learning. We will also draw on Dewey's idea that it is not only production, but equally the quality of creative and consummatory experience that "supplies a criterion for evaluating any particular economic state and operation" (MW 15: 251). Ultimately, we may only measure the worth of any economic regime by the quality of the life of every individual in it.

Before examining capitals in the contemporary economic context, let us look at how Dewey derives his criterion of economic evaluation. Economic demands emerge from biological needs, although they soon extend beyond the bound of needs into potentially endless desires and satisfactions that "gather attention, interest, and effort to themselves" (MW 15: 250). Likewise, tools supplement bodily activity in the continual readaptation of the environment to the novel needs and demands of living organisms: "These cultural or 'artificially' modified environments persist from generation to generation, and radically transform the modes in which life-process manifests itself" (MW 15: 250). Here, the "transformation of activity into *occupation* is the primary fact" where each occupation requires its specialized technology including symbol systems (MW 15: 251). This differentiation leads to the need for economic exchange.

As economies emerge and evolve, it is possible to live far beyond the Darwinian demands that we survive and mate to reproduce our species. With the emergence of increasingly complex economic interactions, human life acquires emergent properties. It is here that Dewey offers his criterion:

> The limit of the biological cycle is something that may indifferently be termed productive consumption or consummatory production. When this becomes a conscious object or meaning, it supplies a criterion for evaluating any particular economic state and operation. Does it tend toward integration of production—(energy expended in modification of environment) and consumption—(the return consequence of the external modification into life-activity)—or toward their separation?
>
> (MW 15: 251)

From a democratic point of view, individuals should experience economic production as creative self-expression, while they should experience economic consumption as productive and expansive growth—that is, as enhancing life-activity. In this way, we may avoid confusing having more with being more.

Dewey observes that when production and consumption are not integrated, "perversion" becomes evident in the "economic process," and we see such things as "drudgery," separation of mind (supervisors) from body (workers), "[p]ower and irresponsibility," "[c]ast and outcast," "excessive specialization," enormous concentrations of capital, and control confined to "media of exchange" (MW 15: 253). Morally, consummatory productive consumption (to combine Dewey's two phrases) is "subordinated to processes of distributive exchange" (MW 15: 254). Wants are multiplied, but often not subject to personal cultivation and control: "Many capacities, scientific and artistic, are not converted into wants for lack of opportunity, and because of excess stimulation of wants connected with money and material success" (MW 15: 261–262). Further, there is "no art in consumption" while the "field of consumption" is "hardly touched by technology and science" and psychology is "developed so far only in reference to production and selling" (MW 15: 262). Worse still is the "failure of education" for the "consumer" (MW 15: 261). We may learn to consume, but not how to consume with aesthetic taste, moral reflection, or cognitive comprehension. In view of ecological crises and debates of our time, this approach to consumer awareness may seem visionary.

While the passages from Dewey's writing quoted so far were written in the early 1920s, he later intensified his critical observations about the tensions and contradictions between capitalism and democracy, especially after the experience of the 1929 Great Depression. Dewey is not denying the achievements of capitalism, although he sharply critiques many of its contemporary characteristics. Among other things, he expands and refines his advocacy for the idea of a planning society versus the planned society of state socialism or the unplanned society of laissez faire capitalism. Likewise, he argues that the social production and application of intelligence as an instrument for democratic reform is necessary:

> The essential fact is that if both democracy and capitalism are on trial, it is in reality our collective intelligence which is on trial. We have displayed enough intelligence in the physical field to create the new and powerful instrument of science and technology. We have not as yet had enough intelligence to use this instrument deliberately and systematically to control its social operations and consequences.
>
> (LW 6: 60)

Dewey further believes that reform and reconstruction must operate on the concrete level of everyday working life:

> It makes a difference whether his work is relatively regular and his reward dependent upon his own exertions, or whether it is uncertain and dependent largely upon market conditions over which the individual worker has no control. And finally it makes a difference whether his relations with his fellow workers or employers are of a family or neighborly or friendly character, or whether the relation is purely impersonal and the motive for work is the acquisition of money in some form as wage or salary or profits.
>
> (LW 7: 374)

Dewey already observed (cf. MW 5: 149) and criticized the enormous gap between rich and poor in his time. Since then, this gap has increased immensely on local and global levels (see Stiglitz, 2012; 2015). Therefore, social and economic relations can only be restructured toward the democratic ideal of greater justice with the help of measures of redistribution:

> We have seen that capitalism has proved to be an effective method of increasing the total wealth and income of the countries in which it has had its fullest trial. The question which has been raised with increasing insistence is, how are the wealth and income distributed among the different members of the various peoples under this system? This is to raise the question of justice.
>
> (LW 7: 406)

In part, this democratic project or vision of a third way between and beyond laissez faire capitalism and state socialism implies, for Dewey, that capitalism may have many faces and that it is possible to confine its excesses and inhuman brutalities by democratic means: The challenge is to deepen democracy and modify capitalism in ways "in which the democratic principle, embodied in our political and educational systems, shall have increasing recognition, and in which liberty, efficiency, and justice shall be combined so far as possible" (LW 7: 428).

Regarding social philosophy, Dewey believes we cannot develop the actions we need from fixed dogma. A society may only achieve democratic reconstruction by continuous planning and experimentation. This conviction applies to all social institutions including government, parliament, courts, marketplace, media, communities, schools, the family, the public, etc.

> There is an undoubted objective clash of interests between finance-capitalism that controls the means of production and whose profit is served by maintaining relative scarcity, and idle workers and hungry consumers. But what generates violent strife is failure to bring the conflict into the light of intelligence where the conflicting interests can be adjudicated in behalf of the interest of the great majority. Those most committed to the dogma of inevitable force recognize the need for intelligently discovering and expressing the dominant social interest up to a certain point and then draw back. The "experimentalist" is one who would see to it that the method depended upon by all in some degree in every democratic community be followed through to completion.
>
> (LW 11: 56)

In capitalist societies, such reconstruction necessarily involves conflict of interests and the restriction of the few with powerful resources by articulating the interests of the great majority while making their claims and needs effective.

In his influential 1935 book *Liberalism and Social Action*, Dewey argues that the democratic reconstructions necessary for new forms of individual and social self-government in twentieth-century societies must imply the socialization and effective intelligent public control over the main productive forces. He believes that liberalism becomes a delusion if it just repeats the old individualistic phrases of early modernity and does not take into account the complex and immensely interrelated conditions of life in twentieth-century capitalism:

> But the cause of liberalism will be lost for a considerable period if it is not prepared to go further and socialize the forces of production, now at hand, so that the liberty of individuals will be supported by the very structure of economic organization.
>
> (LW 11: 61–62)

The tension between democracy and capitalism, as Dewey saw it, was essentially a tension between lived experience and market mechanisms. On the one hand, we have values as experienced and used; on the other hand, we have values as standardized, traded, exchanged. On the one hand, we have diversity, uniqueness, and incommensurability; on the other, we have homogenization, measurement, and comparison. Dewey reflects this basic tension in many details when he, for example, discusses the price system in the market. This system "specifies demands in exchange and makes them comparable to one another; exchange values are subject to quantitative measurement." There are no such "measures for values-in-use or consumption." Hence, "the system of values-in-use gets accommodated to the system of exchange values" that results in a "conflict of quantitative measurement of objects and services, and qualitative character of wants and actual satisfactions" (MW 15: 262). Of course, we may try to indirectly assess use value in terms of exchange value, but the results are always reductive. You may love someone dearly, but flowers given per unit of time is a comically, or perhaps tragically, reductive measure.

Dewey distinguishes human values from economic values. While the tension between experience and the market is inevitable, this must not be understood in the simple form of a dualism between two fixed oppositions. Rather, they are mutually related and the important thing is the interaction between them. Dewey argues that human values do not exist ready-made, but are subject to the vicissitudes of context, which include market conditions in a capitalist society. Both sides are alterable, subject to reflection, social intelligence, and democratic measures.

Challenge for Today: Surplus Values and the Capitalization of all Spheres of Life

We now turn to a contemporary view on the role of capitals in democracy and society. We begin by formulating a working definition of capitals. Capitals have value (such as real estate, tools, and raw materials as means of production) that we utilize to maintain and increase value. To increase capital as private property requires labor, raw materials, a site of production or provision of service, and a market in which we may exchange the increased value and convert it into money. It is either a possession (someone has capital) or a value intended to generate new values (an investment promising the investor a profit). Originally, the Latin lexeme *caput* (= head) referred to herds of cattle, where the number of cattle head indicated the owner's direct wealth. However, over the course of time, the scope of what capital economically designates has immensely enlarged. From head of cattle, it came to designate all means of production employed in producing commodities and goods or services aimed at generating profit. Such means of production are the property of the capitalist, of those who put their capital to use by utilization of tools, machines, and wage-labor to produce or maintain something or offer a service. All capitals are finite, hence scarce and unequally distributed. Since their possession or lack affects life opportunities of individuals and societies, every person in capitalist society faces the unavoidable necessity of engaging with capital in all its forms—including critical and creative ways of using and exchanging it.

In the interactions of an ever more complex capitalist society increasingly determined by the employment of capital, economic capital morphs into many different forms to achieve a profit. In commercial transactions we consider money as capital when it represents possibilities for investment in means of production and the hiring of wage-labor to extract profit. Strictly speaking, only by such use does money become capital. Profits can derive from a wide and constantly expanding range of categories, like bank savings, stocks and bonds, funds, entrepreneurial activity, provision of credit, and such. Against this background, we must recognize that capital always realizes itself in forms of exchange values and, fundamentally, has to do with the growth of surplus values.

However, the very distinction between use and exchange values is not confined to strictly material goods but extends considerably—since social living together constitutes a net of interrelated and interdependent activities—to potentially all resources of experience and the social. Such resources obviously have use value for those who employ them in their activities. But in a capitalist society, the market is the place where they will become exchange values. It is part of the development of capitalism in modern society that more and more resources of living get involved in the market mechanisms. Therefore, we can observe diverse forms of capital.

In his *Forms of Capital*, Pierre Bourdieu (1986) distinguishes economic capital from social and cultural capital, thereby asserting that economic capital is the fundamental form for determining capitalistic production. Constantly striving toward an expanding surplus, economic capital has complex emergent effects because it provides a framework for structuring the social world. Human communication and cooperation are constantly under the constraints of economic capital. However, for Bourdieu, the concept of economic capital is no longer sufficient for describing contemporary forms of capital. He became aware of these alternatives while doing empirical studies. He noticed, for instance, different levels of achievement in school by children from different family backgrounds. He discovered that the equality so loudly proclaimed in capitalist societies proved illusionary regarding the actually achieved level of schooling or career (cf. Bourdieu & Passeron, 1988).

An adequate understanding of Bourdieu's three forms of capital requires the companion ideas of habitus and field. Habitus depicts an individual's behavior, demeanor, and manner in dealing with entities and relations. It is a distinguishing feature among different social and cultural groups. According to Bourdieu, habitus encompasses an individual's particular dispositions, capacities, and competencies as a result of socialization. It provides a distinctive comportment in action including lifestyle, language, clothing, taste, and more. Field refers to the play of power within a social space among agents with diverse ends and means. It is characterized by "rules of the game" that are subject to multiple interpretation. Since the field is dynamic, economic, social, and cultural capitals are also dynamic.

Cultural capital exists in three states: embodied (capacities and dispositions of mind and body), objectified (cultural goods), and institutionalized (educational certification). It amplifies the differences between individuals' unique potentials and their life opportunities. According to Bourdieu, social classes differ significantly in cultural capital and habitus. In his study on *Distinction* (1987), he empirically describes how fields form a distinct habitus that distinguishes individuals culturally on various levels of economic wealth. To what extent cultural capital has an effect depends on available resources, individual appropriation, and modes of circulation. Successful appropriation of cultural capital imparts favorable starting positions. For example, appropriating formal educational goods (degrees, credentials, etc.) allows one to develop a habitus representative of the middle or upper class (stratum, milieu), which is a key prerequisite for the maintenance and further acquisition of economic capital that other strata cannot so easily achieve. In Bourdieu's view, the invisible modes of operation in the formation of cultural capital lie in the long-term development and shaping of this capital, which we cannot acquire from economic capital alone.

Social capital arises through membership in more or less institutionalized groups and social networks such as families, circles of friends, colleagues, and acquaintances that assist each other in a shared field of action. At birth, individuals find themselves positioned in such patterns of relations in keeping with the position attained by the family.

The individual and collective investment strategies of cultural and social capital depend significantly on the economic form of capital already present. The trend of modern institutionalization of cultural capital within educational institutions is that families alone no longer suffice to provide and amass enough cultural capital. Equally, the family no longer suffices to offer and secure the necessary social capital. To that extent, it has become increasingly important in modernity to have a "good address" in the right neighborhood to create favorable basic prerequisites of social networks for oneself and one's children.

For Bourdieu, economic, cultural, and social capitals are forces leading to strong positions of power in relation to the distribution of forces in the field. Persons rely on their habitus in acquiring and maintaining relatively stable dispositions of outlook, social perception, feeling, and desire. In practice, persons always operate on the basis of experiences and actions that utilize the habitus. It generates orientations as well as positions in a field, and works as a marker of distinction to other positions, often in hierarchical relations.

This also includes the generation and communication of immaterial symbolic differences like forms of speech, language, manner, and behavior. The symbolic dimension is potentially connected with all forms of capital. We can use our economic capital directly on the market, but we can also express it symbolically to others by the way we dress, the cars we drive, the forms in which we organize and represent our social relations and cultural aspirations. Symbolic capital can thus express and represent economic, cultural, or social capital as well as their interactions with each other. It manifests itself in obvious symbolic representations that partition social and cultural space. For example, the letters of an academically conferred title (BS, MBA, PhD, JD, MD) provide a symbolic expression of cultural capital, thereby conveying status. All components embodied or contained in forms of capital have a symbolic dimension by which they publically express themselves. Symbolic capital thus confers prestige, reputation, and recognition that help procure positions and privileges. It also implies the inferior status of those lacking such symbols, which means they are subject to hierarchical social relations in which they may undergo exploitation, for example, through economic dependence.

It is always possible, but often difficult, to exchange other forms of capital into economic capital. Conversely, we may not acquire cultural and social capital and their symbolic forms solely by means of economic exchange (e.g., money). The conversion of money into these forms of capital requires time, patience, and effort, because even if money initially facilitates access (e.g., education), follow-up costs like the investment of time and work in learning arise that money alone cannot meet. Examples also include the time and effort invested in establishing social networks, academic exchange, and such.

Bourdieu recognizes that cultural and social capitals are clearly more dynamic and uncertain in their management and handling than economic capital. We may acquire and maintain non-economic capital by sustaining sufficient effort. This includes expenditure of labor-time as in the acquisition of economic capital. According to the classical Marxist concept of capital, the value of a commodity is determined by the amount of average expended labor-time necessary for its production. Bourdieu thinks of social and cultural capital partly on the basis of this model. However, everything we cannot directly transform back into economic capital is susceptible to loss. Educational success, diplomas, and academic titles offer some protection insofar as they are usually not exposed to quick decay. Yet, if we fail to implement them economically, they may lose their exchange value over time and thus lead into dead-ends. For example, a degree in art or music from a respected academy may be a worthwhile qualification for the educated middle class, but such degrees often bring economic disadvantage (e.g., paying off student debt) if a person does not already possess sufficient economic capital. Often even hard-earned skills cannot readily and successfully establish and repay themselves in the highly competitive labor market.

Summing up, we can say that assessing the time and work expended to acquire cultural and social capital is very difficult. We can only measure its exchange value indirectly when someone exchanges it for economic capital. People don't like to boast they have their well-paid job thanks to their connections or those of their family. Rather, they tend to interpret their success as their own exceptional achievement in competition with others. They like to point to the objective diplomas and degrees earned, marking their own education.

In a supposedly liberal and just society, each individual may appear to have equal chances, but on closer examination, it is evident just how unequal the cultural, social, and economic opportunities are from the start. It is decisive for the highest possible degree of just and fair distribution whether the state takes on the role of trustee for all social interests, or whether it mainly protects and promotes the privileges of the better-off. In every case, the tendency of owners of capital is to secure and expand their privately amassed wealth while defending their cultural and social capital, their possessions, power relations, and even to represent them as necessary for human welfare in general. It is not enough to place economic capital solely in the center of focus to appropriately describe current conditions of living even if it always lies at the very core of capitalism. Other forms of capital supplement it and designate separate spheres of interest and power that we should not underestimate. This is all the more true because other forms of capital often convert the power of economic capital into supplementary resources, thus helping either to strengthen or mask it.

In Bourdieu's view (1977: 178), the logic of economic calculation essential for utilizing forms of capital extends to all material and symbolic commodities independently of whether they appear frequently or rarely in a specific social field. His interest is to analyze the conditions and practices oriented toward maximizing material or symbolic profit (Bourdieu, 1980: 209). He is not solely concerned with material exchange of goods, but also includes personal characteristics and competencies as symbolic expressions of profit maximization. However, this entails a general problem: to what extent do all social or cultural capacities and competencies become capitalized?

In this connection, it is instructive that already Dewey used the term "social capital" at the beginning of the twentieth century, for instance, in his well-known book *The School and Society*. There he addressed the wealth of social capital that exceeds and lies beyond each individual's personal experience. What he has in mind here are resources like knowledge, skills, discourses, capacities, methods, as well as social networks such as neighborhoods, the laboratory, and the workplace (MW 1: 77). He argues that the gateway to this immense wealth of social capital is through the experience of individual learners. Later he employed the same concept to designate the responsibility of society and the state to provide sufficient resources for the development of capacities especially of those at a social disadvantage (cf. MW 4: 158). Whether in the early or later period, Dewey always considered capitals as closely related to capacities for acting, participating, learning, and growing—on the individual and the social level likewise. Against this background, we believe that there is a great affinity between Dewey's and Bourdieu's approaches and that both traditions today can learn a lot from critically connecting and reconstructing their mutual perspectives.

Let us come back to the general problem mentioned above. If we speak occasionally with Dewey and systematically with Bourdieu of "social capital" or other forms of capital, in how far, then, do we imply that human resources like capacities, competencies, skills, knowledge, learning, etc., are already capitalized in current society? Must we consider everything as economically capitalized simply because a person acquires certain qualifications by learning? Is there a desire for material or symbolic benefit and profit maximization lurking behind all social transactions? Is not the inevitable consequence of thinking about use value (like capacities, qualities, and so on) as always connected with exchange value a narrow utilitarianism that reduces experiences, interaction, communication, habits, and growth to mere instrumentality? If we answer these questions positively, we arrive all too easily at what today is called "human capital" theory (cf. Becker, 1993).

Not to confuse use value like experience and exchange value like the market-place, we must have a clear criterion to distinguish non-capitalized from capitalized values. In a critical perspective, we may detect a subtle utilitarian tendency in Bourdieu's work. He observes a pervasive profit motive in all human transactions that is especially manifest in economic actions, but also appears in social and cultural fields. He does not establish a precise distinction between capitalized and non-capitalized forms of action. Rather, he always sees capitalization already manifest in the power and potency of interests and the power structure that results as the consequence of action. Bourdieu does not indicate precisely when a given socially or culturally motivated action changes into something economic, calculable, and geared by profit. The advantage of this position is that it allows one to better recognize important relationships within the field, to discern interdependencies, and to better identify and grasp the diversity of capitalized actions in the present. Yet, the concomitant disadvantage is that we easily lose the theoretical power to distinguish between different types of action. In a more comprehensive perspective, we may contrast capitals with other elements in society and culture alongside the capitalized regime of the market.

With the tension between experience and the market order we return to our earlier discussion about Deweyan perspectives on production and consumption. There is an unresolved ambiguity in the theories regarding the various forms of capital. They point in two directions:

(1) They aim to overcome narrow economic conceptions by broadening our perspectives beyond narrow market interests toward more universal human orientations. They wish to overcome the simple dualism between labor and capital, the exploited and the exploiters, by analyzing the far more diverse and culturally complex positioning of different individuals in the con-temporary fields of interest and power. At the same time, they try to unmask the illusions of value-free and objective disinterest in such fields, illusions

that are geared by liberal metaphors like the "market order," "the invisible hand," "freedom of exchange," and so on. By opening up economic capital toward other forms, it becomes possible to examine human qualities, capacities, potentials, and competencies, including, in particular, human desire (cf. Bourdieu & Wacquant, 1992; MW 15: 257).

(2) However, this deconstruction and broadening of perspectives also often leads to an imprecise view of capitalization itself. We may ask: Where is the decisive point of transformation of a human quality, competence, desire, or social power position, into an economic interest, a material or symbolic capital to produce profit? This question needs a precise answer.

The challenge is to remedy the deficiency connected with (2) without having to abandon the advantages accruing from (1). Part of the remedy draws on Dewey's criterion for evaluating any particular economic field of operation by how well it integrates production and consumption. By observing economic capital and market processes in the contexts of other forms of human interaction in culture, we can imagine how human qualities, capabilities, potentials, and competencies are being used as values for a life of expanding meaning. This includes that they are not completely reducible to economic exchange values. The decisive point of transformation of a human quality etc. into capital is the transition from use value to exchange value.

Let us take a closer look on how surplus value increases capital. We may explain the production of surplus value in detail for all forms of capital in analogy to studies of economic capital. It is important to understand that the production of surplus value always springs from a disparity of costs and profits. But how can we calculate this disparity precisely? Table 10.1 presents four forms of surplus value in a simple diagram.

TABLE 10.1 Forms of Surplus Value

Forms of surplus value	Origin of the surplus in disparity
Surplus value from wage-labor	Surplus value of wage-labor extracted from the disparity between values from appropriated labor and wage costs (costs for maintenance of the worker)
Surplus value from supply and demand	Surplus value springs from the disparity between own costs and results from the sale, influenced by supply and demand
Surplus value from delusion, deception, fraud	Surplus value springs from the disparity between the real value (costs) and fictional value through delusion, deception, or fraud.
Surplus value from parasitic gains	Surplus value as profit arising from the disparity between achievements and attainments of others' and one's own parasitic partaking (e.g., through inheritance, marriage, gifts)

Reich (2013) sees four principal origins in the formation of surplus value. They can operate individually, but are for the most part in mutual interplay in producing surplus value:

(1) A classic strategy is to employ an individual in wage-labor and then remunerate his or her labor-time such that, after the deduction of all further costs, a surplus value remains from the production of goods or services that can be realized in the market as an exchange value.

(2) The market obeys the law of supply and demand. If one can temporarily monopolize a market in the production of specific goods or services, one can deliberately render supply scarcer or manipulate demand so that one can achieve greater surplus value. In addition to production of goods or services through wage-labor, often even independent of it, there are diverse forms of surplus value based on property laws in the form of stock exchange, derivate trading, speculation, and so on.

(3) It is a general characteristic of capitalist production of surplus value that the market does not only function as a plain and transparent place of exchange. Strategies of delusion, deception, and fraud (as in the case of advertising, misinformation about contracts, or faked documents) always accompany the exchange of all goods and services.

(4) The complex structures of socially and economically unequal status positions in contemporary capitalist societies are supported by, as well as support, the acquisition of surplus value through parasitic gains. The more capital is available, the greater is the amount to pass it on by inheritance or marriage.

There is always a disparity involved in looking at surplus value. It is the disparity between invested costs (or in a given case, non-costs, as in inheritance) and later profits gained that allows us to define surplus value, pointing at the same time to the conversion of money or monetary costs into *capital*. Money only becomes capital if increase is the aim, in accordance with one of the four disparities. Likewise, personal qualities or competencies alone do not yet constitute capital. We might simply content ourselves with having and developing them as use values temporarily taken out of the circulation of capitals. However, such use may potentially enhance social and/or cultural capacities that we may later convert into exchange value. Only if we can determine costs that are measurable and lead to an increase in gains (for example, as higher wages, income, and other such benefits), can we speak of a capitalization or a form of capital. This distinction is fundamental, because we only become capitalists, on a smaller or larger scale, if we strive for and achieve such surplus economic exchange value. That is why our qualifications and competencies, our human qualities, habitus, etc., are not simply capital or human capital by themselves. We must first utilize them in forms of production of surplus value. This includes tallying up costs over and against gains and returns. The distinction of use values—that contain all human capacities and qualities of experience—and exchange values as a market practice to reduce almost everything into capital and profit, helps us to establish a clear distinction between capacities and capitalization. Agents in a capitalist society long for surplus values. They can get them in the process of capitalizing every use value they have. However, to capitalize use values you must succeed in the market of exchange values.

We have mentioned potentials, capacities, and capabilities in every chapter of our book. Developing capacities that allow us to become more productive is a good thing; developing them to become freer and more creative is even better. The problem with most theories of capitals arises from conceiving them almost entirely from the side of production and in the view of exchange values, which is dangerously reductive. Theories like "human capital" ignore consummatory and creative use values, thereby creating a corrosive dualism. From a Deweyan perspective, this is the very core of the inevitable tension between capitalism and democracy. The necessary critical measure of an economy in a just democratic society involves distributing all values equitably so that everyone may live a life of expanding meaning and value.

Today, one of the greatest threats in education is economic reductionism, which seeks to maximize productive energy or service so that the market may extract quantitative surplus value from each individual without concern for qualitative moral, aesthetic, and cognitive consummatory use value. It constructs the individual as an actor endowed with her or his dispositions (i.e., competencies, resources, and personal qualities, etc.) like a small firm that enters the market driven solely by the profit motive. These personal qualities include informally or formally acquired competencies, social networks, cultural resources, preferences, attitudes, interests, communication styles, and such. In a market-oriented culture, people are driven by exchange values. Exchange is a social reality, but at the same time it is an imagination of desired success and prestige. It is part of the dangers of a consumer society that the individuals become oblivious of or even dis-interested in the broader use values for their lives.

Individuality *de jure* means achieving a broad qualification at one's own costs, thereby becoming employable. But many competitive companies in the markets have to care about the use values of their employees. It is becoming ever more important to successfully compete with other firms in the global marketplace by means of qualified and motivated employees, which is why employees are no longer seen simply as cost factors. Rather, firms have to calculate how employee selection can strengthen their resources in a bid to maximize profits. In the new global service- and innovation-driven economy, non-quantifiable qualities of human creativity are especially prized. "Humanization" of the workplace expresses a new demand; it stands for increases in productivity, labor intensity, supervision, the best selection of potentially creative personnel, their continued further training, and life-long learning. Companies design "human resource management" divisions to organize such processes. It is increasingly important that employees find their job and continuing education personally rewarding, not simply connected with exchange values such as salary and benefits. Laborers may enjoy experiencing the very act of their productive labor as creative and self-expressive. This opens up new possibilities of reintegrating production and consumption. But against the background of what has been argued throughout this chapter, it is clear that such reintegrating aspects of "humanization" stand under the pressure of capitalization of all use values into exchange values. Even the most "humane" workplace may easily be dismantled if it does not produce sustainable profit.

From a democratic perspective, moral equality demands equitable distribution of the ability to experience human qualities. It is the only way to actualize everyone's unique potential. "Novelty 'creation,' qualitative 'progress'," Dewey notes, "depends upon surplus" (MW 15: 266). This surplus capital may have quantifiable exchange values; nonetheless, "it is this marginal region which in the concrete is least calculable, measurable, comparable" (MW 15: 266). What Dewey here calls "the marginal region" is that region of culture where individual, idiosyncratic, mostly non-quantifiable consummatory and creative use values predominate. A properly regulated production of surplus exchange values may enable expansion of this marginal region for all:

> This fact, often used as a justification of a capitalistic system, while it justifies *capital*, really points to the need of a wider distribution of capital so that the wants and energies of *every* individual may, by means of a surplus, contribute in him to new wants and values.
>
> (MW 15: 266)

Educators must strive to help their students become more as well as have more. That means interrogating the meaning of capitalization at our current conjuncture to better integrate production and consumption. It is an existential question for the development of democracy and education as a key driving force for a fair and equitable democratic society. Too many educators naïvely adhere to discourses about competencies and capacities without taking larger economic contexts critically into account. Therefore, they remain helpless and speechless when confronted with the mainstream talk about "human capitals." To combine the creation of capacities with the criticism of capitalization, they have to ask questions like the following: How far do our individual experiences, capacities, and resources appear as capitalized? Where and why and from what perspective? What are the limits of such capitalization? Who decides? Do we experience capitalization as a means or as an end? How far is the development and cultivation of use values a free decision of individuals and groups in education and how far are they preconditioned by market orientations? How realistic are the opportunities of learners to secure access to the relevant avenues of the market and be able to exchange their developed capacities, competencies, and resources with fair chances? How far must we strengthen and empower the capacities, competencies, and experiences of all learners against the reduction to market logics lest we abandon our claims to democracy and education?

Our Summary

Dewey had a clear awareness of the importance of the category "capitals" for economic, social, cultural, and political theories and practices. In capitalism, as he already anticipated, potentially all institutions tend to be connected with or influenced by market mechanisms. This especially applies to educational institutions and practices. Dewey's repeated and powerful criticisms of reductionist programs for vocational education that respond merely to narrow business interests, while neglecting broader public interests in democratic growth and participation for all, are examples of his concern that the accumulation of capitals as resources of power and influence in society was basic to his understanding of education. Contemporary theories in the economic and social sciences have developed a theory of forms of capitals. Terms like "social capital" and "cultural capital" have become widespread and well known through the work of Pierre Bourdieu. We have argued that, for a philosophy of education in our time, Bourdieu's approach is helpful but should be extended by more specific distinctions between use value and exchange value and between different forms of producing surplus value. We have argued that it is always important to take the critical tension between experience and the marketplace into account. More specifically, in our time, this includes observing the complex relation between tendencies towards "humanization" of work and tendencies towards capitalization of human life. This responds to the commonplace observation that today all institutions in society (including schools, universities, and such) are increasingly regarded as players in the marketplace. Democracy and education in our time must consider these developments and produce constructive as well as critical responses to them.

Note

1   Dewey's brother, Davis Rich Dewey, was one of the most influential economists of his generation.

11
THE WAY TO DEMOCRATIC INCLUSION

Against the background of what has been said in Chapters 9 and 10 about exclusion, marginalization, and inequality, we now turn to a more constructive and prospective view on opportunities and chances for realizing stronger forms of democratic participation and educational growth under existing social conditions. If we consider the Universal Declaration of Human Rights passed by the United Nations in 1948, we can say that there is the general tendency in Dewey's educational approach to construct an education for every unique individual without special emphasis on special needs. One can easily apply fundamental insights and beliefs of Deweyan democracy and education to questions of inclusion in the broadest sense of democratic participation. What we said in Chapter 4 about moral equality meaning the incommensurability and uniqueness of individuals profoundly applies here. Among other things, Dewey had a very clear understanding of the democratic necessity to take participation as well as diversity seriously in all affairs of life.

Dewey defined democracy as "a belief in the ability of human experience to generate the aims and methods by which further experience shall grow in ordered richness" (LW 4: 229). He also considered the logics of inclusion and exclusion on many different levels, from the linguistic to the conceptual to the logical to the discursive and social level. Typically, when discussing the logics of conceptions and statements in his 1938 *Logic*, Dewey would also point to the effects of such logics when they are acted upon in social life:

> [C]ommon sense consists, in its generalized phase, of a body of such standardized conceptions which are regulative (or are rules) of the actions and beliefs of persons as to what is proper and improper, required, permitted and forbidden in respect to the objects of the physical and social environment. Thus things and persons are sorted out into distinctive kinds

on the ground of allowable and prohibited modes of acting toward and with them: a practical foreshadowing of operations of inclusion and exclusion in the logical sense.

(LW 12: 264)

With regard to his theory of schooling, Dewey was well aware already in the period of his Chicago Laboratory School at the turn of the twentieth century that in a democracy, the school must be open for all and support educational growth for all learners:

> The school, as an institution, must have a community of spirit and end realized through diversity of powers and acts. Only in this way can it get an organic character, involving reciprocal interdependence and division of labor. This requires departure from the present graded system sufficient to bring together children of different ages, temperaments, native abilities, and attainments.
>
> (EW 5: 225)

One core assumption of Dewey's *The School and Society*, which reflected the intentions and experiences of his Laboratory School project, consists in the belief that the school should represent the social diversity of individuals, groups, and communities in the larger society (cf. MW 1: 87). He even observes in his *Democracy and Education* some years later that it is no longer appropriate in his time to speak of society in the singular. We must recognize that a society is actually many societies, because it has substantially become diversified in social, economic, cultural, political, and other respects (cf. MW 9: 25). Representation of diversity in schools not only concerns heterogeneous backgrounds of learners but also diversity in contents, methods, and relationships of learning. Dewey understands that the role of mere instruction on the side of teaching and mere imitation and reproduction on the side of learning is limited in education for a diverse society:

> Mere imitation would never even make a beginning of a society, because it would only give a number of persons doing the same thing at the same time. A society involves diversity of activities on the part of different persons (division of labor, in a wide sense of that term) and cooperation of different acts to a common end. But in addition to this coadaptation of different acts to a single result (which is found in machinery), there must be also an intellectual and emotional appreciation of the common end and of the relation of the diverse individuals to it.
>
> (MW 7: 236)

Diversity in education and society necessarily involves plurality of roles and attitudes, which is to say that we need an understanding of human practices and interactions that involves plural selves and diverse others. It is here that the need to recognize and cultivate incommensurable capacities becomes critical. In the transition to modernity and today's liquid modernity, we can no longer conceive of the human self as a "rigid unity" (MW 7: 342). Diversity implies that one person includes different "minor selves" (MW 7: 342). Dewey is well aware of the origins of diversity that have emerged from the development of modern societies:

> The widening of the area of shared concerns, and the liberation of a greater diversity of personal capacities which characterize a democracy, are not of course the product of deliberation and conscious effort. On the contrary, they were caused by the development of modes of manufacture and commerce, travel, migration, and intercommunication which flowed from the command of science over natural energy. But after greater individualization on one hand, and a broader community of interest on the other have come into existence, it is a matter of deliberate effort to sustain and extend them.
>
> (MW 9: 93)

His educational approach insists that the diversity unintentionally produced by social, economic, and political developments is only the unavoidable condition of democracy and education in our time. It is not sufficient to have laissez faire politics and the market drive the process. Rather, we need deliberate political, social, and educational efforts to create and construct diversity intentionally in every possible way that provides for democratic cooperation, communication, participation, and inclusion of everyone. Against the narrow utilitarian interests of capitalism, Dewey was eager to protect education from arbitrariness and social forgetfulness. To avoid the reduction of learning to mere utility, he argued for "greater diversity of capacities" as a regulative ideal for education in modernity. "The idea of a fixed and single end lying beyond the diversity of human needs and acts rendered utilitarianism incapable of being an adequate representative of the modern spirit" (MW 12: 184). *Democracy and Education* claims we must strengthen the modern potential for diversity and participation against the equally modern tendencies to uniformity, order, and utilitarian conformity. The tension between both sides, we may add, is something that we still can observe in our time of liquid modernity.

> The best guarantee of collective efficiency and power is liberation and use of the diversity of individual capacities in initiative, planning, foresight, vigor and endurance. Personality must be educated, and personality cannot be educated by confining its operations to technical and specialized things, or to the less important relationships of life. Full education comes only when there is a responsible share on the part of each person, in proportion to capacity, in shaping the aims and policies of the social groups to which he belongs. This fact fixes the significance of democracy.
>
> (MW 12: 199)

This significance of democracy gives us a clear orientation for the project of constructing democracy in school. Therefore he concludes: "The responsibility of the school in coordinating into an orderly whole the diversity of social tendencies which, in the complexity of contemporary life, tend to dissipate and distract self-hood, is constantly increasing" (MW 7: 343). The necessary task of balancing out diversity in society and diversity in learning is therefore a constitutive challenge for school in modern society (cf. MW 13: 319). Dewey believes that the modern sciences, especially, could provide a model for using diversity and participation for the deliberate purpose of solving relevant problems. He says:

> It is of the nature of science not so much to tolerate as to welcome diversity of opinion, while it insists that inquiry brings the evidence of observed facts to bear to effect a consensus of conclusions—and even then to hold the conclusion subject to what is ascertained and made public in further new inquiries.
>
> (LW 13: 135)

He repeatedly criticizes the naïve optimism held by many of his contemporaries about the progress of modernity. His meliorism combined the idea that we must cultivate hope for betterments in the future while remaining critical of the dangers and threats to important elements of democracy. Modern conditions of capitalism that build on inequality and hamper the well-being of all especially put diversity, pluralism, participation, and inclusion at risk (cf. LW 13: 182 ff.). Regarding progress in modern society, it remains a profoundly ambivalent and unfinished project as long as there is a deep divide between those who can and those who cannot partake in its benefits (cf. Stiglitz, 2015). Similarly, modern forms of capitalism jeopardize sufficient and sustainable realization of diversity in their tendencies "to reduce heterogeneity to homogeneity, diversity to sheer uniformity, quality to quantity" (MW 8: 7).

Construction and criticism in Dewey's sense imply that different, controversial, and even contradictory opinions and reflections are cultivated in educational processes, and that difference and diversity are appreciated as necessary contributions to a democratic way of life. This presupposes a different concept of schooling and a different role for teachers:

> The teacher who does not permit and encourage diversity of operation in dealing with questions is imposing intellectual blinders upon pupils—restricting their vision to the one path the teacher's mind happens to approve. Probably the chief cause of devotion to rigidity of method is, however, that it seems to promise speedy, accurately measurable, correct results.
>
> (MW 9: 182–183)

We must overcome rigid orientations on fixed results and expectations lest our learning cultures become mere sites of reproduction and imitation. In a democratic way of living together, there must be opportunities for creativity and new constructions as well as participation on the part of all learners. Dewey argues:

> Variety is the spice of life, and the richness and the attractiveness of social institutions depend upon cultural diversity among separate units. Insofar as people are all alike, there is no give and take among them. And it is better to give and take.
>
> (MW 10: 288)

Challenge for Today: Exclusion and Inclusion

Taking Dewey's approach to education seriously in our time obliges us to give creative and critical responses to the controversial and contested field of claims to diversity and homogeneity. In education, the tension is between orientations towards experience versus "one-size-fits-all" strategies. It is a deeply modern paradox that society—in its solid or liquefied forms—ventures to construct order and thereby homogeneous standards for all, on the one hand, and conceives of difference and diversity as necessary social conditions and resources in increasingly pluralistic societies, on the other hand. Dewey believes that in a democracy we must acknowledge both poles of the tension and meet their requirements. This is the very idea behind his democratic ideal of "ordered richness" (LW 4: 229). Since Dewey's day, the tension has not disappeared and the potential as well as actual solutions still respond to the same challenges. We may ask ourselves why it is that, even in times of liquefied modernity, we still have many quarrels and problems around diversity. We can still observe powerful tendencies to reduce the tension to one-sided orientations on one pole only and forget about the other. Reductive claims to homogeneity are as detrimental to democracy and education as arbitrary deregulation and destruction of social orientations and standards that guarantee democratic living together.

Against this background, there is no denying that contemporary societies need to accept and appreciate diversity. We live in an "age of migration" (Castles, Haas & Miller, 2013) that increasingly entails social, cultural, political, etc. diversity in capitalist societies all over the world. But still the dream of homogeneity manifests a deep-seated longing in many social groups because it represents and protects their selective interests. In modernity, this dream has taken different concrete forms. Many of them build on the influential tradition of "survival-of-the-fittest" thinking that is often attributed to Darwin but rather constitutes what is called Social Darwinism. Such theories support the belief that there is a ranking of differences in nature and that it is the function of natural and social selection to subject all individuals to fixed standards. Such logic implies that some are better fitted for survival and growth than others, and that it is in the very service of nature to multiply and enlarge the fitting on the level of society.

We here encounter a trivialization of Darwin's theory of evolution that has produced real and serious consequences in societies from the middle of the twentieth century until today. Darwin provided a description and explanation of the emergence and developments of species, including mankind, as a result of processes of environmental adaptation in connection with selection. His idea of evolution involves diversity of genetic resources and selections that include mutations, recombinations, and genetic drifts. The trivialization of his ideas that has produced the ideology of Social Darwinism rests on a number of conceptual twists. First, the term *Survival of the Fittest*, introduced by Herbert Spencer in 1864, has been transformed from a descriptive term of natural observations into an intentional and deliberate social and political program. It seems unfortunate, in this respect, that Darwin himself appropriated this term in his later works and thereby, to some extent, supported the ideological transformation himself. Second, the Social Darwinist program maintains a very rigid understanding of the term *fittest*. It can literally be translated into *strongest* and thereby denies the very diversity that the Darwinian term includes. Evolution in the comprehensive Darwinian sense implies the success of species on the basis of their advantages in their specific natural environments, which includes that many different species can be successful at the same time and live in mutual interdependency with each other. The turn to Social Darwinism consists in the idea that the important thing is not success of the multitude of life but elimination of those who are less fortunate and advantaged. It reduces evolution to a rigid and hierarchical scheme in which the "strong" and powerful dominate and subjugate and ultimately even eliminate the "weak." Accordingly, fitness loses its biological Darwinian sense of adaptation to an environment and becomes a social and cultural affair of ranking that often builds on forms of symbolic or physical violence. Whereas Darwin thought of fitness in terms of adaption, specialization, mutation, and reproduction, the Social Darwinist appropriation of the term focuses on physical strength, health, robustness, force, assertiveness, and violence (cf. Gould, 1989).

In accord with what we have seen in Chapter 1 concerning the relationship of nature and culture, Dewey provides a penetrating criticism of Social Darwinism's exclusionary and antidemocratic implications when he occasionally turns to social interpretations of disabilities:

> It is sometimes argued that Darwinism carried into morals would abolish charity: all care of the hopelessly invalid, of the economically dependent, and in general of all the weak and helpless except healthy infants. It is argued that our current standards are sentimental and artificial, aiming to make survive those who are unfit, and thus tending to destroy the conditions that make for advance, and to introduce such as make towards degeneration. But this argument (1) wholly ignores the reflex effect of interest in those who are ill and defective in strengthening social solidarity—in promoting those ties and reciprocal interests which are as much the prerequisites of

strong individual characters as they are of a strong social group. And (2) it fails to take into account the stimulus to foresight, to scientific discovery, and practical invention, which has proceeded from interest in the helpless, the weak, the sick, the disabled, blind, deaf, and insane. Taking the most coldly scientific view, the gains in these two respects have, through the growth of social pity, of care for the unfortunate, been purchased more cheaply than we can imagine their being bought in any other way. In other words, the chief objection to this "naturalistic" ethics is that it overlooks the fact that, even from the Darwinian point of view, the human animal is a human animal. It forgets that the sympathetic and social instincts, those which cause the individual to take the interests of others for his own and thereby to restrain his sheer brute self-assertiveness, are the highest achievements, the high-water mark of evolution.

(MW 5: 335)

Against this background, it seems clear that in Dewey's as well as in our time the discourse of the *survival of the fittest* is not only reductionist, but deeply incompatible with democracy and education. Social Darwinism appears on the global level and has many historical ramifications like colonialism, classism, racism, patriarchate, nationalism, chauvinism, etc. that have as a common denominator the ordering and ranking of the social world according to a scale of strong and weak (cf. Hall, 1996). In contemporary education, we find many instances and conditions of homogenization that show traces of the *survival of the fittest* discourse. When we delimit and simplify the diversity of experiences by exclusion of differences, the tendency to sort out and rank learning processes as well as outcomes according to a common and hierarchical order often prevails. We then have apparently clear-cut distinctions between the successful and unsuccessful, the winners and losers, the enabled and disabled, etc. In many cases the socially constructed order and ranking will then appear as self-evident and insofar "natural," especially to those who are immediately involved in the process like teachers and students. Another inevitable consequence is the emergence of orientations towards a common average as constitutive of educational expectations and practices. The average as the mainstream standard is precisely and in all respects the opposite of what Dewey meant by "ordered richness." In education, the *survival of the fittest* discourse finds expression most commonly in a *one-size-fits-all* attitude that, ironically, is often even interpreted as a universal standard of justice. Apparently, *one-size-fits-all* positions everybody under equal conditions, while actually it increases inequalities because not everybody starts with the same preconditions, resources, and capabilities. When equality of opportunity and educational opportunity means developing a limited number of capacities to fit into the already existing social order rather than making unique contributions to enhancing that order, the result is not at all fair in respect to human rights and capabilities (cf. Nussbaum, 2000, 2006). For it overtly neglects the uniqueness and special contexts of diverse experiences.

If we look on educational systems worldwide, we find that the quest for homogeneity is illusionary, anyway, on all levels including so called elite-groups. Given the interdependences of communication, transaction, and cooperation between all levels of society in liquid modernity, the quest for homogeneity constitutes a deliberate defense of privilege and difference that places its hope on the construction of borders that in the democratic project itself have become obsolete. Liquid modernity implies that even for elite groups the construction of such borders has become a deeply ambivalent and contradictory task. In the long run, even elites cannot completely and sustainably achieve this task, and to the degree in which they succeed in achieving it, they themselves delimit and hamper their own life chances by protecting themselves with borders. The rich try to safeguard their advantages by gating access to education as much as they try to safeguard their houses and neighborhoods in gated communities (cf. Bauman, 2000: Chapter 5). There is a growing trend that Dewey would certainly have criticized as increasing social compartmentalization, because it hampers participation for all and puts the democratic project at risk. If we take a more specific look on the educational situation in the United States and in Germany, as examples of relatively rich societies, we find that the unequal distribution of wealth and social status shows a dramatic correspondence on the level of educational chances and success. Both countries have become champions in connecting poor life conditions with poor education (cf. the PISA results). And what seems to be especially dangerous for the prosperity of democracy is that the gap is still growing further (see Stiglik, 2015).

Against this background, to make inclusion effective in education, we need a determined political will, and we need to take specific measures especially on the levels of educational policies, educational administrations, as well as schools. For example, Booth & Ainscow (2011) have developed an "index for inclusion" that is a very helpful and pragmatic instrument. We need to complement concrete measures of inclusion with an equally important general attitude on the part of public deliberation, as well as educational communities in schools and other contexts, that welcomes diversity, appreciates differences, cultivates participation, and develops sensitiveness for individual and social ways of growth. To construct and sustain such shared attitudes, educational institutions first of all need a clear mission statement based on principles of democracy and education.

To avoid the temptation to conceive of inclusion as an ideal and decontextualized counterworld, however, it is necessary to take into account the tension between the standards we discussed at the end of Chapter 9 and conditions of actual social life in capitalist societies. This is another core insight of pragmatic and constructivist social intelligence, because we can only develop our ends, visions, and standards out of social experience as it is concretely lived. It is therefore necessary to recognize at least three major challenges on the way to democratic inclusion:

(1) *The context of capitalism*: It is part of the very logics of capitalist practices that selective interests of individuals and groups compete with each other, thereby entailing the formation of powerful agents in society who dominate the life of others in asymmetric ways. Capitalist inequalities have a strong tendency to divide groups, privilege some and marginalize others, appropriate resources and market advantages for some at the cost of others, etc. This is a main part of the actual social background behind systems of exclusion in society as well as in education. In many countries worldwide, we observe today the emergence and increase of private and elite schooling, which is a clear symptom that the capitalist logic of inequality, division, and exclusion is powerfully at work in education.

(2) *The context of marginalization*: Despite the general democratic claim in many societies that public life is open to everybody and all diverse groups of society, we still observe in all nominally democratic societies worldwide that minority groups live under conditions of economic, social, cultural, and also public marginalization. They experience real and massive difficulties to articulate their voices on their own behalf. This is a risk and challenge for democracy, especially if we conceive of democracy as a way of life that is built on the belief that only the people in the multitude themselves know where the shoe pinches and therefore need to have sufficient opportunities to articulate their own experiences. In respect to democratic well-being and prosperity for individuals as well as the public as a whole, Wilkinson and Pickett (2010) argue that even on a merely economical level, capitalist inequalities produce additional unnecessary costs for society. Consider the immense funding of social systems required to compensate for the negative consequences of the practices of exclusion. If we think of the actual situation in fields like employment, health care, social security, pensions, and others, we find that the public in capitalist societies must compensate the effects of exclusion with financial resources that could have better been invested in prevention like well-funded educational systems. In any case, we can say that the costs of the capitalist logic of exclusion for democratic living together are much too high. The worldwide wave of neoliberal market politics around the millennium turn has increased these processes. As a countermovement, this has also provoked public debates and demands for government politics that delimit the excessive dominance of specific interests by state-funded investments and strategies to control the redistribution of wealth from the public to the few (cf. Stiglitz, 2012).

(3) *The context of precarious sustainability*: We have to remind ourselves that against these backgrounds the way to inclusion is a long travel that often traverses narrow and dangerous roads. Until now there are relatively few cases worldwide where societies have ventured to proceed on that way with a comprehensive and well-balanced program that sufficiently responds to all challenges. Well known for their advantages in inclusive education, the

example of the Scandinavian countries comes quickly to mind. A striking feature in these examples is that inclusion is not only piecemeal work. Rather, it builds on a comprehensive scheme and communicates a comprehensive and general attitude. We suggest that these observations account not the least for the fact that in these cases inclusive practices in education have measurable effects on the reduction of social inequalities. Their school systems, generally speaking, have been successful in giving all individuals and groups, including people with disabilities or disadvantages, relatively good opportunities for participation.

We have spoken throughout this chapter of inclusion as a necessary attitude. This clearly involves general orientations toward solidarity and support for those less advantaged than others. It further requires cultivating sensitivity toward inchoate voices across differences as well as critical awareness of and struggle against instances and conditions of excessive greed, rigid competition, discrimination, marginalization, and exploitation that have been aptly labeled by some as "predatory capitalism."

Our Summary

Dewey was a Darwinist, but he was by no means a Social Darwinist. He already criticized and rejected the notorious slogan and idea of "the survival of the fittest," which has produced so many cruel forms of discrimination and even elimination of others since the nineteenth century. In education, we are still learning that ways that follow the ideals of human rights, social justice, and equity have to do away with the historical heritage of "survival of the fittest" thinking. It is clear that Dewey, with his formulation of fundamental criteria of democracy, which focus on diversity and participation, helps us to understand that education needs to appreciate differences and regard them as resources for the enrichment of the experience of all who work and learn together. A twin idea that usually accompanies the "survival of the fittest" strategy is the educational orientation of "one size fits all" that explicitly or implicitly influences so many current practices. We have argued that on the way to inclusion a series of steps is necessary in order to reconstruct current practices, institutions, and theories. In the first place, the important thing in inclusion is that the idea itself must be a generous one that reflects basic implications of democracy and education. Therefore, the standards of inclusion apply equally to all humans, and we must not confine them to any specific situation or group. However, as we saw in Chapter 9, some groups have been deliberately targeted historically for discrimination and exclusion. Thus, we have to take pains that the application of the ideal of inclusion to all humans does not lead to the forgetfulness of the unique needs of marginalized individuals or groups in special situations. Inclusive education in this sense always has to respond constructively and critically to the tensional relation between distinction and separation.

12

PHILOSOPHY AS EDUCATION

From Pragmatism to Constructivism

In this chapter, we invite the reader to a theoretical meta-reflection on the educational and philosophical approach we have so far developed in the book in the wake of Dewey. We will proceed in three steps: First, we briefly address Dewey's own philosophical meta-reflection given in Chapter 24 of *Democracy and Education*. Like him, we believe it is necessary to have a philosophical method to provide sufficient grounds for discussing democracy and education in ways that allow for a broad and comprehensive understanding. Only then can we avoid arbitrariness and unjustified reductions. Second, we argue this meta-theoretical reflection in our time should take a constructivist turn. We remind the reader that Dewey already had an elaborated implicit constructivism that anticipated many later developments and on which we can draw today. Third, we bring different themes and aspects proposed in the challenge for today sections from throughout this book into a final reflection that focuses on the distinction of observer, participant, and agent perspectives in interactive constructivism.

Philosophy as Education

Dewey writes: "If we are willing to conceive education as the process of forming fundamental dispositions, intellectual and emotional, toward nature and fellow-men, philosophy may even be defined *as the general theory of education*" (MW 9: 338, original italics). He distinguishes philosophy from scientific knowing: "Philosophy is thinking what the known demands of us—what responsive attitude it exacts. It is an idea of what is possible, not a record of accomplished fact. Hence it is hypothetical, like all thinking . . . Its value lies . . . in defining difficulties and suggesting methods for dealing with them" (MW 9: 336).

Dewey tells us that by the time we reach Chapter 24 of *Democracy and Education*, "we have completed the circuit and returned to the conceptions of the first portion of this book" (i.e., Chapters 1–14). He also tells us, "these conceptions are consistent with the philosophy which sees intelligence to be the purposive reorganization, through action, of the material of experience; and they are inconsistent with each of the dualistic philosophies mentioned" (MW 9: 332). Dewey understands philosophy "in terms of the problems with which it deals; and we have pointed out that these problems originate in the conflicts and difficulties of social life" (MW 333). This is a dramatic departure from modern epistemological approaches to philosophy as uncovering the ultimate metaphysical foundations of all existence. Traditionally, philosophies have sought "certain totality, generality, and intimateness of both subject matter and method" (MW 9: 224). Regarding subject matter, Dewey finds that philosophy seeks "to gather together the varied details of the world and of life into a single inclusive whole" that is either a unity or, "as in the dualistic systems, shall reduce the plural details to a small number of ultimate principles" (MW 9: 334). As we have seen, Dewey rejects all the forms of reductionism along with the philosophies associated with them. Nonetheless, he does appreciate that all philosophies attempt "to attain as unified, consistent, and complete an outlook upon experience as possible," although all too often to attain unity, consistency, and completion philosophies employ reductive analysis inadequate to respond to the endless complexity of existence and daily life.

Dewey makes it clear he wishes to pursue philosophy in its original etymological sense as love (or friendship, *philo*) of wisdom (*sophia*), which "would influence the conduct of life" and that always lies beyond knowledge alone. One may have a great deal of knowledge and still act the fool. Therefore, Dewey concludes, "philosophy cannot be defined simply from the side of subject matter." A notion of "generality, totality, and ultimateness is most readily reached from the side of disposition toward the world" (MW 9: 334). He writes:

> When science denotes not simply a report of the particular facts discovered about the world but a *general attitude* toward it—as distinct from special things to do—it merges into philosophy. For an underlying disposition represents an attitude not to this and that thing nor even to the aggregate of known things, but to the considerations which govern conduct.
>
> (MW 9: 335)

Almost everyone knows they are going to die, but people take many different attitudes toward it. As affected by socialization and education in multiple ways, we all have many different kinds of dispositions including, but not limited to, conscious and unconscious mental (intellectual), emotional, moral, reflective (deliberate), and imaginative dispositions. Further, "any person who is open-minded and sensitive to new perceptions, and who has concentration and responsibility in connecting them has, in so far, a philosophic disposition" (MW 9: 335). Philosophy is not only for people in philosophy departments, who are too often only in love with knowledge of ultimate things, but for anyone, including teachers, administrators, parents, and children who would pursue wisdom in action.

All we may hope for is a wise, relatively stable, consistent, and unified response to an ever-changing world:

> From this point of view, "totality" does not mean the hopeless task of a quantitative summation. It means rather *consistency* of mode of response in reference to the plurality of events which occur. Consistency does not mean literal identity; for since the same thing does not happen twice, an exact repetition of a reaction involves some maladjustment. Totality means continuity—the carrying on of a former habit of action with the readaptation necessary to keep it alive and growing. Instead of signifying a ready-made complete scheme of action, it means keeping the balance in a multitude of diverse actions, so that each borrows and gives significance to every other.
>
> (MW 9: 335)

From Pragmatism to Constructivism

In a radically contingent universe where nothing ever happens exactly the same way twice, "totality" does not mean something finished, complete, final, and exclusive (see Garrison, 2012b). In Dewey's pluralistic universe, everything has external relations. Indeed, the only reason we might call it a universe is that everything is in potential or actual relations. Otherwise, we would get what Dewey, following William James, calls a totalized and closed "block universe" (LW 4: 167). It is a core assumption of Dewey's implicit constructivism that we experience our world as an irresistible mixture of the precarious and the stable (see LW 1: Chapter 2). This fundamental insight contains the following constructivist implications: Experience is a constant flow of experiencing and the experienced. Already Dewey anticipated that the ways in which we articulate experiences depend on our positions as observers, participants, and agents in cultural contexts (see Chapter 7 of this book). Long before explicit constructivisms of our time described the varied ways of world-making in a contingent cultural universe, Dewey already saw that human experience is always involved in tensional relations between stable constructions and precarious events. He even anticipated an appropriate criticism against radical constructivism or other forms of subjectivist constructivisms that overemphasize the side of individual constructions of versions of reality that seem to be arbitrary. To overcome arbitrariness and one-sided subjectivism in constructivism, we may use Dewey's rich cultural approach to show that the viability of reality constructions is never only a matter of mere subjective perspectives, but is deeply embedded in cultural contexts, including constructions of past generations in all their diversity and contradictions. Against this background, experience has always a stable dimension as construction, but precarious events show that constructions are always open to further deconstructions and reconstructions. In this connection, Dewey very often himself uses concepts like construction and reconstruction in his writings (see Garrison, Neubert & Reich, 2012).

From our perspective, Dewey's implicit constructivism is philosophy as a method of achieving some unity of response as a tool of wisdom and not philosophy as the impossible quest for indubitable knowledge of existence. For him, continuity—in the tensional relation between the precarious and the stable—takes the place of what in traditional metaphysics was totality and certainty. Continuity means the ability to connect the present with the past and thereby to learn from experience by forming useful dispositions toward the world going forward. This is the very definition of individual and social growth given in Chapter 4. Dewey draws an important meta-theoretical conclusion when he observes that "the wholeness characteristic of philosophy is a power to learn, or to extract meaning, from even the unpleasant vicissitudes of experience and to embody what is learned in an ability to go on learning" (MW 9: 335). The meaning of life is to go on making meaning. That is the most profound meaning of what we call "constructivism." The goal is to construct (deconstruct and reconstruct) meanings that allow all of us to live long and prosper down through the generations. In an evolving pluralistic universe, the quest for unity, continuity, and consistency of response remains forever halting, precarious, uncertain, incomplete, and permanently postponed.

Dewey insists that imagination as the ability to see the possible in the actual is "the chief instrument of the good" and therefore a necessary component not only in scientific knowing but also in philosophical reflection and social reconstruction (LW 10: 350). It is important for the sciences as sources of testable hypotheses regarding knowledge, and even more important for philosophy where we may seek to create something truly novel in the universe. Dewey is not so much offering a philosophy of education or even a philosophy of life as a philosophy *for* life, a philosophy for those that want to live long, prosper, and grow in an unfinished and unfinishable pluralistic universe.

We have made many references to dispositions and capacities in earlier chapters, so by now the reader should have a good understanding of what Dewey means by them. Capacities and dispositions are expressions of habits, and Dewey developed an elaborate social philosophical account of the role of habits in culture (see MW 14). His implicit social constructivism comprehends habits as "second nature" in the sense of providing the culturally embodied basis of learning. Dewey is especially interested in social habits: "Only by engaging in a joint activity, where one person's use of material and tools is consciously referred to the use other persons are making of their capacities and appliances, is a social direction of disposition attained" (MW 9: 45). We have seen that Dewey believes social habits constructed and reconstructed by participating in democratic communities and institutions are the most plastic and responsive to the needs of diversity, otherness, and difference in a pluralistic universe. Indeed, part of what it means to have a critical-creative democratic disposition is to be open to continuous reconstruction of the habits that constitute our individual selves in response to changes in our environment.

Observers, Participants, Agents in Democracy and Education: Some Final Reflections

The Cologne program of interactive constructivism deliberately connects with Dewey's philosophical experimentalism and his implicit cultural constructivism. Like Dewey, we believe that the most inclusive goal of philosophy as education is to cultivate social intelligence as a resource for broadening and deepening democracy not only in theory but in practice. In this connection, Dewey's many critical and constructive perspectives on democracy and education still apply, but require recontextualization and reconstruction. Interactive constructivism suggests that we may enhance our understanding of the role of social intelligence in culture by distinguishing the perspectives of observers, participants, and agents. We have seen in Chapter 7 that this distinction is already anticipated in Dewey, but we argue it deserves further explicit consideration. Why is the distinction so important?

From the perspective of interactive constructivism, observers are at the same time understood as cultural participants and agents. Observers are not merely detached spectators; rather, they partake in cultural practices, routines, and institutions before becoming able to observe and to produce descriptions of the observations they make. Here we have to overcome the tendency in constructivist approaches to overestimate the position of observers in ways of constructing freely their views of the world. As observers, we see, hear, sense, perceive, and interpret our world. We do so in a subjective way, but never only as individuals. We construct our versions of reality based on social and cultural beliefs and expectations, of selective interests, culturally influenced and regulated habits. For interactive constructivism, observers are always involved in interactive relationships within specific cultural contexts. The aim of establishing a constructivist observer theory is to refer the construction of meanings and knowledge to the *perspectives* of observers and to reflect the selective interests, the foci of partaking, and the blind spots in our actions. Interactive constructivists consider all meanings and knowledge claims as viable and provisional cultural constructions that on principle must remain open to further re-/de-/constructions by other observers. For constructivism in all its forms, an observer turn in the meta-theoretical reflection is typical. But what are the challenges of such a turn?

Let us have a closer look at some examples based on recent discourses about social, political, economic, and cultural developments in emphasizing the observer perspectives.

Freedom of Observer Positions and Individual Use Values

In liquid modernity, social life conditions are increasingly individualized. There is the appearance in many situations that decisions about selective interests of observers depend merely on free will and individual choice according to personal ways of living. There are always multiple options for observer positions. No one individual can survey all possible observer positions. Therefore, choice often occurs under conditions of limited transparency. There is a tendency to reduce the complexity of possible perspectives to a more simple and exclusionary interpretation. By doing so, educators easily become trapped in narrow conventional interpretive frameworks like traditional Enlightenment ideas of individuality, innate rationality, and autonomy, forgetting the necessity of exchange values, the power of markets, and the embeddedness in social and historical contexts.

Diversity and the Power of Exclusion

In our time we may easily observe that diversity is growing. Because of globalization, increasing diversity has become inevitable in almost all societies. At the same time, the predominant powers in globalization create many new forms of exclusion to protect the privileged interests of powerful groups. This makes the observer position highly ambivalent, because, on the one hand, there is the democratic claim of including all observers (at least in nominally democratic societies). On the other hand, we find even in the most democratic and pluralistic societies that dominant group interests constrain and shape social contexts in hegemonic ways of living that tend to marginalize and exclude the experiences and interests of others from full and free articulation and recognition (cf. Chapter 11).

Tradition and Translation

Cultural diversity also includes challenges for cultural identities because what formerly seemed culturally given contexts now increasingly appear as the fluid task of positioning, constructing, and articulating oneself with regard to cultural traditions and changing social-cultural contexts. While we observe others, they observe us as our cultural traditions intersect. How do we respond to these often ambivalent, contradictory, and potentially conflicted intersections? We may identify two opposed strategies in our global scene (cf. Hall, 1992). On the side of tradition, there are strong tendencies towards apparently closed and fixed cultural identities. Such tendencies are characteristic of essentialist movements like religious fundamentalism, nationalism, chauvinism, ethnocentrism, and racism. On the side of translation, we observe the emergence of new forms of cultural contexts, interactions, and identities. The formation of identities appears as a complex process of constructions, de- and reconstructions, including unexpected forms of cultures in-between we cannot reduce to one predetermined pattern.

Consumer Society and Public Democracy

The conditions of a consumer society pose new challenges to the effective realization of public democracy in Western societies. Consumption is the main driving force in contemporary capitalism, but unlike production, consumption does not easily establish bonds of solidarity. Therefore, today the practices of capitalism increasingly lead to individualized and dispersed interests that hardly communicate with each other. Gated communities and lifestyles of the upper middle-class and wealthy or marginalized neighborhoods of the poor constitute contemporary forms of compartmentalization and reciprocal alienation. This places communicative and participatory democracy at risk.

Freedom of Observation and the Spectacle of the Media

Observers today have hardly a chance to escape the omnipresence of mass media in their different and emerging forms. The revolution in media technologies has led to a virtualization of observer perspectives. Public media sell and subtly shape observer positions by creating the illusion of free will. The virtualization involves distortion and even fraud by manipulation of selective interests that direct our attention. Even if there is a diversity of media representations—which is too often not the case even in democratic societies—such diversity is always framed and confined by hegemonic mainstream interpretations. Freedom of observation is a claimed democratic principle, but the dangers of manipulation and systematic distortion of public opinion are a continuing threat to the very ideals of pluralistic democracy.

Every observer is also a participant. As participants, we partake in the larger contexts of multiple and often heterogeneous communities of interpreters who provide basic orientation in our cultural universe. We participate in social groups, communities, and networks including the Internet, among other institutions. Our partaking is an indispensable cultural resource, but it also implies commitments, responsibilities, loyalties, and limitations. As we argued in Chapter 7, our observer perspectives and actions deeply depend on contexts of cultural participation, i.e., the involvement in interpretive communities. Let us again consider some important challenges.

Democracy and Capitalism

As we saw in Chapters 9 and 10, there is a continuing tension between democracy and capitalism. At its core lies the ambivalent relation between experience with its qualitative and consummatory axis and the marketplace with its quantitative and calculative axis. Both are necessary in social life but difficult to balance properly in order to provide fair opportunities for partaking and growth for all in society.

Freedom and Justice

Participatory and pluralistic democracy is threatened by the expanding gap between the rich and the poor. To secure a sustainable balance of free choice and justice, democracy needs equitable wealth distribution and equal educational opportunities for all. These are imperatives for realizing democratic conditions of participation in the social commonwealth.

The Need for More Direct Democracy under Conditions of Representative Democracy

The ideal of democracy is full and unrestrained participation in as many direct ways as possible. Representative democracy is not a contradiction to direct or participatory democracy. Actually, we need structures of representative democracy like the division of power to realize chances of direct democratic participation for all in a complex modern society. However, there is always an ineliminable tension between representative and direct democracy. Against this background, it is the challenge of organizing and empowering communities that constitutes the heartbeat of lived democracy. Education is an important dimension of organizing and empowering communities in this sense.

Democracy and Education

The school therefore is an essential locus of democracy. Only if it becomes an all-inclusive site of participation under equal opportunities and moral equality can it do justice to its democratic ideal. Schools everywhere must strive to maximize inclusion while minimizing the gap between the rich and the poor, the well-educated and non-educated.

As agents, we act and experience. We communicate and cooperate, we devise plans, we try to realize interests, to overcome resistances, investigate possibilities, and cooperate and struggle with others. In acting, we are always involved in selective perception according to our needs, desires, and interests thereby forgetting or even ignoring diversity of perspectives—not only of others but also our own. Likewise, involved in acting we often become oblivious to the conditions of participation in contexts of power, truth, knowledge, and so on (cf. Chapter 7). Once more, let us consider some examples.

Acting Always Involves Blind Spots

Social research like gender studies, intersectional studies, ethnological studies, critical whiteness studies, Africana studies, and social class and milieu studies all show that the construction of differences is a powerful cultural strategy to produce a comprehensive, systematic, and ordered view of the social world. This includes the construction of categories and ways of acting, participating, and observing that render certain perspectives more visible while at the same time creating blind spots.

Ambivalence of All Actions

In an unfinished, dynamic, and open cultural universe, we cannot escape the contingency of events and all actions. In liquid modernity, this contingency is even more apparent than in former times of relatively solid modernity. Acting always includes a view to the future. A typical modern perspective of acting towards a future has been the ideal of unambiguous and permanent progress. History has shown, though, that progress is always tentative and indeterminate and often has its dark sides. Every project potentially involves unintended consequences.

Self-contradictions and Incoherence of Roles

In our observations, participations, and actions we often experience contradictions due to insufficient consistency of the different roles that we take. For example, we observe conflicts in society like the ecological crisis of our time. Simultaneously, we participate in a consumer society that is using up recourses as we act pursuing our own personal interests.

With regard to phenomena like the ones just mentioned, we must reflect on what it means when we interpret Dewey for our time. To this end, we have to distinguish between self- and distant-observer perspectives. The self-observers perceive and reflect themselves and others from the *inside* of the practices and interactions in which they immediately partake. The distant-observers observe others in their practices and interactions from the outside. For every self-observer, the presence of (potential) distant-observers implies a constant challenge to relativize their own observation by trying to grasp the alien view. If we consider democracy and education today, we do so as self-observers in our time while looking as distant-observers to the historical context of Dewey, whom we may only interpret from our own contexts of interests, involvements, and concerns. There is an inevitable tension and ambivalence involved here that we might nonetheless use critically and constructively.

On the critical side, rethinking Dewey helps us to reconsider the challenges of democracy and education today. We have started to analyze these challenges by distinguishing the three roles of observers, participants, and agents. When we look more closely at the distinction of self- and distant-observers, we begin to consider some of the differences between Dewey's and our time. For example, one difference concerns the unfinished work of constructing new links in the democratic chain of equivalences. Democracy means to criticize all contexts in which equal rights are suspended or denied. The articulation of equivalent rights has further developed since Dewey's time. Consider for instance the equality claims of LGBT, native peoples, and individuals with special needs. Another example involves our understanding of the complexity of power relations and the effects of power in the diverse experiences of humans. While it was typical in Dewey's time to scrutinize power relations especially in contexts of class and economic dependence, the horizon in our time has considerably broadened to include other differences. Also, there is a changed and extended awareness of the necessary diversity of human experiences including the lives and biographies of those who live in contexts of marginalization. A third example addresses the relation of complexity and reductionism that we explained throughout the book.

On the constructive side, we think that an important strength of using Dewey today lies in his comprehensive and generous approach to connecting the political and educational, the social and the individual, culture and learning, theory and practice, social intelligence and reconstruction. He helps us to think more profoundly about the interconnections between (1) structures of representative democracy, (2) the intermediate realm of public debates, deliberations, and opinions, and (3) the immediate face-to-face encounters of human beings in all areas and institutions of social life. In times of liquid modernity, we definitely need this combination of perspectives in order to see education creatively and constructively in its necessary political, economic, cultural, and social contexts. What is more, Dewey provides an approach to reconsider the deep roots of democracy in human experience and communication. Democracy in a deeper sense is not only the observation of a political system but also the consummatory experience of partaking and the creative and critical potential of acting.

Dewey's enduring legacy lies in having provided us 100 years ago with a comprehensive philosophy of democracy and education. His philosophy of reconstruction is open and inviting to further reconstructions by every generation. It shows why philosophy of education remains an indispensable component of every educational theory and practice. The challenge of his legacy is to make use of his constructive and critical insights in a continuing democratic conversation. Our book is a contribution to this conversation about democracy and education.

Dewey's Summary

After a review designed to bring out the philosophic issues implicit in the previous discussions, we defined philosophy as the generalized theory of education. Philosophy was stated to be a form of thinking, which, like all thinking, finds its origin in what is uncertain in the subject matter of experience, which aims to locate the nature of the perplexity and to frame hypotheses for its clearing up to be tested in action. Philosophic thinking has for its differentia the fact that the uncertainties with which it deals are found in widespread social conditions and aims, consisting in a conflict of organized interests and institutional claims. Since the only way of bringing about a harmonious readjustment of the opposed tendencies is through a modification of emotional and intellectual disposition, philosophy is at once an explicit formulation of the various interests of life and a propounding of points of view and methods through which a better balance of interests may be effected. Since education is the process through which the needed transformation may be accomplished and not remain a mere hypothesis as to what is desirable, we reach a justification of the statement that philosophy is the theory of education as a deliberately conducted practice.

(MW 9: 341–342)

Our Summary

Dewey's philosophy of *Democracy and Education* provides a perspective that takes problematic situations seriously and considers the tensional relationship of risks and opportunities they imply. In his day, the name for a philosophy of reconstructing problematic situations in the broader social and cultural sense was pragmatism. Many today still follow this line of work. While some continue to call this program pragmatism, others point to the implicit constructivism contained in Dewey's approach. We belong to the constructivist side and have, therefore, tried to develop arguments in this book that make this approach strong and productive in our time. Like Dewey, we believe that from a constructivist perspective philosophy in the broadest and most generous sense is education. More specifically philosophy and education so understood consist of the formation of dispositions and constructive as well as critical responses to the world. This kind of philosophy is a strong appeal against reductionisms of all forms in philosophy, the sciences, education, and society. In this sense, what we need is a new and reconstructed program of democracy and education that draws on the many strengths and powerful resources that we find in Dewey and uses them as instruments for construction and criticism today.

REFERENCES

Citations of the works of Dewey are to the critical edition, *The Collected Works of John Dewey, 1882–1953* published by Southern Illinois University Press, Carbondale. Volume and page numbers follow the initials of the series. For instance, MW 9: 1.

Abbreviations for the volumes used are:

EW   *The Early Works* (1882–1898)
MW   *The Middle Works* (1899–1924)
LW   *The Later Works* (1925–1953)

Additional material can be found in the section: *Supplementary Volume 1* (1884–1951)

Alexander, T.A. (2013), *The Human Eros: Eco-Ontology and the Aesthetics of Existence*. New York: Fordham University Press.
Barber, B.R. (1992), *An Aristocracy of Everyone: The Politics of Education and the Future of America*. New York: Ballantine Books.
Bauman, Z. (1997), *Postmodernity and its Discontents*. New York: New York University Press.
Bauman, Z. (2000), *Liquid Modernity*. Cambridge, UK: Polity Press.
Bauman, Z. (2004), *Wasted Lives. Modernity and its Outcasts*. Cambridge, UK: Polity Press.
Becker, G.S. (1993), *Human Capital*. (3rd edition). Chicago: University of Chicago Press.
Bhabha, H.K. (1994), *The Location of Culture*. London, New York: Routledge.
Bhabha, H.K. (1996), "Culture's In-Between". In: Hall, S. & Du Gay, P. (Eds.), *Questions of Cultural Identity*. London, Thousand Oaks, New Delhi: Sage, 53–60.
Booth, T. & Ainscow, M. (2011), *Index for Inclusion*. (3rd edition). Bristol, UK: Centre for Studies on Inclusive Education, CSIE.
Bourdieu, P. (1977), *Outline of a Theory of Practice*. Cambridge, MA: Cambridge University Press.
Bourdieu, P. (1980), *Le sens practique*. Paris: Edition de Minuit.
Bourdieu, P. (1986), "The Forms of Capital". In: Richardson J. (Ed.), *Handbook of Theory and Research for the Sociology of Education*. New York: Greenwood Press, 241–258.

Bourdieu, P. (1987), *Distinction: A Social Critique of the Judgement of Taste*. Cambridge, MA: Harvard University Press.

Bourdieu, P. & Passeron, J.-C. (1988), *Reproduction in Education, Society and Culture* (Theory, Culture & Society). London: Sage.

Bourdieu, P. & Wacquant, L.J.D (1992), *An Invitation to Reflexive Sociology*. Chicago: Chicago University Press.

Bradley, H. (1992), "Changing Social Divisions: Class, Gender and Race". In: Bocock, R. & Thompson, K. (Eds.), *Social and Cultural Forms of Modernity*. Cambridge, Oxford: Polity Press and Open University, 11–67.

Campbell, J. (1992), *The Community Reconstructs. The Meaning of Pragmatic Social Thought*. Urbana and Chicago: University of Illinois Press.

Castles, S., Haas, H. de & Miller, M.J. (2013), *The Age of Migration*. (5th edition). New York: Guilford Press.

Clifford, G.J. (1984), *Edward L. Thorndike: The Sane Positivist*. Middletown, CT: Wesleyan.

Cope, B. & Kalantzis, M. (2013), "Multiliteracies: New Literacies, New Learning". In: Hawkins M.R. (Ed.), *Framing Languages and Literacies: Socially Situated Views and Perspectives*. New York: Routledge, 105–135.

Cox, H. (1999), "The Market as God". *Atlantic Monthly*, March 283 (3), 18–23.

Crouch, C. (2004), *Post-Democracy*. Cambridge and Oxford: Polity.

Crouch, C. (2011), *The Strange Non-death of Neo-liberalism*. Cambridge and Oxford: Polity.

Cunningham, C. (1994), "Unique Potential: A Metaphor for John Dewey's Later Conception of the Self". *Educational Theory*, 44 (2), 211–224.

Danforth, S. (2008), "John Dewey's Contributions to an Educational Philosophy of Inetellectual Disability". *Educational Theory*, 58 (1), 45–62.

Deleuze, G. & Guattari, F. (1988), *Thousand Plateaus: Capitalism and Schizophrenia*. London: Athlone Press.

Dennett, D.C. (1995), *Darwin's Dangerous Idea: Evolution and the Meaning of Life*. New York: Simon & Schuster.

Dewey, J. (2012), *Unmodern Philosophy and Modern Philosophy*. Deen, P. (Ed.). Carbondale: Southern Illinois University Press.

Eldridge, M. (2004), "Dewey on Race and Social Change". In: Lawson, B.E. & Koch, D.F. (Eds.), *Pragmatism and the Problem of Race*. Bloomington and Indianapolis: Indiana University Press, 11–21.

Fallace, T.D. (2011), *Dewey and the Dilemma of Race: An Intellectual History 1895–1922*. New York: Teachers College Press.

Fesmire, S. (2011), Not Alone on the Third Plateau: Animals in American Pragmatism. *The Pluralist*, 6 (3), 44–49.

Foucault, M. (1978), *The History of Sexuality. Volume I: an Introduction*. New York: Vintage Books.

Foucault, M. (1979), *Discipline and Punish: The Birth of the Prison*. Trans. Alan Sheridan. New York: Vintage/Random House.

Foucault, M. (1981), "The Order of Discourse". In: Young, R. (Ed.), *Untying the Text: A Post-structural Anthology*. Boston: Routledge & Kegan Paul, 48–78.

Foucault M. (1988), Technologies of the Self. In: Martin, L.H., Gutman, H. & Hutton, P.H. (Eds.), *Technologies of the Self*. Amherst: University of Massachusetts Press, 16–49.

Fraser, N. (1998), "Another Pragmatism: Alain Locke, Critical Race Theory, and the Politics of Culture". In: Dickstein, M. (Ed.), *The Revival of Pragmatism. New Essays on Social Thought, Law, and Culture,* Durham & London: Duke University Press, 157–175.

Gardner, H. (2000), *Intelligence Reframed: Multiple Intelligences for the 21st Century*. New York: Basic Books.

Garrison, J. (1995), "Deweyan Pragmatism and the Epistemology of Contemporary Social Constructivism". *American Educational Research Journal*, 32 (4), 710–740.

Garrison, J. (2002), "Dewey, Derrida, and 'the Double Bind.'" *Educational Philosophy and Theory*, 35 (3), 349–362. Reprinted in Trifonas, P.P. & Peters, M.A. (Eds.) (2004), *Derrida, Deconstruction and Education*. Oxford: Blackwell, 95–108.

Garrison, J. (Ed.) (2008), *Reconstructing Democracy, Recontextualizing Dewey: Pragmatism and Interactive Constructivism in the Twenty-First Century*. Albany, NY: State University Press of New York.

Garrison, J. (2009), "Dewey's Constructivism: From the Reflex Arc Concept to Social Constructivism". In: Hickman, L.A., Neubert, S. & Reich, K. (Eds.), *John Dewey Between Pragmatism & Constructivism*. New York: Fordham University Press.

Garrison, J. (2012a), "Individuality, Equality, and Creative Democracy—The Task Before Us". *American Journal of Education*, 118 (3), 369–379.

Garrison, J. (2012b), "Dewey and Levinas on Pluralism". In: Green, J., Neubert, S. & Reich, K. (Eds.), *Pragmatism and Diversity*. New York: Palgrave, 99–126.

Garrison, J. (2014), "Review Article—Unmodern Philosophy and Modern Philosophy". *Educational Theory*, 67 (3), 195–203.

Garrison, J., Neubert, S. & Reich, K. (2012), *John Dewey's Philosophy of Education. An Introduction and Recontextualization for Our Times*. New York: Palgrave Macmillan.

Gavin, W.J. (1988), *Context over Foundation: Dewey and Marx*. Dordrecht: Reidel.

Glaude, E.S. Jr. (2007), *In a Shade of Blue: Pragmatism and the Politics of Black America*. Chicago: University of Chicago Press.

Goleman, D. (1995), *Emotional Intelligence*. New York: Bantam Books.

Gould, S.J. (1989), *The Panda's Thumb*. New York: W. W. Norton.

Gould, S.J. (1996), *The Mismeasure of Man* (2nd edition). New York: W. W. Norton.

Green, J.M. (1999), *Deep Democracy*. Lanham, Boulder, New York, Oxford: Rowman and Littlefield.

Green, J.M., Neubert, S. & Reich, K.(Eds.) (2012), *Pragmatism and Diversity*. New York: Palgrave.

Gregg, C. (2010), "Parental Control over the Brain". *Science*, 330 (605), 770–771.

Habermas, J. (1984), *The Theory of Communicative Action*. Volume 1. Boston, MA: Beacon Press.

Habermas, J. (1987), *The Theory of Communicative Action*. Volume 2. Boston, MA: Beacon Press.

Hall, S. (1973), *Encoding and Decoding in the Television Discourse*. Birmingham, UK: Centre for Cultural Studies, University of Birmingham, 507–517.

Hall, S. (1992), "The Question of Cultural Identity". In: Hall, S., Held, D. & McGrew, T. (Eds.), *Modernity and Its Futures*. Cambridge, UK: Polity Press.

Hall, S. (1996), "The West and the Rest: Discourse and Power". In: Hall, S., Held, D., Hubert, D. & Thompson, K. (Eds.), *Modernity: An introduction to modern societies*. Malden, MA: Blackwell.

Hattie, J. (2009), *Visible Learning. A Synthesis of over 800 Meta-Analyses Relating to Achievement*. London, New York: Routledge.

Hattie, J. (2012), *Visible Learning for Teachers. Maximizing Impact on Learning*. London, New York: Routledge.

Heckman, J.J., Stixrud, J. & Urzua, S. (2006), "The Effects Of Cognitive and Noncognitive Abilities On Labor Market Outcomes and Social Behavior". *Journal of Labor Economics*, 24 (3), 411–482.

Hickman, L.A. (1990), *John Dewey's Pragmatic Technology*. Bloomington: Indiana University Press.

Hickman, L.A. (2006), "Socialization, Social Efficiency, and Social Control: Putting Pragmatism to Work". In: Hansen, D.T., *John Dewey and Our Educational Prospect*. New York: Teachers College Press, 67–79.

Hickman, L.A., Neubert, S. & Reich, K. (Eds.) (2009), *John Dewey—between Pragmatism and Constructivism*. New York: Fordham.

Hofstadter, R. (1944/1992), *Social Darwinism in American Thought*. Boston: Beacon Press.

Hollinger, R. (1996), *The Dark Side of Liberalism*. Westport, MA: Praeger.

Joas, H. (1996), *The Creativity of Action*. Chicago: University of Chicago Press.

Johnson, M. (1993), *Moral Imagination: Implications of Cognitive Science for Ethics*. Chicago: University of Chicago Press.

Johnson, M. (2007), *The Meaning of the Body: Aesthetics of Human Understanding*. Chicago: University of Chicago Press.

Kalantzis, M. & Cope, B. (2008), *New Learning*. New York: Cambridge University Press.

Kitcher, P. (2005), "The Hall of Mirrors". *Proceedings and Addresses of the American Philosophical Association*, 79 (2), 67–84.

Kuhn, T.S. (1962), *The Structure of Scientific Revolutions*. Chicago: University of Chicago Press.

Lacan, J. (2006), *Ecrits*. The First Complete Edition in English. New York: Norton.

Lankau, R.A. & Strauss, S.Y. (2007), "Mutual Feedbacks Maintain Both Genetic and Species Diversity in a Plant Community". *Science, New Series*, 317 (5844), 1561–1563.

Larochelle, M., Bednarz, N. & Garrison, J. (Eds.) (1998), *Constructivism and Education*. Cambridge: Cambridge University Press.

Lawson, B.E. & Koch, D.F. (2004), *Pragmatism and the Problem of Race*. Bloomington, IN: Indiana University Press.

Lekan, T. (2009), "Disabilities and Educational Opportunity: A Deweyan Approach". *Transactions of the Charles S. Peirce Society*, 45 (2), 214–230.

McDermott, J. (1992), "Isolation as Starvation: John Dewey and a Philosophy of the Handicapped". In: Tiles, J.E. (Ed.), *John Dewey: Critical Assessments, Vol. III: Value, Conduct, and Art*. London: Routledge Press.

Mead, G.H. (1934/1967), *Mind, Self, and Society: From the Standpoint of a Social Behaviorist* (edited by Charles W. Morris). Chicago: University of Chicago Press.

Meyer, H.-D., Tröhler, A., Laberee, D.F., & Hutt, E. L. (2014), "Accountability: Antecedents, Power, and Processes". *Teachers College Record*, 116, 1–12.

Neubert, S. (2008), "Dewey's Pluralism Reconsidered—Pragmatist and Constructivist Perspectives on Diversity and Difference". In: Garrison, J. (Ed.), *Reconstructing Democracy, Recontextualizing Dewey: Pragmatism and Interactive Constructivism in the Twenty-First Century*. Albany, NY: State University of New York Press, 89–117.

Neubert, S. (2012a), "Dewey's Pluralism Reconsidered—Pragmatist and Constructivist Perspec-tives on Diversity and Difference". In: Neubert, S., *Kultur und Erziehung im Pragmatismus und Konstruktivismus*. Muenster: Waxmann.

Neubert, S. (2012b), *Kultur und Erziehung im Pragmatismus und Konstruktivismus*. Muenster: Waxmann.

Neubert, S. (2012c), "Democracy and Education in the 21st century – Deweyan Pragmatism and the Question of Racism". In: Neubert, S. (Ed.) *Kultur und Erziehung im Pragmatismus und Konstruktivismus*. Muenster: Waxmann.

Neubert, S. & Reich, K. (2006), "The Challenge of Pragmatism for Constructivism—Some Perspectives in the Programme of Cologne Constructivism". *Journal of Speculative Philosophy, New Series*, 20 (3), 165–191.

Neubert, S. & Reich, K. (2008), *Perspectives of Pragmatism—The Cologne Video Project and the Dialogue between Pragmatism and Constructivism*. Available at: www.hf.uni-koeln.de/dewey/31679. Accessed November 4, 2015.

Neubert, S. & Reich, K. (2012), "Reconstruction of Philosophy and Inquiry into Human Affairs—Deweyan Pragmatism in Dialogue with the Postmodern Sociology of Zygmunt Bauman". In: Green, J., Neubert, S. & Reich, K. (Eds.), *Pragmatism and Diversity*. New York: Palgrave Macmillan.

Nussbaum, M. (2000), *Women and Human Development. The Capabilities Approach*. Cambridge: Cambridge University Press.

Nussbaum, M. (2006), *Frontiers of Justice. Disability, Nationality, Species Membership*. Cambridge/London: Belknap.

Noddings, N. (2012), *Philosophy of Education*. Boulder, CO: Westview.

Noddings, N. (2013), *Education and Democracy*. New York: Teachers College Press.

OECD (2009), "Policy Guidelines on Inclusion in Education". Paris (UNESCO) (Doc.Code: ED-2009/WS/31).

OECD (2010), "The High Cost of Low Educational Performance. The long-run economic impact of improving PISA outcomes" Available at: www.pisa.oecd.org/dataoecd/11/28/44417824.pdf. Accessed October 28, 2015.

Pigliucci, M. (2001), *Phenotypic Plasticity: Beyond Nature and Nurture*. Baltimore, MD: The Johns Hopkins University Press.

Pongrácz, P., Miklósi, Á., Molnár, C. & Csányi, V. (2005), "Human Listeners Are Able to Classify Dog (*Canis familiaris*) Barks Recorded in Different Situations". *Journal of Comparative Psychology*, 119, 136–144.

Provine, R.T. (2005), "Yawning". *American Scientist*, November/December, 532–539.

Putnam, H. (2002), *The Collapse of the Fact/Value Dichotomy*. Cambridge, MA: Harvard University Press.

Quine, W.V. (1969), "Ontological Relativity". In: Quine, W.V., *Ontological Relativity and Other Essays*. New York: Columbia University Press, 26–68.

Rabinow, P. (2011), Dewey and Foucault: What's the Problem? *Foucault Studies*, 11, 11–19.

Reich, K. (2007), "Interactive Constructivism in Education". *Education & Culture*, 23 (1).

Reich, K. (2008), "Democracy and Education—Pragmatist Implications for Constructivist Pedagogy". In: Garrison, J. (Ed.), *Reconstructing Democracy, Recontextualizing Dewey: Pragmatism and Interactive Constructivism in the Twenty-First Century*. Albany, N.Y: State University of New York Press.

Reich, K. (2009), "Observers, Participants, and Agents in Discourses—A Consideration of Pragmatist and Constructivist Theories of the Observer". In: Hickman, L., Neubert, S. & Reich, K. (Eds.), *John Dewey—between Pragmatism and Constructivism*. New York: Fordham.

Reich, K. (2012), "Diverse Communities–Dewey's Theory of Democracy as a Challenge for Foucault, Bourdieu, and Rorty". In: Green, J., Neubert, S. & Reich, K. (Eds.), *Pragmatism and Diversity*. New York: Palgrave.

Reich, K. (2013), *Chancengerechtigkeit und Kapitalformen*. Wiesbaden: VS Springer.

Rilke, R.M. (1990), *Selected Poems*. New York: Routledge.

Rorty, R. (1979), *Philosophy and the Mirror of Nature*. Princeton, NJ: Princeton University Press.

Rorty, R. (1999), *Philosophy and Social Hope*. New York, London: Penguin.

Sassen, S. (2008), *Territory, Authority, Rights: From Medieval to Global Assemblages*. Princeton, NJ: Princeton University Press.

Segerdahl, P., Fields, W. & Savage-Rumbaugh, S. (2005), *Kanzi's Primal Language: The Cultural Initiation of Primates into Language*. New York: Palgrave.

Seigfried, C.H. (2002), "John Dewey's Pragmatist Feminism". In: Seigfried, C.H. (Ed.), *Feminist Interpretations of John Dewey*. University Park, PA: Pennsylvania State University Press, 44–77.

Sen, A. (1985), *Commodities and Capabilities*. Amsterdam: North-Holland.

Sen, A. (1992), *Inequality Reexamined*. New York: Russell Sage.

Sen, A. (1993), "Capabilities and Well-Being". In: Nussbaum, M.C./Sen, A. (Eds.) *The Quality of Life*. Oxford: Clarendon Press.

Shusterman, R. (1999), "Dewey on Experience: Foundation or Reconstruction?" In: Haskins, C. & Seiple, D.I. (Eds.), *Dewey Reconfigured*. Albany, NY: State University of New York Press.

Shusterman, R. (2008), *Body Consciousness: A Philosophy of Mindfulness and Somaesthetics*. New York: Cambridge University Press.

Slavin, R.E. (2006), *Educational Psychology. Theory and Practice*. Eighth edition. Boston, MA: Pearson.

Stiglitz, J.E. (2012), *The Price of Inequality*. New York, London: Norton.

Stiglitz, J.E. (2015), *The Great Divide*. New York, London: Norton.

Sullivan, S. (2003), "(Re)construction Zone: Beware of Falling Statues". In: Gavin, W. J. (Ed.), *In Dewey's Wake. Unfinished Work of Pragmatic Reconstruction*. Albany: State University of New York Press, 109–127.

Sullivan, S. (2006), *Revealing Whiteness: The Unconscious Habits of Racial Privilege*. Bloomington, IN: Indiana University Press.

Tomasello, M. (2008), *Origins of Human Communication*. Cambridge, MA: The MIT Press.

Toronto District School Board (2011), "Equity Foundation Statement". Available at: www.tdsb.on.ca/wwwdocuments/programs/Equity_in_Education/docs/EquityFoundation_Statement.pdf. Accessed November 12, 2011.

Von Foerster, H. (2003), *Understanding Understanding: Essays on Cybernetics and Cognition*. New York: Springer.

Von Glasersfeld, E. (1995), *Radical Constructivism: A Way of Knowing and Learning*. London: Falmer Press.

Westbrook, R.B. (1991), *John Dewey and American Democracy*. Ithaca & London: Cornell University Press.

WHO (2014), "Disability". Available at: www.who.int/topics/disabilities/en/. Accessed March 6, 2015.

Wilkinson, R. & Pickett, K. (2010), *The Spirit Level. Why Equality is Better for Everyone*. London: Penguin.

Wittgenstein, L. (1953), *Philosophical Investigations*. New York: The Macmillan Company.

INDEX

Taylor & Francis eBooks

Helping you to choose the right eBooks for your Library

Add Routledge titles to your library's digital collection today. Taylor and Francis ebooks contains over 50,000 titles in the Humanities, Social Sciences, Behavioural Sciences, Built Environment and Law.

Choose from a range of subject packages or create your own!

Benefits for you

» Free MARC records
» COUNTER-compliant usage statistics
» Flexible purchase and pricing options
» All titles DRM-free.

REQUEST YOUR FREE INSTITUTIONAL TRIAL TODAY

Free Trials Available
We offer free trials to qualifying academic, corporate and government customers.

Benefits for your user

» Off-site, anytime access via Athens or referring URL
» Print or copy pages or chapters
» Full content search
» Bookmark, highlight and annotate text
» Access to thousands of pages of quality research at the click of a button.

eCollections – Choose from over 30 subject eCollections, including:

Archaeology	Language Learning
Architecture	Law
Asian Studies	Literature
Business & Management	Media & Communication
Classical Studies	Middle East Studies
Construction	Music
Creative & Media Arts	Philosophy
Criminology & Criminal Justice	Planning
Economics	Politics
Education	Psychology & Mental Health
Energy	Religion
Engineering	Security
English Language & Linguistics	Social Work
Environment & Sustainability	Sociology
Geography	Sport
Health Studies	Theatre & Performance
History	Tourism, Hospitality & Events

For more information, pricing enquiries or to order a free trial, please contact your local sales team:
www.tandfebooks.com/page/sales

 Routledge
Taylor & Francis Group

The home of
Routledge books

www.tandfebooks.com